Counseling Children and Adolescents through Grief and Loss

Jody J. Fiorini
Jodi Ann Mullen

Research Press
2612 North Mattis Avenue
Champaign, Illinois 61822
[800] 519-2707
www.researchpress.com

Printed in the United States of America

5   4   3   2   1   06   07   08   09   10

In this volume, excerpts may be printed in connection with published reviews in periodicals without express permission. No other part of this book may be reproduced by any means without the written permission of the publisher.

Copies of this book may be ordered from Research Press at the address given on the title page.

Composition by Jeff Helgesen
Cover design by Linda Brown, Positive I.D. Graphic Design, Inc.
Printed by United Graphics, Inc.

ISBN-13: 987-0-87822-553-8
ISBN-10: 0-87822-553-6
Library of Congress Catalog Number 2005936299

This book is lovingly dedicated to children and adolescents: to our own beautiful children, Samantha Fiorini, Emily Fiorini, Leah Mullen, and Andrew Mullen

To the children and adolescents with whom we have worked over the years who have taught us so much

And to the children and adolescents who are struggling through grief and loss issues: May your voices be heard and your burdens be lifted.

Contents

Part II: Types of Losses and Interventions

Chapter 4: Intangible Losses   53

Chapter 5: Losses through Death   75

Chapter 6: Interpersonal Losses   97

Part III: Grief Lasts a Lifetime

Part IV: Interventions

Preface

Dr. Jodi Mullen and I have worked in schools, agencies, and private practice for a combined total of more than 25 years. Throughout our time in the field, we have worked with many children and adolescents who have experienced grief and loss. We both counsel children and adolescents using a variety of modalities in addition to traditional talk therapies such as play therapy, narrative therapy, and music and art therapies. Although there are a few texts about grief and bereavement in children that deal with losses that occurred through death, few are available that discuss non–death-related losses, such as moving, changing schools, and break-ups. The texts that were available were geared toward parents and caregivers and did not discuss clinical interventions. Other texts did not take a developmental approach to working with both children and adolescents through loss issues and seemed to adapt adult strategies for use with children. Although we were able to locate pertinent information in the available texts and the current research literature, nowhere did we find a comprehensive resource that we could have at our disposal.

In addition, when we decided to teach a course in counseling children and adolescents through grief and loss on the campus at which we work as assistant professors, our options were limited in terms of appropriate texts to adopt. This book grew out of the dearth of counseling materials we encountered related to counseling children through grief and loss. The intended audiences of the text are professional counselors in the field, including school counselors; counselors-in-training; and counselor educators who are looking for a comprehensive text to use in teaching students about grief and loss issues in children and adolescents. This text will also appeal to other helping professionals, such as social workers, psychologists, and school psychologists.

The layout of the text is intended to be user-friendly. The book is broken into four parts. Part I defines terms and discusses the relevant research related to counseling children through grief and loss. It also discusses family and cultural features related to loss and the developmental aspects of working with children and adolescents through grief and loss. The typical cognitive, emotional, and behavioral responses to loss that children experience at different ages are stressed. The secondary and intangible losses experienced by this population are also highlighted. This is very exciting because very few texts focus on the secondary and intangible losses that we feel are the most clinically significant in our work.

Part I of the text forms the structure and foundation for subsequent chapters in Part II. Part II examines different types of losses encountered by children and adolescents. The chapters reflect the types of losses we typically encounter with children and adolescents in our own practice. Each chapter presents case studies that will be examined using the assessment strategy laid out in Part I. Cases will be examined in terms of primary, secondary, and intangible losses, and in terms of cognitive, emotional, and behavioral responses. Using this method, counselors and counselors-in-training will be able to learn how to assess for and conceptualize the different types of losses as well as formulate possible counseling responses to each. We have found that our own students respond best in learning through the case-study approach.

Part III discusses the lifelong impacts of losses experienced in childhood and adolescence as well as how losses experienced by therapists in their own childhood may reemerge as a consequence of working with this population. Therapist self-care is therefore stressed. Part IV of the text provides a variety of interventions counselors can use in working with children and adolescents on loss issues. This section provides a how-to approach and even includes a list of required materials and supplies. This section of the book will be valuable to both practicing counselors and counselors-in-training. In short, we have given you the book that we wish we already had on our shelves: a book that synthesizes what is currently known about the approaches that work in counseling children and adolescents through grief and loss, provides a method for assessing such clients, and most important, provides guidance in selecting creative interventions that are tailored to the needs of children and adolescents and do not merely treat them as mini-adults.

—Jody Fiorini

Acknowledgments

This text grew out of our mutual respect, friendship, and passion about our work as counselor educators, supervisors, and clinicians. Over these past ten years, our relationship has afforded us friendship, support, and a lot of laughter. We recognize now that our friendship has also provided us with wonderful opportunities for professional and personal growth. Growth is a result of nurturance, care, and love. We would like to thank the people who have supported us in this endeavor.

We would like to extend our deepest thanks to Dr. Dibya Choudhuri, professor at Eastern Michigan University, for contributing chapter 2. There was no one else we would have had write a chapter on the cultural implications of grief and loss. Dibya, your enthusiasm and expertise are unparalleled. Our friend and former student, Melissa Luke, also contributed to this text. Thank you, Melissa, for sharing your creative ideas and insights in chapter 3. Two words: Molly Wallace. Molly, thank you for doing everything we asked. Your detective work was absolutely essential to the completion of this project.

Our gratitude also goes to the following students and alumni at SUNY Oswego, each of whom contributed an intervention for counseling children or adolescents who have experienced loss: Penny Clark, Janet Clendenen, Mary D'Amico, Debbie Haynes, Stephany Keans, Tracy Towndrow, Sharon Van Lieu, and Sarah Watts. Our special appreciation goes to Jeremy Hollenbeck, Melissa Luke, Bonnie Marini, and Barbara Owen, for their contribution of the "Survival Kit for Moving," included in chapter 3.

Thanks also to the other members of the Counseling Children and Adolescents through Grief and Loss course at SUNY Oswego. You all nurtured our ideas and supplied us with the energy to embark on this journey. We are delighted to share your projects from our course with the readers of this book.

Karen Steiner, managing editor of the project, was not only an incredible source of support, but also a mind reader. We were elated to have an editor who knew what we wanted to say, even when we said it poorly. We are indebted to Karen for her meticulous and thoughtful feedback. We would also like to thank Dennis Wiziecki for planting the idea that we could write this book.

Jody Fiorini would like to thank several members of her family for their undying support and enthusiasm: For my brothers and sisters—Debi White, Jim Luciani, Jamie Rusnak, and Doug Luciani—who encouraged me every step of the way. To my parents, Jim and Dee Luciani, who constantly remind me of how proud they are of me. To my in-laws, Pete and Ruth Fiorini, who have promised to buy a copy of this book for everyone they know. And last, to my husband, Mark Fiorini, and my daughters, Samantha and Emily, for being patient while I poured so much of my time and attention into this book. My life would mean nothing without you.

Jodi Mullen would like to say that you can do anything when you are surrounded by people who love and believe in you: I would like to thank my mother, Gail Hernandez, for being proud of me and letting me know at every instance. My father, Marty Weinstein, has been a constant source of encouragement. (I would like to ask for forgiveness from the people to whom my parents have unapologetically bragged.) I am blessed to have siblings who are such an integral part of my life. My sister, Andrea Constantis, and my brother, Rory Weinstein, not only care unconditionally for me, but also care about the work that I do—you guys rule! Most important, I would like to thank my husband, Michael Mullen, and children, Leah and Andrew, for being chronically understanding and patient with me and the time I put into this book. There is no way words can express how I love you all. Finally, I want to honor my Grandma Leah, who died during the writing of this text. Your spirit continues to inspire me.

PART I

Introduction

CHAPTER 1

What Is Loss?

THE LAND OF MYTH AND MAKE-BELIEVE

Once upon a time, there was a land where death was never mentioned. In this land, children were always happy and resilient, and they bounced back from any loss or trauma they experienced. In fact, children were thought to be particularly incapable of feeling depressed or of truly understanding or experiencing loss. Children in this land held their heads high and were "strong little troupers" when faced with issues like death, divorce, or other life transitions. In this land, parents and other adults decided it was best not to talk about traumatic events with their children because it might "confuse" them or make them feel upset. The less said, they thought, the better. In fact, the parents of these children as well as the other adults decided that they should hide their own feelings so as not to upset the children. The adults were very surprised then, when the children began to behave differently, act sad or angry, and engage in risky behaviors after they had experienced a traumatic event or life change. "How could this be," the parents thought, "when we have tried our best to insulate our children from pain? Could we have been wrong all along? Do children grieve?"

SOCIETAL MYTHS ABOUT GRIEF AND LOSS

The passage above illustrates a fundamental problem in the way our society handles grief and loss issues with children and adolescents. We live in a very death-phobic culture. We use a variety of euphemisms, such as "passed away," to describe death; even using the word *died* is taboo. We admire people who are "strong" when

3

faced with adversity. Many of us remember the image of two-year-old John F. Kennedy Jr. saluting as his father's coffin rolled past during the president's funeral. "How very strong and stoic John-John was," we said to ourselves. This image serves as an example of the way we expect children to respond to adversity. We want them to be "brave little soldiers" because it makes it easier for us.

In a society in which people average only three days off work to mourn the loss of a relative—and then only a close relative, such as a spouse, parent, or child—how can we expect children to understand and work through their losses (Eyetsemitan, 1998; Sunoo & Solomon, 1996)? Also, if topics as crucial as death are off limits, then so-called minor losses, such as a breakup or a move to a different city, will be treated as downright trivial and inconsequential. These minor or trivial losses are, however, a source of great pain and anguish for our children and adolescents.

MYTHS ABOUT GRIEF AND LOSS IN CHILDREN

In their book *When Children Grieve*, James and Friedman (2001) discuss major myths that society holds about children and how they should and often do handle grief. These myths strongly contribute to adults' overlooking or underestimating the pain children experience as a result of loss. James and Friedman cite the following myths about the way children handle grief: (a) children don't grieve, (b) it is possible to replace the object of loss, (c) grief is private, and (d) helpful strategies include being strong, keeping busy, and allowing time to heal all wounds. These are only some of the many myths surrounding grief and loss that negatively affect the way adults interact with children and adolescents who have experienced loss. Let's explore more fully some of these and other myths our society holds regarding children and grief.

Children Don't Grieve

In all our years of working with children and adolescents, it has never failed to amaze us that adults from a wide variety of backgrounds, socioeconomic groups, education levels, and ethnicities share an underlying belief that children and adolescents are incapable of grief. We believe that children are resilient and capable of bouncing back from any loss. The notion that children cannot understand death or loss is simply not true. Children do feel grief and experience loss in profound ways. They understand death but not in the way that adults do. Children can handle strong emotions for only short periods of time, and then they will put their grief aside (Fitzgerald, 1992). They may be very upset yet soon afterward play with toys as though nothing were wrong. This reaction is confusing to parents and may lead them to believe that their children are doing just fine when, in actuality, they are not. Children may engage in egocentric or magical thinking and assume losses are their fault or that people can come back, but these belief systems do not isolate or shield them in any way from the pain of loss. Children's inability to verbally express themselves and their feelings, coupled with our reluctance to engage children in dialogue about their losses, contributes to the myth that children cannot and do not feel grief or understand loss.

Adult resistance to and denial of belief that children experience loss is particularly evident when discussing the rise in child suicides in the United States. Many adults simply refuse to believe that children are capable of committing suicide. However, the increasing numbers of children who purposely commit these acts and leave notes has provided us with irrefutable evidence that children are capable of such depths. The rate of suicide in children under the age of 14 is alarming. According to the American Academy of Child and Adolescent Psychiatry, suicide is the sixth leading cause of death nationwide of children ages 5 to 14 (Weaver, 2002, July 23). Because children have less access to the most lethal means of committing suicide than adults, they may resort to riding a bike in traffic, hanging themselves, and so forth. These acts may be and often are construed as accidents. In our own home region of central New York, "a 13-month study in Onondaga County in the late 1990s found 39 cases of children 10 or younger who ended up in an emergency room because they had either threatened or intended to harm themselves," and in two cases children died by hanging themselves (Weaver, 2002, pp. A1, A6). This situation can no longer be ignored. Societal denial is impeding our ability to help children who are seriously at risk.

It's Not Okay to Feel Bad

Another common myth that complicates the grieving process of children and adolescents is the message that they shouldn't feel bad (James & Friedman, 2001). We have repeatedly heard adults say to children, "Don't feel bad." Our initial reaction as adults is to want to eliminate the pain that children are experiencing. We will often say things like "Don't worry, it's okay" or "You're really lucky—it could be worse" or begin phrases of intended comfort with sentiments such as "Well, at least . . . ." Although the intended result is to make children or adolescents feel better, responses such as these actually minimize and invalidate their feelings. Such reactions can be responsible for producing a sense of numbness in children because the message received is, in essence, "Don't feel."

You're Supposed to Feel Bad

At the same time adults are telling children not to feel bad, they may add to their confusion by also sending the message that they *are* supposed to feel bad. There are certain expected responses to grief in our society. One is that a person should feel sad after experiencing a loss, when in actuality a person may feel nothing or may even feel relieved after experiencing a loss. An example from one author's (J. F.) experience may help illustrate this phenomenon:

> When my grandmother died, I was 10 years old. My parents, very serious, took me aside in private to "break the bad news to me." Although I had known my grandmother, I felt no great attachment to her. I saw my grandmother only a few times a year and did not have an emotional bond with her. When my parents told me about the death, I literally felt nothing. My predominant feeling was concern for my father. I remember the look my parents exchanged, as if something were wrong with me. Because I was a sensitive child, they had expected me to have an emotional reaction. I remember feeling at the time that I was letting them down—that I *should* feel bad. Although such an expectation was never voiced, it was there nonetheless. I remember vividly trying to recall a sad incident in my life so that I could produce tears. When I did begin to cry, both my parents visibly relaxed. I had done my job.

We have seen similar reactions when we are providing crisis response counseling services in schools following the death of a student or teacher. Many times, we have seen a number of children or adolescents who feel that there is something wrong with them or that they are bad or heartless people because they have no emotional reaction to the loss. Just the presence of crisis response counselors signals to students that they "should" be feeling bad. Very often children need reassurance that it is okay to feel nothing, it is okay not to feel bad.

Replace the Loss

One of adults' favorite strategies in responding to loss felt by their children is to try to replace the lost object (James & Friedman, 2001). The most common example is the parent who responds to the death of a beloved pet by running out and buying the child another pet. This strategy is faulty on at least two counts. First, it doesn't allow time for the child to assimilate the loss and go through a mourning process. Losing a pet is a learning experience for children. It allows them to come to an understanding that all things die, and it allows us to model healthy grief. By quickly replacing the lost object, we are signaling to children that grief is "awful." Second, such strategies as "We'll just buy you another one" minimize the child's experience by assuming that the object or animal is replaceable. It is often the emotional attachment to the object that causes the feelings of loss, not the object itself. It is important to note that we use replacement strategies with other types of losses as well. When an adolescent experiences a breakup with a girlfriend or boyfriend, we may say, "There are other fish in the sea." Such advice is a variant of the replace-the-loss theme.

Don't Talk about It

One of the most common messages we send to children and adolescents is that grief is a private matter (James & Friedman, 2001). When we send the message to children that they should not talk about their grief, we are really saying, "Don't make me think about it." When children talk about their grief, it makes us feel uncomfortable, sad, and, most of all, helpless. Keeping our children from talking about their losses saves us from our own pain and discomfort. The implicit message children receive is that no one cares about their loss and that they are utterly alone in their grief. We believe that squelching children's discussion of their feelings of loss is responsible for the reemergence of loss issues later in life. The pain does not simply go away. It is repressed and stored away until another loss triggers an emotional response down the road. Ironically, at this point, a child may not realize why he is reacting so strongly to what he considers a relatively minor loss. Suppressing thoughts and feelings surrounding childhood losses can have serious long-term repercussions on a person's mental health.

Brave Little Soldier

In the introduction to this chapter, we discussed the notion of the "little trouper" or "brave little soldier." Our society sends the message loud and clear that we value people who are strong in the face of adversity. We admire people who put up brave fronts and who show a stiff upper lip. How many times have we witnessed deathbed scenes in movies where mourners were told to "be strong" and "don't cry"? Trozzi (1999) refers to this as "buck-up therapy." Children and adolescents receive these messages loud and clear. We have counseled families who had experienced a loss who were so busy putting on brave fronts for one another that there was no communication going on at all. People were going through their days like automatons, trying to keep up appearances for each other's sake, all the while heavily laden with grief and pain. In many ways, the myth of being strong is the most insidious and dangerous of all.

You'll Get Over It

One of the classic myths related to grief and loss is the notion that time heals all wounds (James & Friedman, 2001). This myth is detrimental in many ways. First, it is in itself a faulty statement. Time does not heal all wounds. Some wounds are very deep and leave a lasting impression and accompanying feelings of sadness. The loss of a parent, for example, is not a loss that goes away. Each time Mother's Day or Father's Day rolls around, each time there is a father/daughter banquet or a mother/son dance, when a child does not have her father to walk her down the aisle at her wedding, the feelings of loss come to the forefront. Even non-death losses are slow to heal. When I (J. F.) broke up with my high school boyfriend, I was told, "Give it time, you'll forget." I can still feel the pain associated with that experience. It was the first major loss I had experienced, and I was basically told, as many teens are, that it really wasn't a big deal.

Children and adolescents may also be highly resistant to the notion that they will get over their loss. To many people, getting over it implies forgetting about the lost object or person. Children and adolescents do not want to get over their loss if it means giving up their relationship with the lost person or object. "You'll get over it" may be one of the most hurtful, minimizing phrases anyone can use with a child or adolescent who has experienced a loss.

You're Overreacting

As we have already seen, adults are masters at minimizing children's loss experiences. When a child has a strong reaction to parting with an old toy that she hasn't played with in years, we tell her things like "You're making a big deal out of nothing." To the child it is certainly not "nothing" to be asked to give away a prized possession that has personal meaning. That object may bring back fond memories or may have made the child feel safe in the dark. It may signal that the child is leaving childhood and growing up—and this may be a very scary thought and a transition the child is not ready to face. We would caution any adult who feels that his or her child is overreacting or just seeking attention to consider the underlying hidden losses that the child may be associating with the primary loss.

Just Don't Think about It

A favorite adult strategy for dealing with loss is to distract or deflect. When we are overwhelmed with emotion or experiencing loss, we may resort to "keeping busy." If we keep ourselves busy enough, we will not have time to dwell on our feelings of loss and will exhaust ourselves so we can sleep at night. Because this strategy is often successful for us as adults, we often suggest this strategy to children and adolescents who have experienced loss. "Keep your mind and body occupied," we tell them (James & Friedman, 2001). This strategy, however, robs children of the opportunity to work through their feelings of grief. It does not take the feelings away; it merely postpones them until the child finally runs out of things to do or energy to do them. The "keep-busy" strategy is a Band-Aid that may lead to more complicated grief feelings down the road. It is simply another mechanism to deny the reality of children's grief.

It's Time to Move On

Our society has little patience with the grieving process. As mentioned previously, corporations typically allow people little time off to attend the funeral of a close loved one. Many consider anything beyond a couple of months of emotion "milking it" or a sign of a mental problem. In fact, there is no time limit on grief. Each person experiences grief in his or her own unique way, and the length of the grieving process differs based on a variety of circumstances. For example, if the loss is one in a series of several losses, the grieving process may take longer. Other factors that may affect the length of the grieving process are the personal attributes of the griever, the support network available to the grieving person, and the severity of impact on the person's life.

If You Don't Cry, You Don't Care

Children are often fed the faulty notion that there is a right way to grieve, but not everyone grieves in the same way. We always cringe when we watch crime shows on television if the police officers assume a person's guilt, based on the emotional reaction to the news of a loved one's death. The notion is that if people show no emotion or do not cry, there is something wrong with them. We see the same expectations applied to children and adolescents who have experienced grief and loss. The false tears one of the authors (J. F.) felt forced to produce at the news of her grandmother's death, and the pressure put on adolescents to feel sad when a fellow student dies are examples of society's expectations about what grief is supposed to look like. The last thing a grieving child needs is to be made to feel that he is not grieving correctly. The very notion that there is a right way to grieve is a dangerous myth.

We have discussed only some of the many myths about grief that pervade our society and impede our ability to work with children and adolescents who have experienced loss. It is imperative that counselors examine their own beliefs surrounding grief and loss to be sure that their own biases will not prevent them from helping their child clients through their loss experiences.

DEFINING LOSS, GRIEF, AND MOURNING

Because there are many definitions of grief, we challenged our students, as a group, to come up with an all-encompassing definition of grief and loss. We were impressed with the result:

> Grief is an inevitable, never-ending process that results from a permanent or temporary disruption in a routine, a separation, or a change in a relationship that may be beyond the person's control. This disruption, change, or separation causes pain and discomfort and impacts the person's thoughts, feelings, and behaviors. Although loss is a universal experience, the causes and manifestations of it are unique to each individual and may change over time.

This definition suggests that grief and loss occur not only as a result of an end to something (for example, a death or the end of a relationship) but also as a result of a change or disruption in the person's life (for example, moving or divorce). The definition accurately implies that even the happy events in our lives—such as going to school, getting married, and graduating from high school—are life-changing circumstances that can and often do produce feelings of grief and loss. Our definition of loss also suggests that the experience of loss is unique to each person and that grief can be expressed in an infinite number of ways.

These facts should not be overlooked in working with children. We very often expect certain events in a child's life to be exciting or happy when the child actually responds with fear and anger. For instance, a parent might assume that moving to a nicer, larger home within the same school district would be a rather exciting, positive opportunity for their child; the disruption seems from their perspective to be minimal. Therefore, when the child responds with anger or sadness, the parents are dumbfounded. Each of us has had experiences that bear this out. When J. M. removed a tree from her front yard, her daughter responded with tears and fury. It seems that the tree was her friend. She talked to it and played with it every day. J. M. had no way of knowing either that her daughter had this connection to the tree or that she would be upset by its removal. Likewise, when J. F. moved from an apartment to a house, her daughter, who was then two years old, would not take a bath in the new tub. Bath time was a favorite ritual in the family, full of singing songs and playing games. She expressed her displeasure with the move by refusing to participate. Again, the old tub was her friend, and although the new tub was bigger and shinier, to her it was cold and unfamiliar.

Mourning used to be seen as a task that required detaching from a lost loved one or object. For example, Worden (1991) defined mourning as a "process of separating from the person who has died and adapting to the loss" (p. 10). More recent definitions suggest, however, that mourners do not just move on and relinquish the relationship to the lost person but continue to have a relationship with that lost person or object throughout their lives (Webb, 2002). This approach is a much more hopeful and satisfying one for counselors who work with children and adolescents who have experienced grief and loss. Instead of insisting that children and adolescents work through and "get over" their feelings of grief, counselors are able to help them redefine their relationship with their lost loved one or object and hold on to meaningful memories.

To this end, Dr. Sandra Fox (1985) outlined four tasks that children work through as they mourn a loss. These tasks include understanding, grieving, commemorating, and moving on. One of the first questions asked when a person has experienced a loss is "Why?" During the task of understanding, a child or adolescent seeks to understand what caused the loss and why it happened (Trozzi, 1999). In chapter 3, we will discuss the ways and extent to which children can understand loss at different developmental and cognitive stages.

The second task of mourning, the task of grieving, means allowing children and adolescents to experience the painful feelings associated with a loss (Trozzi, 1999). As we have already discussed, adults often try to protect their children from common feelings of grief, such as sadness and anger, or reward them for being strong. In reality, however, children need to be allowed an opportunity to feel and express their emotions about the loss in order to process their experience.

The third task of mourning is commemorating the person or loss (Fox, 1985). During this task, children and adolescents are encouraged to develop a personally meaningful way to affirm and remember the lost person or object. For example, in the case of J. M.'s daughter, the loss of the tree could have been commemorated by planting a new tree with the seeds from her old friend. In chapter 11, we will examine many strategies for assisting children and adolescents in commemorating their losses.

The last task in the process of mourning is the task of moving on (Fox, 1985). During this task, children and adolescents discover new ways to "maintain an inner connection with and representation of the deceased as they develop other friendships, attend school, play, and perform all the things that shape their daily lives" (Trozzi, 1999, p. 67). It is important to note that the task of moving on does not imply getting over the loss, but instead refers to the process of defining a healthy, new relationship with the lost person, object, or experience.

SUMMARY

As a society, we have not done an effective job of helping our children and adolescents through their grief and loss experiences. Our children are hurting because we are reluctant to confront issues of loss within ourselves, let alone within our children. In the name of protecting our children, we keep information from them and deny them the opportunity to feel their grief. Helping children through their loss experiences requires that we actually accept that children feel grief and are bright and capable enough to understand many aspects of loss.

There are serious consequences of overlooking or minimizing loss issues in children and adolescents. Children who are given incomplete information are likely to fill in the gaps of their knowledge by using their imaginations. Very often, what children imagine is much worse and far scarier than the reality of the situation. For example, the child who is denied an opportunity to attend a funeral to say goodbye to Grandma may envision funerals as frightening encounters. Children are left to imagine death as they have seen it portrayed in cartoons or other television shows. These images can have a lasting impact on children and may contribute to the continuation of our death-phobic society.

Similarly, adolescents who are told, "Don't worry, there are other fish in the sea" after a breakup are learning two lessons. First, their feelings are being minimized because, in essence, they are being told that their loss is "no big deal." Second, they are being encouraged to squelch their feelings by entering into a new relationship to replace the lost one. This advice may make friends or parents feel better. It allows the teen an opportunity to be active and stop wallowing in her feelings. As anyone who has ever experienced a rebound relationship knows, however, such help is fleeting and only temporarily prevents people from experiencing the pain of their loss. The result may be that the teen never develops true coping skills for handing the grief feelings associated with loss.

Counselors have an opportunity to play an important role in assisting parents and other adults in understanding the way grief and loss are manifested in children and adolescents, helping them to provide comfort and support to their children, and providing them with useful interventions that will allow their children to work through their feelings of grief without minimization or denial. The remainder of this book will explore the developmental and cultural implications of grief and loss in children and adolescents; present a framework for assessing clients who have experienced loss; offer case studies to help counselors understand the issues related to grief and loss in children and adolescents; and demonstrate strategies and specific interventions for working with this population.

CHAPTER 2

Cultural, Religious, Familial, and Gender Factors Related to Grief and Loss

Earth and metal . . . . although my breathing ceases,
time and tide go on.

—Atsujin, Japanese Death Haiku

INTRODUCTION

Across the range of cultures, people hold varying beliefs about life and death. These beliefs can be both resources and obstacles in providing support in times of grief and loss. A cross-cultural perspective shows an infinite variety in people's responses to death, in how they mourn, and in the nature of their internalization of the lost object. Instead of being viewed as a process, mourning is seen as an adaptive response to specific task demands arising from loss that must be dealt with regardless of the individual, culture, or historical era (Hagman, 2001). Culture, religion, family, and gender identities shape the impact of grief in terms of what is felt, what type of loss elicits those feelings, the implications of having such feelings, how such feelings are expressed, the appropriateness of various feelings, and strategies for dealing with feelings that may not be directly expressed (Rosenblatt, 1993). For instance, in Egyptian culture, bereaved persons are encouraged to dwell on their pain and sorrow in the company of others; in Bali, mourners are enjoined to contain their sorrow and pretend to be cheerful (Wikan, 1990). In Egypt, therefore, the bereaved are discouraged from watching television for a year after the death of someone close, but in Bali, the grief-stricken family is encouraged to do so in order to help them forget their sorrow and "manage the heart."

You might ask, "If death is a universal, inevitable characteristic of human existence, wouldn't all human beings react in essentially similar ways?" On one level of understanding, the response is yes, in that every person has access to fear and sadness as universal human emotions. Beyond that, however, there are particular mind-sets, belief systems, and understandings of the phenomena of grief and loss that are rooted in how we locate ourselves within a culture, religion, and social identity. While the experience of grief and loss is intensely personal and unique, these experiences cannot be separated from the complex sum of who we are and the cultures that nourish and surround us.

> *Give sorrow words; the grief that does not speak whispers to the over-wrought heart and bids it break.*

> —Shakespeare, *Macbeth*

In this chapter, you will begin to explore the complex factors that influence our beliefs and feelings. With examples from various cultural systems, you will discover the range of attitudes and beliefs about death, bereavement, loss, and grief. You will also receive an overview of the beliefs of some major religions about death and dying that affect the mourning process.

In working with grief and loss, counselors need to assess and understand the impact of such identities to be able to work effectively. Unawareness of the influence of cultural or religious factors may lead to the misapplication of standardized grief models, resulting in potential misdiagnosis and ineffective treatment, with the end result being little benefit to the client.

Understanding your own orientation to issues of sickness, death, and loss is the first step for any helper. As you read this chapter, reflect on the following questions to identify the cultural and spiritual beliefs that frame your own perspective.

1. As a child, how were you treated when you were ill? How do you use or not use such methods now?

2. What were the conversations that you recall from your family of origin regarding death?

3. What causes you to become ill?

4. If you were very ill, would you like to know everything about your condition, including the possibility that you might die from your illness?

5. What will happen to you after you die?

6. Identify the primary relationships that are important to your well-being.

7. Briefly identify or describe the spiritual path or faith community that nurtures and sustains you.

Death, feared as the most awful of evils, is really nothing. For so long as we are, death has not come, and when it has come we are not.

—Epicurus, 341–270 B.C.

CROSS-CULTURAL APPROACHES TO GRIEF

A Chippewa girl was in the hospital for spinal fusion surgery, and she wanted to pray for strength to deal with the possibility that she might never walk again. When she tried to burn sage in her room for purification, the hospital guards came in and forcibly stopped her, citing it as a fire hazard rather than an issue of religious significance.

The body of a four-year-old Iranian girl who had accidentally drowned was to be shipped back by plane, with her parents accompanying the body. The airline, however, refused to accept the parents as passengers at departure because they were perceived to be hysterical and a potential problem to other passengers.

A children's hospital center in an area with a substantial Hispanic population displays attractive flower beds filled with marigolds at the building's main entrance each season. Because the orange blossoms are considered a symbol of death in Mexican culture, many Mexican Americans choose not to come.

Because our understanding of grief is often culturally constructed, we need to be careful even in defining the construct of grief. For instance, grief work implies a cognitive process of confronting a loss, going over the events before and at the time of death, focusing on memories, and working towards detachment from the loss (Neimeyer, 2001). Fundamental to such conceptions is the view that the griever needs to bring the reality of loss into his or her awareness as much as possible and that suppression is a pathological phenomenon. Among the Navajo, however, mourning is limited to four days; then the bereaved are expected to return to normal life and not speak of the deceased person or discuss their feelings of loss. These prescriptions are closely linked to the Navajo belief in the power of the deceased person to do harm to survivors (Miller & Schoenfeld, 1973). In addition, there is considerable variation in belief across cultures regarding the process of death—who is considered to be dead and in what sense. For instance, in northeastern Brazil, children we would consider merely ill are often counted as dead (Scheper-Hughes, 1985). Infants and children are typically only mourned for a few days. However, these children are counted as part of the family, and after their deaths mothers are expected to join them in heaven.

Rosenblatt (1993) suggests that, given the range of anthropological studies on bereavement and grief, it is inappropriate to suggest one theory of grief that can be universally applicable. Across cultures, beliefs regarding ordinary and normative grief, repressed grief, excessive grief, and somatization of grief vary considerably. In Balinese culture, emotional agitation is discouraged because prayers will not be heard if the one who prays is agitated (Wikan, 1988). Thus a Balinese person who is bereaved will make great efforts, using jokes and distractions, to redefine death as not bad or even desirable. Overt grieving in this cultural context is therefore not normative.

In the United States, grief is often considered a psychological process, while in many other cultures, it is somatacized. For example, in China and many other societies, one of the predominant ways to articulate problems in living is through physical ailments (Kleinman, 1986). An American counselor may understand some metaphors of physical ailments as an index of emotional pain so that *Men*, a Chinese term for pressure on the heart, may be interpreted as the heart breaking, but there may well be other metaphors that are experienced but not understood.

Anger, another component of loss, is also an integral part of mourning in many cultures. In the United States, mourning is not necessarily associated with aggression, but anger may be a normative component of grief in cultures that believe loss is caused by someone, even in situations where the death would be deemed accidental or natural in our own culture.

In understanding and working with grief cross-culturally, it is necessary to step outside your own frame of reference. Educating yourself about the cultural aspects of your clients is a first step. However, you must treat educational sources with care. Cultural insiders or referents may not have the same cultural viewpoints or experiences as the client. Written sources are risky too because descriptions of grief and mourning may not apply to the individual with whom you are working. These sources are helpful, though, in pointing out your own presuppositions and opening the way for you to be able to listen fully to the client and his or her experience (Weidman, 1975).

Loss is defined by the meaning we give it. For instance, in cultures where children have multiple parents and caretakers, the loss of a parent may have different meanings than in a culture where parents in a nuclear family are the designated caretakers. Depending on the personal connections, a parent's death may or may not be a major loss. The ease of replacing the lost object also affects the experience of the loss. Losses that are considered appropriate are often easier to deal with. Among the Yoruba, for instance, the idea that a child might predecease a parent is considered so unnatural that when a child dies, the parents are restrained from attending the funeral because they might go mad with grief (Moloye, 1999). You should also consider whether death means the end of a relationship with the attendant loss that belief entails or whether the relationship is thought to continue in a different form. All of these differences in interpretation may well lead to differences in grieving.

> *Death, be not proud, though some have called thee*
> *Mighty and dreadful, for thou art not so. . . .*
> *One short sleep past, we wake eternally,*
> *And death shall be no more; Death, thou shalt die.*
>
> —John Donne, 1572–1631

RELIGIOUS AND CULTURAL ELEMENTS

Culture and religion are often intertwined. Many cultures also have a particular religious or spiritual understanding that informs the worldview and values. Particularly around issues of grief and loss, human beings have often sought spiritual explanations for comfort and to make meaning of the loss. However, religions change in the context of culture. An example is the differences in mourning rituals among Mexican and Irish families; both families may be staunchly Catholic.

On the first days of November, Mexicans celebrate *Los Dias de Los Muertos* (Days of the Dead), focusing on both remembrance of the deceased and the continuing lives of the survivors. Salvador (2003) describes the rituals of the family's visiting the graves of relatives at the cemetery, carrying a sumptuous picnic, sharing reminiscences about the departed, and conversing with other relatives and family who have congregated. Children will eat *calaveras* (sugar candy in the shape of skulls) and a special bread called *pan de muerto* (bread of the dead). Marigolds and chrysanthemums are used to decorate gravesites, and often gifts of alcohol and cigarettes are brought for the deceased's enjoyment. At home, the family may make an altar with offerings of flowers and food as well as photographs and memorabilia of the deceased. Traditionally, departed children are remembered during the first day of the festivity, termed *Día de los Angelitos* (the Day of the Little Angels), and adults are remembered on the second day.

While an Irish family has no equivalent annual memorial, the Irish wake is a way of meeting the family's needs at the time of the funeral. Sheehy (1994) says that, in Irish culture, strong emotional attachments develop between family members so that each member of the family is unique and irreplaceable. The loss of a family member often prompts relatives from far away to congregate and return for the funeral. These occasions also provide ways for the family to reorient themselves and renew the strength of the family networks. At the funeral itself, up until the 1970s or so, it was common for the body of the deceased to be laid out in a coffin in the living room of the home in which he or she had lived. The body was often washed and prepared by the women and dressed in a habit with a rosary and a crucifix. After this, there would be a period of keening and wailing to mourn the death. In the preparations made for the wake, there would be lots of food and drink, and the focus would be on remembering the life of the deceased through family members' socializing. The body would be conveyed to the church on the evening before the burial. While the content and extent of the rituals have changed, the symbolic rites integrate the culture of the living with the culture of the dead. These practices remain an integral part of the Irish answer to the threat to identity posed by death (Sheehy, 1994).

The next sections describe elements from some of the major religions regarding death and bereavement to demonstrate the interweaving of religion and culture. These important factors influence children's conceptions and experiences of death (Candy-Gibbs, Sharp, & Petrun, 1984).

Judaism

In Judaism, two important values include *kavod hamet*, which is required to honor the dead, and *nichum avelim*, or comforting the mourners (Cytron, 1993). These twin values are present through all the rituals associated with death and bereavement, in which respect must be shown for the deceased while striving to bring solace to the bereaved. Therefore, the integrity of the deceased body must be respected, disallowing autopsies, for instance, as well as using burial as a means of disposal. Cremation is seen as an unnatural way of treating the body, and it is closely associated with the Holocaust. Burial is often in a family plot, or arrangements may have been made to bury the body in Israel.

In Judaism, official mourning is determined by one's relationship to the deceased, in the following order: father, mother, brother, sister, spouse, and son or daughter of the deceased. These official mourners are excused from many ritual obligations to be able to attend to the funeral arrangements. In the first rite, a black garment or ribbon is symbolically used to demonstrate the deceased's being cut away from loved ones. For children, the cut is made above the heart; for adults, it is made on the right side. At the service, the rabbi will often give a eulogy. The interment takes place in the cemetery, and many family members participate in the act of placing earth on the coffin. In the final step, the family recites the Jewish prayer called the *kaddish*, a prayer that makes no overt reference to death, but affirms life (Cytron, 1993). Following the service, the family mourns for a week. During *shiva*, visitors come and help to draw out the family's grief with reminiscences of the departed. The bereaved may use acts of self-sacrifice—such as not shaving for men, not wearing new clothes, not sitting on furniture, or not using mirrors—to demonstrate the disruption the death has brought. This period also brings the family together in their grief to share their sorrow and recollections of the deceased member. At the end of the *shiva*, family members say their final prayers and then go for a short walk outside. This simple act symbolizes the need to take up acting in the world, turning from the preoccupation with loss to the responsibilities each mourner carries.

After this period, Jewish families may participate in *sheloshim*, marking the first month after the funeral, as well as the *yahrzeit*, the first anniversary of the death. In this anniversary, the family lights a special candle and recites the *kaddish*. During the Jewish ceremonies of Yom Kippur, Passover, Shabuoth, and Sukkoth, a significant part of the worship service is set aside for remembrance, and family members make collective prayers and individual meditations.

The part played in the rituals and ceremonies changes, depending on whether they are boys or girls and whether they have completed the adulthood rites of the bar or bat mitzvah, typically in the early teen years. The extended period of ritual mourning in Judaism may help the children to see the death as permanent, while the funeral rituals may help the child see the nonfunctional and universal aspects of death, grief, and loss that are often difficult to accept (Ayash-Abdo, 2001).

Christianity

The term *Christianity* covers a wide array of practices and belief systems, but most center on resurrection and the continuation of the human soul, which usually depends on how life on earth has been lived. Many Christian churches have specially written funeral services, as well as special readings, prayers, and hymns. It is traditional to wear dark clothes to funerals and black ties with suits, but sometimes people prefer to wear bright clothes as a celebration of life and resurrection. A public memorial may follow funeral services, particularly if the family prefers a simple, private funeral. The memorial service provides the opportunity to celebrate the life of the deceased with a wider group of friends and colleagues.

Part of the Catholic tradition is the laying on of hands and healing through touch. This is the origin of the "anointing of the sick," which used to be known as the last rites. When Catholics see the priest coming, they are to be concerned because it signals to them that the end is near. The touch is meant to restore the sick one to health if God desires it or to help them bear the illness bravely. The oil used is blessed by the bishop. When a person is dying, prayers are spoken into the ear of the dying person to encourage an act of faith.

After death, biblical words and phrases from the scriptures are said. The priest's task is to be immediately with the family. The mass consists of readings, the use of candles and incense, and the Eucharist. This special service recalls the last supper that Jesus Christ shared with his disciples before his death. The funeral liturgy is a chance to grieve and offer hope. After the funeral and the cemetery, there is usually food for the mourners. The church prefers burial in the ground but now permits cremation, which was forbidden because this practice historically began as a way to express a lack of belief in an afterlife. However, it is more practical now, and urns are allowed into the church. A cloth is placed over either the casket or the urn as a reminder of baptism. Donation of organs or the body is considered an act of charity and is permitted. Following the burial, churches offer masses in people's names to remember them. There is a strong belief in the afterlife in which the deceased is united with God. However, there is still a sense of connection with the living.

Protestant rites lack the ritual and symbolism of Catholic services, usually being simpler and more straightforward. Although many denominations of Protestantism exist, each of which has a unique approach and rituals in dealing with death, one common factor is the idea of a loving and caring relationship with Jesus Christ (Gilbert, 1995). Through faith symbols such as the sacrament of baptism, believers are reassured of an eternal relationship with a loving God that cannot be broken by death. Statements of faith, such as the hymn "Abide with Me," affirm the presence and support of God for the dying and provide comfort for the grieving

In Protestantism, importance is placed on meeting the family's wishes in composing the funeral service. The site of the service may be a church, a funeral home, or the graveside, and the body may or may not be present for the ceremony. If the body is present, the clergy of certain Protestant denominations (such as Lutherans) ask that the casket be closed, if it is open, before the service begins. Protestant services may include prayers, music, eulogy, a sermon, and readings of Biblical scripture. The focus of the service tends to be on celebrating the life of the deceased and affirming belief in the deceased's having achieved everlasting life. Mourners may also be invited to pray at the burial site, and those near the grave may throw handfuls of earth onto the casket as it descends. A gathering where food is served typically occurs after the burial, usually hosted at the church or in the home of a friend or family member.

Islam

There is a great focus in Islamic tradition on the afterworld where believers can be rewarded for their virtuous actions on earth. During the process of dying, verses from the Koran may be recited to remind the dying one of his or her eventual release. The dying person will often seek forgiveness for acts and attempt to settle debts. Similar to Judaism, the sanctity of the body is observed. After death, the body is turned to face Mecca and not left alone while relatives and friends recite prayers. The prayer for the dead, *salat ul janaza*, is performed. The body, always prepared by persons of the same sex as the deceased, is carried to the place of burial on a bier while the carriers recite prayers. Some close relatives may view the face of the deceased before burial. Spouses, daughters, and sons are not permitted to see the face, but sons-in-law may (Gilanshah, 1993). At the funeral, weeping and the release of sorrow is encouraged, although women may wail and men may be more restrained. Tea, sugar, and syrup are available to tend to mourners who faint from grief. Muslims believe the physical body is relieved by crying, helping the process of healing to begin (Gilanshah, 1993). Because the deceased is now with Allah, extravagant funeral practices are frowned upon.

Following the burial, friends and relatives gather at the deceased's family house, where they may stay as long as a week. This constant socializing is encouraged to prevent mourners from being isolated in their grief. A prayer ceremony is held on the third day following burial, and prayers continue to be said for at least seven days. After seven days, fresh flowers and a prepared stone are placed on the grave. Close relatives are required to wear black for 40 days, although widows may wear black for up to a year. Tradition suggests that mourners do not cook during this period and that friends and relatives supply them with food. This symbolizes the need to focus on the grief process and the necessity of community support for the bereaved. At the anniversary of the death, another ceremony is held to pray for the deceased, give charity to the poor in the deceased's name, and ask for blessings (Gilanshah, 1993).

Given the Islamic beliefs about death, death is not considered a terrible event for the one dying; it is more a loss for those left behind. Gilanshah (1993) remarks that children often experience death and are taught about it much more frequently than children in the Western world because of the harsher conditions that are often present in Muslim countries. Islam teaches that death is an integral part of life, and while one may mourn the passing of a loved one, death itself is not a stranger.

Hinduism

For Hindus, death represents the transition of the soul from one embodiment to the next and is the means by which the spirit can ascend in its journey towards heaven, or nirvana. Ideally, a Hindu should die while lying on the floor in contact with the earth. The body is washed and dressed and is often laid out for visitors. Family members will perform prayers and, although touching the corpse is considered polluting, many mourners will need to do so to say farewell. Children are often brought to view the body. Hindus cremate their dead, and the burning of the dead body signifies the release of the spirit. The belief in reincarnation means that a Hindu funeral can be as much a celebration as a remembrance service. The flames themselves are important as they represent the presence of the god Brahma, the creator. White is the traditional color of mourning.

Prayers are usually said at the entrance to the crematorium and may be offered en route. Flowers or sweetmeats may also be passed around, and noise is also part of Hindu rituals, which may be made by horns and bells. The chief mourner, usually the eldest son or eldest male in the family, represents the whole family in saying goodbye to the deceased. Male members of the family may shave their heads as a mark of respect. Women typically do not attend the cremation. At the crematorium, Vedic scriptures are read, and the chief mourner traditionally lights the pyre, although in modern times it is more usual to push the button to make the coffin disappear and then go below to ignite the cremator. After the cremation, the family may come together for a meal and prayers and begin a period of 13 days of mourning, when friends will visit and offer condolences.

Buddhism

Death is considered a transition within Buddhism, a reminder of the impermanence of life (Truitner & Truitner, 1993). The story of Kisa Gotami is used to emphasize this teaching. According to this story, a young woman, Kisa Gotami, lost her only child and insisted on carrying the corpse around and asking the Buddha to bring her child back to life. The Buddha said it might be possible, but she needed to gather mustard seeds from her neighbors. The caveat was that the mustard seeds should come from a house where no one had died. She found mustard seeds everywhere, but not a place where death had not occurred, so she realized that death touches everyone.

At the time of dying, meditation is helpful, as is chanting *sutras* into the ear of the dying person because hearing is the last sense to go. The body is kept for three days because that is how long it takes the soul to leave the body. However, if the organs are to be donated, compassionate action in the service of life is allowed. The body is cremated and a funeral service is held in which mourners speak from their hearts, and the urn is displayed at the service. Filial pity and local custom may often cause a display of grief at the service, where the surviving close relatives wear white and wail. Ashes are sprinkled at a place specified by the departed person and the family. The funeral is not only meant to pay respects to the deceased and to help support the bereaved in their grief, it also supports the deceased to come to a true awakening. After 49 days, further rites are held to help the family members affirm their karmic link to the deceased. A one-year anniversary commemoration is also held.

The philosophical and ritual aspects of Buddhist practice may be both comforting and confusing to children. On the one hand, they are enjoined to be calm and centered, striving to be free from attachment. However, Confucian elements in the culture may prompt grief and mourning towards deceased adults and the continuation of the filial relationship even after death. These expectations may be confusing to children, who are developmentally unsure of the permanence of death and confused about ways to hold on to and detach from the deceased simultaneously.

> For in and out, above, about, below,
> 'Tis nothing but a Magic Shadow-show,
> Play'd in a Box whose Candle is the Sun,
> Round which we Phantom Figures come and go.
> Into this Universe, and Why not knowing
> Nor Whence, like Water willy-nilly flowing;
> And out of it, as Wind along the Waste,
> I know not Whither, willy-nilly blowing.

> —Omar Khayyám, 1048–1122
> *The Rubaiyat,*
> translated by Fitzgerald

IMPACT OF LOSS ON THE FAMILY SYSTEM

Given the diversity of family coping styles, there are few fixed and defined processes by which a family copes with grief. However, there are many familial factors, influenced in turn by the culture, community, and religious base in which the family is sustained, that impact the grieving process. Brown (1988) described the importance of real contact with death, particularly in terms of children and their inclusion in that process. He believed it is crucial that children not be excluded from participation in rituals surrounding the death in the hopes of sparing them pain. Funeral rituals, visits to the grave, memorial services, and open acknowledgment of loss and the circumstances of death serve a vital function in allowing the mourning process to be coherent. The loss must be put in meaningful perspective to fit with the family's belief system and experiences.

Another major familial factor is the disruption that occurs when a family member dies, dislocating established patterns of interaction and equilibrium. In the immediate aftermath of a loss, families may have to make further changes that increase the upheaval. For instance, a child who loses a parent might also have to grapple with a new school if the surviving parent is compelled to relocate for financial or emotional reasons.

Again, mourning can vary as each new season, holiday, or anniversary in the life of a family—who attached particular roles, functions, or aspects to the deceased family member—reinvokes the loss (Wortman & Silver, 1989). If new family members seek to enter the family system, they may be refused acceptance and be seen by some family members as an unsatisfactory replacement for the deceased. Sometimes the fear of loss or idealization of the deceased makes for obstacles in forming new attachments and commitments. Thus a child may refuse to accept a new adult partner in her surviving parent's life, believing it a betrayal of the deceased parent.

In terms of loss in the family life cycle, the important factors to consider are (a) the timing of the loss, (b) the simultaneous occurrence of other major life changes, (c) a past history of unresolved loss and mourning, (d) the kind of death that occurred, and (e) the role played by the deceased in the family (McGoldrick & Walsh, 2005). Untimely deaths are those that confound social and chronological expectations; the death of a grandparent is expected, but the death of a young spouse and parent is not.

In untimely deaths, because of the lack of preparation and search for meaning, the mourning can go on for years. Siblings, spouses, parents, and children can have survivor guilt about being alive when the deceased is not. The loss of a mate can be complicated by responsibilities towards children. Children, in turn, may try to take care of the remaining parent, both to distract the bereaved parent and to manage their own anxiety about their survival. With the death of a parent, children may have difficulties forming intimate attachments in the face of fears of abandonment and repeated loss. McGoldrick and Walsh (2005) also suggest that children may have later difficulties in parenting if the same-sex parent was lost in childhood. Assessing the emotional state of the surviving parent and the availability of other adult caregivers is crucial to being able to assist children and adolescents who have experienced the death of a parent.

When loss occurs at the same time as other major life-cycle changes, a family may become overloaded. For instance, a child who is born at a time of significant loss may assume a family replacement function. A girl who is born on the anniversary of her grandmother's death may be seen as her stand-in, expected to serve the family in similar ways. Transgenerational family patterns are also important in the ways in which a family has historically attended to loss. These histories, if unattended to, can be acted out in covert family scripts. An example of this is the father who becomes depressed in early mid-life as he approaches the anniversary of his own father's untimely death. If the death was inadequately grieved, the son may observe it at this point in the life cycle, and if the pattern is not highlighted and clarified, it may end up repeating itself across generations.

Hidden losses—such as miscarriages, secret abortions, or infertility—can represent the loss of family dreams. The death of a child can be the worst of untimely losses, which destroy generational expectations. The position of the child complicates the loss, particularly the death of the firstborn or only child, only child of a particular sex, child with particular talents, or child who was difficult or with whom family members have had ambivalent relationships.

The kind of death that occurred can be another complicating factor. Parental difficulties with such loss may be acted out in the symptomatic behavior of siblings. In a case study described by McGoldrick and Walsh (2005), a four-year-old boy refused to go to nursery school. Investigation found that his older brother had died at the age of four, and the parents had explained that the death had resulted from a virus that he had picked up at nursery school. In the death of a child, the needs of siblings and other relatives are often neglected. Siblings may experience intense anniversary reactions and prolonged grieving, exacerbated by guilt from having had normal sibling rivalry. Because parents are often preoccupied by grieving, the surviving child may feel as if he has lost the parents as well. In the case of a family member with a protracted illness, there may be diminished attention to the surviving children's needs. On the other hand, after the accidental death of a child, parents may become overprotective and hypervigilant of the other children and have difficulty with separation.

Accidental adolescent death associated with impulsive, risk-taking behavior may lead to intense anger and frustration mixed with the attendant grief as parents and siblings deal with the senseless loss.

Alcohol and/or drug-related automobile accidents account for a high percentage of teenage deaths (McGoldrick & Walsh, 2005). Adolescents of color, particularly from working-class and poor families and communities, are especially at risk for violence, with the hopelessness and depressed expectations about the future contributing to a focus on immediate gratification and self-destructive behavior (Burton, 1995). Adolescents who experience a parent's death may develop considerable guilt as they may have wished to be free of parental authority and control. Peer models also contribute to acting-out behavior to cope with the pain, including stealing, fighting, sexual activity, or withdrawal. Such behavior in turn increases stress on the family and may draw in larger extrafamilial systems, such as the school or judicial system. In some ways, adolescents can serve as the barometer of family losses, drawing attention to problems that are unresolved.

> *Soon, I feel the time comes near to leave. With sunset shadings screen the parting day.*
>
> *Let the hour be silent; let it be peaceful. Let not any pompous memories or meetings create a sorrow's stance. May the trees at the gate raise the earth's chant of peace in a cluster of green leaves. May the night's blessings be in the light of the seven stars.*
>
> —Rabindranath Tagore, 1861–1941

ASSESSMENT OF CULTURAL, RELIGIOUS, AND FAMILY VALUES AFFECTING THE GRIEVING PROCESS

Helping children cope with the death of a loved one includes showing respect for the family's cultural heritage. According to McGoldrick et al. (1991), these are some important questions that will help inform how best to work with the grieving child:

1. What are the culturally prescribed rituals for managing the dying process, the deceased's body, the disposal of the body, and commemoration of the death?

   Here, you can get an understanding of the cultural as well as religious aspects that will be present. It is important to get a sense of the level of acculturation of the family, of whether the family closely follows traditional rituals or incorporates new ones or is coping with confusion about the kinds of rituals and procedures available that can best meet the family's needs. The family's comfort or confusion will be transmitted to the children, whose processing of the information will be influenced by the reactions and responses of adult family members. Acculturation also impacts the degree to which a child might feel alienated from peers in terms of the death. For instance, in Hispanic and Latino cultures, the death of a godparent is extremely important for a child, but it may not be recognized as such by the school system because the person is not considered to be close kin.

2. What are the family's beliefs about what happens after death?

   These messages are transmitted either directly or covertly to the child, and an understanding of the family's beliefs is extremely helpful for the counselor to have in working with the child.

3. What does the family consider an appropriate emotional expression and integration of the loss?

   In many cultures and families, there are different appropriate expressions of grief as well as commonly understood timelines of mourning. Prescriptions range from appropriate expression at time of death, following the death, and at the funeral service, as well as in the weeks, months, and years following the death. Some cultures and families have built-in rituals for dealing with anniversaries, while others do not. If children receive conflicting messages from different family members, the process of grieving is further complicated.

4. What are the family's gender rules for handling the death?

   Prescribed affective, cognitive, and behavioral expressions may also differ by gender. Sometimes, boys may be given the message that they must be stoic and are not supposed to grieve openly. Alternately, boys may translate grieving into acting-out behavior. On the other hand, girls may not be allowed or encouraged to express anger.

5. Do certain types of death carry a stigma (for example, suicide), or are certain types of death especially traumatic for that cultural group (for example, death of a child)?

   This inquiry gives the counselor a sense of the uniqueness of the death and its attendant implications. There may well be "good" deaths and "bad" deaths in the context of cultural and familial readiness.

When I am dead, my dearest
Sing no sad songs for me;
Plant thou no roses at my head
Nor shady cypress tree;
Be the green grass above me
With showers and dewdrops wet;
And if thou wilt, remember
And if thou wilt, forget.

—Christina Rossetti, 1830–1894

USING RITUALS TO ADDRESS GRIEF

There is much agreement among counselors on the efficacy of therapeutic rituals in facilitating healing among clients (Imber-Black, 2005). The primary mental health benefits of ritual are closely tied to the relational aspects of the ritual process. These act to validate and encourage the healthy expression of a wide range of human emotions. According to Reeves and Boersma (1990), a ritual consists of "a joint activity given to ceremony, involving at least one person and the symbol of loss, endowed with special emotion and often sacred meaning, focused around a clearly defined set of social objects, and when performed confers upon its participants a sense of the sacred or out of the ordinary" (p. 282).

Jacobs (1992) concluded that religious ceremony and ritual functions mitigate anxiety and deal effectively with other problematic emotional states. Religious rites have a cathartic effect as emotions are released and expressed through attachment and connection to significant others. Rituals can be used to assist individuals to move from a maladaptive to an adaptive style of grieving.

As an example of the use of ritual to work through grief, the ritual of *Mizuko Ruyo* is used in Japan to deal with the aftermath of abortion (Klass & Heath, 1996). *Mizuko* means child of the water. *Ruyo* is a Buddhist offering. In a ritual drama played out by Jizo, the bodhisattva who suffers for others, the parents' pain and the child's pain are connected. In that connection, the pain of each is resolved. The child is made part of the community and does not become a spirit bringing harm to the family. The parents can fulfill their obligation to care for the child and transform the sense of *kurnon*, sickness unto death, into a realization of Buddhism's first noble truth that all life is suffering.

In a slightly different cultural context, the *Bardo Thodol* (Tibetan Book of the Dead), together with its associated ritual, provides a way to understand how Buddhism in Tibetan culture manages the issues associated with what we call grief in Western psychology. The resolution of grief in the survivors is intertwined with the journey to rebirth of the deceased (Goss & Klass, 1997).

Reeves and Boersma (1990) suggest using three processes of rituals to assist individuals in overcoming maladaptive grieving patterns. These include (a) separation, allowing for detachment from either an earlier fixed point in the social structure, from a set of cultural considerations or both; (b) bridging, or crossing of thresholds, characterized by ambiguity, neither the past fixed state nor the coming state; and (c) aggregation, in which the passage is consummated in a stable state.

Cross-cultural use of rituals means abandoning a search for ideal therapeutic procedures and instead looking for culturally embedded practices, achieved through an open listening to the client's voice, in the reality and values of the sustaining culture (McGoldrick, Hines, Lee, & Preto, 1986). Understanding and accepting the client's definition of health and perception of the world is crucial. Rituals should be suggested only after counselors believe they understand the issues and have developed a working alliance. They should be flexible enough to change and adapt to the client's needs, and to be therapeutic, they must be invested with respect, solemnity, and mysticism (Ishiyama, 1995). Angela's case, adapted generally from Webb (2003), suggests using a therapeutic ritual as a possible intervention.

Case Study: Angela—"Padrino Is Very Sick"

Angela is a 10-year-old Puerto Rican girl who has entered counseling as her parents undergo the process of divorce. She has a younger sister, Linda, who is four years her junior. Ultimately, the father plans to move out of the home while the mother retains custody of the girls. Just recently, the family has received the news that Angela's padrino (godfather) Roberto has been diagnosed with terminal lung cancer. Roberto was Angela's father's mentor and friend when he was a young man coming to the mainland. He is only distantly related, but he has been very much a part of their lives ever since Angela was born. This is the first major death that will occur in Angela's life because both sets of grandparents are alive. The paternal grandparents, who reside in Puerto Rico, are more distant.

In many ways, because Roberto is older, locally available, and has grown children of his own, he has taken on the role of a grandfather with Angela and Linda.

Discussion Questions

1. What methods could you use to discover what thoughts and feelings Angela is experiencing?

2. What kinds of activities and conversations could you have with Angela that might alleviate her fears about her father's departure and her godfather's death?

3. How might Angela be allowed to say goodbye to her padrino?

4. What steps might be taken both before and after the divorce to facilitate a smoother transition for Angela?

Case Analysis

In this situation, the child is already working on the impending loss of her father, who in moving out, will inevitably become a more distant presence. The threatened death of her godfather means that she will be losing two significant men in her life in the same period of time. Her father's grief at the news is also a part of her response. Angela may well have to deal first with fearsome ideas and images she may have about cancer and the dreadful nature of Roberto's suffering and death before she can begin mourning (Nader, 1996).

Various options exist for working with Angela. A family counseling session may be appropriate, including the parents and Linda, to collectively process the news about Roberto's terminal illness. At such a session, it would be important to have toys and activities that can allow the children to express their feelings, rather than just inviting verbal expression from the adults (Webb, 2003). Reviewing photographs and drawing pictures of happy times can be meaningful activities that bring the family together (Romanoff, 2001). One benefit of such an intervention, if the family agrees, may be that Angela gains some understanding that the family has not broken up, even if the parents are divorcing. It will also access the family story about Roberto, including both his life and his death.

Another meaningful intervention is to suggest a therapeutic ritual. In this case, Angela could perform such a ritual with her little sister to commemorate her godfather. Given their varying ages, perhaps a collage of their memories that both can complete and that might be displayed at the memorial service would be appropriate. If completed during the process of the family bereavement session, it can offer opportunities for family members to recall their feelings about Padrino as well as to express negative feelings about their anger at his cancer and even some blame for his smoking.

Another option that may be helpful is a bereavement group for the children. Children may fear being pitied about their losses, and in a bereavement group, they often feel support and a sense of having experiences in common with their peers (Webb, 2003).

SUMMARY

In this chapter, we completed an overview of the cultural, religious, and familial factors that affect the grieving process. However, these are extremely complex issues, and this chapter provides only an introduction. Counselors who work cross-culturally with children and adolescents should approach this task with a maximum of self-awareness and be prepared to deal with their own cultural notions of the counseling experience and relationship. Educating themselves about the unique cultural, religious, and familial factors involved is a critical feature so that counselors neither apply stereotypical or caricatured cultural categories nor overlook the importance of these factors. In her work with members of other cultures, Weidman (1975) pioneered the concept of the "culture-broker"—a well-informed intermediary whose inputs are brought to bear on the counseling process. The client, however, remains the major source of information about those features of his or her cultural experience that might otherwise baffle the counselor.

Children's process of grieving and bereavement needs to be understood on the individual level of cognitive and emotional development. Counselors must also understand the cultural and familial context in which the loss is embedded and made meaningful (Neimeyer, 2001). Counselors who are aware of the array of these influences can work much more effectively with their clients as well as provide a variety of treatment methods and interventions that children may respond to positively. Chapter 3 will discuss developmental perspectives regarding grief and loss in children and adolescents.

Grieving Children and Adolescents: Developmental Considerations

In this chapter, we will make an argument for counselors to conceptualize childhood and adolescence as distinct cultures. Working with children and adolescents from a multicultural perspective, including consideration of their ages, gives counselors opportunities to better connect with their clients and conceptualize their clients' struggles, goals, and overall perspectives.

Counselors who work with children and adolescents by simply adapting skills that they would use with adults are likely to miss the complexity of working with these populations. Schaffer (1988) makes the argument that cultural differences affect a variety of aspects of the counseling relationship: "Cultural differences can affect the validity of assessment as well as the development of therapist-client rapport, therapeutic alliance, and treatment effectiveness" (p. 4).

Erdman and Lampe (1996) assert that it is also important to note that any cultural differences between counselor and client are likely to be compounded by the differences accounted for by the assignment of status as adult or child. Creating a counseling relationship in which the child or adolescent client feels understood may be a more difficult task than in a counseling relationship in which the client is an adult. When the client in the counseling relationship is a child or adolescent, aspects of the relationship are altered (Landreth, 2002; Stern &

Newland, 1994; Thompson & Rudolph, 2000), which may make the task of empathizing with the client more daunting.

Children and adolescents differ from adults developmentally, cognitively, emotionally, physically, and psychologically. These differences require counselors who work with children and adolescents to have specialized knowledge. Researchers indicate that many helping professionals lack proper preparation and education in working with child clients (Corey, Corey, & Callanan, 1993; Erikson, 1985). In fact, in a study of play therapists (Mullen, 2003), therapists suggested that the impetus for their specialized training and preparation in play therapy was grounded in their common feeling that the education and preparation they had received as counselors and therapists did not adequately prepare them to work with children. The process of therapy and counseling with children and adolescents requires at minimum an adaptation of skills used with adults. Moreover, viewing childhood and adolescence from a cultural perspective is the cornerstone of providing children and adolescents with counseling services geared to their particular developmental and cultural experience.

THE CULTURES OF CHILDHOOD AND ADOLESCENCE

Childhood

The culture of childhood refers to the shared experiences children have in particular societies and subcultures and to the social construction of childhood itself. Most of the professional literature that focuses on cultural perspectives has excluded children and childhood (Vargas & Koss-Choino, 1992). When working with children in a counseling context, the counselor will find that the salience of age is readily apparent. A knowledge of the distinct cultures of adulthood (counselor) and childhood (client) is required for the counselor to effectively transverse the cultural barriers presented as a dynamic of the child-counseling relationship.

Therapists and counselors who work with adults are not likely to encounter a client who refuses to come into the office without an accompanying adult, who hides behind a chair in the waiting area, who spends the entire session talking about Care Bears, or who is significantly below the therapist's level of cognitive and abstract reasoning ability (Landreth, 2002). The world of children is vastly different from that of adults. Rules, values, customs, and language exist there that are part of a culture that counselors have left behind long ago. If you are a child, you are generally powerless. You live in a world where size does matter, where your daily accomplishments are judged inconsequential by the dominant culture (drawings, homework, physical tasks like cartwheels), and where what is important to you may not be deemed important by the dominant culture. As a child, your thoughts and feelings are often dismissed and minimized, under the assumption that a little person equals a little problem.

Conceptually, children are mandated clients in the sense that they did not request or seek counseling services; another person (an adult) in their life initiated the relationship. Children, for the most part, do not even know why they are in the counseling relationship, what a counselor is (or does), or what the rules of the relationship are. Children who are experiencing grief and loss may be sensitive about having to meet with a counselor when other children and adults who have shared in the loss do not have to.

Adolescence

Definitions of the word *culture* typically include the notion that a specific group of people hold similar beliefs and customs. Culture can be defined, then, as "any group of people who identify or associate with one another on the basis of some common purpose, need, or similarity of background" (Axelson, 1993, p. 2).

Adolescents represent a cultural group whose membership, like children's, is not permanent. Adolescents maintain similar belief systems and customs that are based on common developmental tasks as well as on their position and relationship with the dominant (adult) culture. Clinically, adolescents often report struggles related to power and responsibility. For example, they are confused as to why they are responsible enough to care for a younger sibling for a few hours but not responsible enough to spend even a moment alone with a peer of the opposite sex. They recognize that the rules of adulthood do not pertain to them, but they observe that neither do the rules of childhood. One teen explained it this way: "I went from needing my parents to pick out my clothes and dress me to being able to do those things for myself. Now that I'm 14, suddenly my parents don't think I can pick out my own clothes and will even pull up my pants or button my shirt higher as I walk out the door."

Commonly held norms concern language, dress, and interpersonal styles. Oftentimes, these norms and beliefs contrast with a counselor's past or present experiences. In clinical practice, we have never had an adult referred for some of the interpersonal reasons our adolescents are referred. One of our adolescent clients was referred for her sexual behavior. Her mother, the referral source, stated, "She needs to talk to a counselor. She's given too many blow jobs." Our perception of this comment changes as the age of the client changes. This example highlights how our experiences with and as adolescents can affect our clinical work. In this example we asked the teen's mother how many is too many, and we also asked the client the same question. Talk about divergence of thought!

The scenario also brings up the counselor's own feelings about teenage sexuality. It is very common for adult counselors to judge the behaviors of their child and adolescent clients in ways that they would never judge an adult's. A case like this could also arouse parental feelings in counselors. In their desire to protect children, counselors may become engaged in a process of preaching or lecturing despite the fact that they know that judging and advising negatively impact the client-counselor relationship.

Adolescents themselves may recognize, but not be able to express, that they are part of a distinct, often marginalized culture. Their pursuit of autonomy and differentiation may lead to their self-identification with membership in a *different* (adolescent) culture. Effective cross-cultural counselors are "open to understanding values that differ from their own, and no longer need to convert others or give up their own values" (McGoldrick, 1998, p. 22). Our experience as clinicians and counselor educators and supervisors highlights the struggles of new and seasoned counselors who work with adolescents. These counselors grapple with maintaining empathy, avoiding a parental stance, and trying to prevent their clients from making the same mistakes they did as adolescents. These are just a few of the challenges counselors deal with when working with adolescents. When counselors are able to recognize the experiences of adolescents as fitting into a cultural context, the risks of insensitivity, advising, lecturing, preaching, minimizing, dismissing, and disrespecting are reduced.

HOW DO CHILDREN AND ADOLESCENTS EXPERIENCE GRIEF?

In children and adolescents, emotional, cognitive, and behavioral symptoms and indicators of loss may be mistaken or explained away as moodiness, raging hormones, a phase, an overreaction, or evidence of being spoiled. Losses differ in their intensity and seriousness. The experience of loss is unique to every individual, and extraneous factors can compound the impact of loss for even the most resilient individual. A child who has experienced many losses simultaneously, for example, may shut down after experiencing a seemingly minor loss. Another child may have moved and therefore have few supports or established friendships available to help cope with these losses. Other children may by nature be more sensitive to change and have difficulty coping with any new experience. Under certain circumstances, even the most common experiences—having a haircut or losing a tooth—can seem traumatic to some children.

The following discussion concerns the emotional, cognitive, and behavioral expressions of loss in children and adolescents. In this discussion, it is important for readers to note the interconnectedness in children's and adolescents' emotional, cognitive, and behavioral experiences of loss.

EMOTIONAL RESPONSES TO LOSS

Loss is unique to each individual, experienced in a multitude of ways with a host of changing emotions. A sense of loss may be related to a change in children's surroundings, aspirations or plans, culture, lifestyle, or routine. Children may feel a loss of control over their life and a loss of their identity. A sense of loss is also affected by the nature of the loss—for example, a relocation or move, a parent's unemployment or promotion, death or illness in the family, or family divorce or remarriage.

It is important to understand that children, unlike adults, do not have an extensive range of labels for the emotions they feel. Therefore, it is crucial to help guide their natural efforts to communicate their loss with methods that can be tailored to their developmental level. Children will experience conflicting emotions caused by this change in their life. They will need to review the loss and convert the emotional energy that the loss has created before being able to complete their grieving process.

Despite the type of loss, children must endure an affective period of grief and coping. The intensity and duration of the feelings may vary, but children and adolescents tend to go through similar stages of grieving as they cope with loss (Mack & Smith, 1991). Whether the loss is connected to death or other types of losses, the loss of a major relationship, object, or routine in a child's or adolescent's life may leave the child feeling empty, frightened, and alone. Feelings of anger, confusion, desertion, and insecurity are common. In addition, they are likely to feel responsible and guilty about the loss.

Guilt is a common emotion associated with loss in children and adolescents, particularly if a death or divorce is involved. According to two separate studies by McEntire (2003) and Worden (1996), children express guilt about remembered misbehavior or missed opportunities to express affection. Unfortunately, the normal developmental tasks of adolescents, including rebelliousness and withdrawal from the family, may prompt guilt feelings after the loss of a loved one. Often, adolescents feel that they should have spent more time with the loved one, not gotten angry with that person, or told the individual that they loved him or her. Young adolescents may feel that somehow they were responsible for the death, thus bringing on guilt feelings (Glass, 1991). Bereaved children and adolescents also become anxious over the safety of other loved ones or themselves.

Teenagers often send mixed messages regarding their needs. Some adolescents may restrict their expression of feelings, giving the impression of being unaffected (Cunningham, 2004; Schoen, Burgoyne, & Schoen, 2004). Furthermore, many teenagers see mortality and death as a natural process that is very remote from their day-to-day life and something they cannot control (Glass, 1991). The emotional consequences of loss are confusion and powerlessness, especially when a peer has died. After a significant loss, older children or young adolescents often will feel helpless and frightened. They may want to retreat to childhood, where they had a sense of protection from death or loss, but they often feel compelled by social expectation to act more like adults. Therefore, they may suppress their emotions (Glass, 1991).

COGNITIVE RESPONSES TO LOSS

Much of the literature regarding how children and adolescents experience loss, particularly how they think about loss, is connected to Piaget's model of child development (Piaget, 1970). Webb (2002) argues that, although Piaget's work did not specifically address children's understanding about death, his theories about the development of children's thinking apply directly to the topic.

Birth to Age Three

According to Piaget's developmental theory, this age range includes the *sensorimotor stage* (from birth to age two) and the beginning of the *preoperational stage* (ages two to seven). During the time from birth to age three, children think in egocentric terms; they cannot understand the concept of "forever," but they will begin to use symbols, words, and mental images to represent reality to themselves.

Emswiler and Emswiler (2000) concluded that, prior to age three, children may sense an absence among persons in their immediate world and may miss a familiar person who is gone, but they are unlikely to understand the difference between a temporary absence and death. Likewise, the National Center for Victims of Crime, after compiling the findings of several professionals who work with grief in children, theorized that before age five, most children do not realize that all people, including themselves, will die (Emswiler & Emswiler, 2000; McEntire, 2003, & Worden, 1996). A preschool child may talk about death but still may expect the person to come back, or a child who has moved may think that she will be going back to their old room soon. An adult should allow the child to cry, regress, and attach to objects and people. We encourage adults to label the child's feelings and connect the feelings to what is upsetting the child.

Ages Three to Five

In the latter part of Piaget's preoperational stage (ages two to seven), children are given to "magical thinking." They believe that they possess powers that allow them to control the world just by thinking. They are unable to distinguish between thoughts and deeds. In this egocentric stage, they are unable to see another's perspective. Attempting to convince a child in this age range that moving far away to a bigger and better house is a good thing because "Daddy got a great new job" or that his recently deceased grandfather "is in a better place" only muddles an already confused picture in their young minds. It is important for the parents to understand the role of such magical thinking.

According to Goldman (2004), children ages three to five can express logical thoughts and fears about death, conceptualize that all body functions stop, and begin to internalize the universality and permanence of death. Fredlund (1984) reported that children between the ages of four and five years are likely to verbalize about death. Regardless of their increasing ability to conceptualize death as real, children who are from two to seven years old often think that death is reversible. A common explanation for death by young children is that the person went to sleep but will eventually awaken (Metzgar, 2002; Schoen, Burgoyne, & Schoen, 2004). Because of their natural egocentricity, children at this stage also tend to believe that they could have changed the course of events and prevented the person from dying (Fry, 1995). These children may exhibit feelings of sadness, anxiousness, anger, fear, and regression. The adults in their lives should listen to their concerns about loss, prepare them for the consequences of the loss, and allow the children as much choice and control as is feasible.

Ages Five to Nine

In this age range, the child is now moving into the *concrete operational stage* and experiences a reduction of egocentricity and an increased capacity for abstract reasoning. As a response to loss, the child is likely to exhibit feelings of sadness, anxiety, withdrawal, confusion, fear, and worries of being ignored or ostracized. The child may respond with aggression or withdrawal, may have nightmares, and may lack concentration, with a decline in school grades, when faced with a loss.

By age nine or ten, most children have developed an understanding of death as final, irreversible, and inescapable (Emswiler & Emswiler, 2000; McEntire, 2003, & Worden, 1996). However, the cognitive manifestation of feelings of powerlessness associated with a loss can result from an inability to have prevented the loss or change the current situation. A child may draw the conclusion, therefore, that the way he treated his mother somehow accounted for the sudden loss (Schoen, Burgoyne, & Schoen, 2004).

Ages Nine to Twelve

In this *formal operational stage,* children begin to develop the capacity for more abstract thinking and independence from parents. Children at this stage place a great deal of emphasis on their relationships with friends and avoid standing out or being different. Given the onset of higher level thinking and focus on peer relationships, children experiencing a loss during this stage will often begin to ask themselves "What if?" questions. What if the kids at the new school won't like me? What if I don't like my new house? What if I had been there when Dad had his heart attack? Children experiencing a loss during this stage of development often have feelings of sadness, depression, and anxiety. Some characteristics to watch for may be withdrawal, avoidance of verbally expressing feelings, acting out, and reduction in academic performance.

Ages Twelve and Up: Adolescence

Piaget's model is also the lens through which adolescent thinking about loss and death is viewed. Adolescents function in the Piagetian stage of *formal operations.* Theoretically, teens should be capable of abstract and formal thinking, problem solving, and deductive reasoning. At this age, personalities are being integrated. Adolescents can comprehend the concept of death, which serves as a vehicle for more in-depth spiritual and conceptual thought (Gorman, 1972;

Schoen, Burgoyne, & Schoen, 2004). It is important to note that children and adolescents progress through the stages of development at varying rates and that some never reach the level of formal operations. It is therefore important to assess children's cognitive abilities and not make assumptions about their capacity to understand and cope with loss.

BEHAVIORAL RESPONSES TO LOSS

Grief responses of children come in many forms and are as diverse as the children who are experiencing loss. When viewed through a child-centered lens, the five stages of grief in adults, as described by Kübler-Ross (1969), could easily translate to behavioral responses in children. Anger may manifest itself as aggression or verbal expression of angry feelings. Denial could also be characterized by behaviors like aggression or withdrawal—or by a continued fantasized relationship with the lost object or person. Behaviorally, denial could easily look like regression. In the bargaining stage, the child may try to atone for perceived misdeeds in order to bring back the lost loved one. She may promise to "be good," if only Mommy and Daddy will get back together. Similarly, in the guilt stage, often while engaged in the process of magical thinking, the child may feel personally responsible for the loss. A child who is experiencing feelings of guilt may suffer from somatic complaints (headaches, nausea); withdraw from friends, pets, or toys; or act out aggressively (hitting, swearing). In acceptance, the child may be able to discuss the lost person or object in a realistic and healthy way, without an overwhelming sense of grief or sadness.

Some children and adolescents internalize their grief. These children may maintain a relationship with the deceased in a fantasized way. Unfortunately, quiet responses such as this often go unrecognized, and because these children do not manifest any obvious outward symptoms, they may not receive the help they need to cope with their losses.

Other children and adolescents externalize their reactions to loss by acting out. The inability to handle feelings of grief may result in angry outbursts, irritability, sleeping and eating disorders, and persistent questioning about the details of the loss. Other frequent expressions of grief in childhood include fear of personal fallibility, hypochondria, and shock (Schoen, Burgoyne, & Schoen, 2004). Expressions of anger often give adolescents a sense of power to counteract their feelings of helplessness and fear (Glass, 1991).

A SAMPLE INTERVENTION

To illustrate how to translate emotional, cognitive, and behavioral aspects of development into interventions designed to help children and adolescents cope with grief and loss, we offer the "Survival Kit for Moving," described in the following pages. The activities in this kit were designed by students in our grief-and-loss course to give counselors a selection of age-appropriate interventions to help children and adolescents cope with losses associated with moving. Interventions related to other types of losses are included in chapter 11 of this book.

SUMMARY

Viewing childhood and adolescence through a multicultural lens can expand child and adolescent counselors' belief systems to include the importance of accepting children and adolescents as individuals who are part of complex cultures, different from the dominant adult culture. Effective counseling with children and adolescents requires more than an adaptation of skills for adults. Counselors must realize that cultural boundaries need to be negotiated in order to engage with children and adolescents.

Likewise, it is crucial to understand children and adolescent experiences with loss from a developmental perspective. Over time, children develop more realistic ways of thinking about and understanding death and other types of losses. Before the onset of adolescence, however, it is not unusual for children to engage in magical thinking and to feel responsible for the loss of a loved one. Preadolescent children also have a difficult time conceptualizing the permanence of death. A counselor must assess each child's developmental level and capacity to understand and cope with loss in order to carry out the most effective interventions.

In Part I of this book, we discussed definitions of grief, common losses of childhood and adolescence, myths surrounding the ways in which children grieve, and multicultural and developmental aspects of grief and loss in children. In Part II, we will delve further into specific types of losses commonly experienced by children and adolescents, and will provide concrete examples through the analysis of case studies.

SURVIVAL KIT FOR MOVING

The Survival Kit for Moving is intended to enlighten adults—both parents and counselors—about the variety of losses associated with moving and the signs to look for in children reacting to them. It includes several proactive, age-appropriate interventions designed to make the moving process less traumatic.

Interventions in the Survival Kit fall into specific developmental stages. Although the suggestions are categorized by age, many are appropriate for more than one age range—and some may be helpful for adults.

Birth to Age Three

On Leaving the Old Home: Ritual of "Goodbye"

- Move around the home and let the child say or wave goodbye to each room and to outdoor areas.

- Do not wash the child's favorite blanket, bed linens, or stuffed toys before you move.

- For a baby: Carry the baby around the room and sing a soothing goodbye song.

- Three-year-olds can put together a memory box to represent or contain items from the old house. The items might include a piece of wallpaper (look underneath a light switch), a twig from a favorite tree, blades of grass, a flower or a rock, or a piece of carpet or flooring. Adults may also help the child to take Polaroid or digital pictures of favorite places in the yard and each room of the house. It is possible to initiate a conversation about leaving the child's old bedroom or favorite place behind. The adult should try to use at least one "feelings" word—for example, "I am feeling *sad* that I will not be able to sit under this tree anymore—I will miss it."

After you have gathered everything, each item may be placed in a box that the child has decorated. Pictures may be placed in the box or glued to a sheet of poster board. The child can then keep the box or poster in the new room.

On Arrival at the New Home: Ritual of "Hello"

- Repeat the goodbye process at the new home, except the child will now say (or wave) hello. For older children, initiate a conversation about the differences between each house and the child's favorite aspects of each home. This will lead a child to think about positive aspects of the new home or to help discover remaining feelings about the old home. It is also possible to begin a conversation about the fun things that can happen with the new home and yard.

If You Have Already Moved

- You can draw a picture with your child of the old house. Discuss your feelings about the old house and encourage your child to discuss his feelings and a favorite memory about each room. You can then discuss the nice aspects of the new house.

- Allow the child to have as much control as possible over the placement of furniture in his room and other important rooms or pieces of furniture.

Other Tips

- If there are pictures on the refrigerator door, save them and try to place them on the new refrigerator in the same way.

- Three-year-olds are capable of moving some of their own items, such as their toy box or bookcase, to a special place in their new room.

Ages Three to Five

On Leaving the Old Home

- Use a play situation to address the child's concerns. Allow the child to pack the furniture from his or her doll house or a cherished set of action figures, Matchbox cars, or the like, wrapping each piece with care with tissues or bubblewrap and placing it carefully in a packing box (an empty shoe box works well), just as Mommy and Daddy have packed their belongings. Allow the child to decide whether to place the box on the moving truck or to carry it to the new house in the car. Watch carefully for items that are given special care, and acknowledge the child's feelings—for example, "You wrapped the little girl's bed with extra tissue so it won't break. That must be very important to you."

On Arrival at the New Home

- Sit on the floor with the child and the empty dollhouse or book-shelf and give her the option of deciding how to arrange the prized possessions. Watch carefully and acknowledge the child's preferences. For example, if the child indicates a specific object, ask, "Where would you like to put it?" When she completes the task, give the child as much control as possible over arranging furniture in her own room.

Other Tips

- If you are moving nearby, you might prepare the child by visiting the new home prior to the move. If it's an option, allow the child as much input as possible into the selection of his own bedroom.
- Visits to the new grocery store, library, and playground will assure the child that the familiar things in life haven't gone away—they are just in a different place.
- Ask the child to talk with her puppets, allowing her to tell the puppets they are about to move. Listen carefully to the concerns the child raises with the puppets—they may be a reflection of the child's concerns.

Ages Five to Nine

On Leaving the Old Home

- Collect the telephone numbers and e-mail addresses of old friends so the children can keep in touch with them. Take pictures of the child's friends at a party or as they participate in activities.
- Call ahead and arrange a visit to the new school.
- Collect seedlings and plantings from around the house and garden.

On Arrival at the New Home

- Arrange for sleepovers (of old friends, if possible).
- Put together a scrapbook of old and new friends.
- Arrange for inclusion in familiar activities at the new school (for example, band, sports, dance).
- Re-root seedlings and plantings around the new house.
- Be proactive in introducing yourself to your new neighbors and their children.

Ages Nine to Twelve

On Leaving the Old Home

- Given the importance of peer relationships to children this age, conduct an activity involving the child's friends. Invite several of the child's best friends over for a going-away sleepover party.

Request that these children bring as many pictures as possible of the kids together from different occasions in the past. At the party, explain that the children may put together a collage of pictures for the departing child. Doing so will allow the child time to talk with friends about memorable experiences in the past and concerns about moving. At the end of the party, have the children exchange e-mail addresses, phone numbers, and home addresses. This will help the child stay in touch with his or her current friends and help preserve the children's peer support system.

NOTE: If you wish, you can have color copies of the collage made and then send them, with a note from the child, to the children who attended the party.

Other Tips

- Bring the child to the new school for a tour and to set up the child's schedule.
- Investigate the existence of activities that include some of the child's current hobbies (for instance, sports, band, clubs).
- Tour the new community for activity and recreation centers (for example, swimming pools, community centers, parks, shopping malls).
- Continue with daily family routines as much as possible.
- Listen and provide answers to the child's questions.

On Arrival at the New Home

- When arriving at the new home, help the child find a special place in her room to hang the collage.
- Continue daily routines.
- Continue to listen and respond to the child's concerns about moving.
- Introduce the child to neighbors.
- Go with the child to sign up for familiar activities at school and in the community.
- Inquire about new student helper programs in the new school district.
- Invite the child's friends to the new home for a sleepover, if possible.

Ages Twelve and Up: Adolescence

On Leaving the Old Home

Photo Album. During the weeks leading up to the move, children of any age can use a disposable or digital camera to take photographs of any familiar sights that have been important to them, including both people and places. It is a good idea for the child to have access to the camera for at least a week so that she can document anything that has significance. This may include the child's home, school, park, or favorite tree, as well as less obvious choices, like the grocery store, mall, library, or mail carrier. One child wanted to remember a particular stretch of highway driven numerous times each day as the family traveled from their home to other locations. Another child's family frequently went sledding down a particular hill. This activity is personal, undertaken from the child's perspective, and as such is highly individualized.

These pictures can be put in a photo album or affixed to the pages of a scrapbook. If the child wishes, leave room for text to explain why this picture has been included: An expression of this private reasoning is perhaps the most important part of the process.

On Arrival at the New Home

Photo Album (Continued). Provide the adolescent with another camera to take more photographs once the move to the new home has taken place. He or she can use the photographs in the original book as a guide and then take pictures of parallel items at the new home and neighborhood. The adolescent can place the new pictures next to the old and describe what is the same and what is different. Expression of both positive and negative comparisons is helpful.

The Next Best Thing. In this activity, the adolescent packages up items that serve as reminders of past events and experiences. The package for "The Next Best Thing to a Sleepover" might include, for example, microwave popcorn, a copy of favorite CDs or videos, and beauty tips torn from old magazines with a few dollar-store makeup items. The adolescent sends the package to a friend at the old location, along with a letter asking the friend to use the disposable camera (also enclosed) to take pictures of herself and other friends having fun with these items. The friend then returns another box, including the pictures taken with the camera, items for a new "Next Best Thing" experience, another disposable camera, and instructions to the original friend to take pictures of the new experience and return a new box. An exchange of packages of this kind allows the friends to remain connected, while creating new and special memories to share. Other ideas for "Next Best Thing" events are a picnic, shopping trip, trick-or-treating, camping trip, rainy-day afternoon, and birthday party.

PART II

Types of Losses and Interventions

CHAPTER 4

Intangible Losses

Eight-year-old Diana and her family returned to their home after a long weekend away with relatives. Diana was exhausted after the long, busy weekend spent playing with her many cousins, so she slept most of the way home. She made her parents promise to wake her up as soon as the lights and skyline of her hometown came into view. Although she enjoyed being away, she loved coming home even more, and the sight of her city coming into view always made her feel happy and relieved. When her family pulled into the driveway, Diana jumped from the car in anticipation of sleeping in her very own bed and petting her cat, Skittles. No one was prepared for what awaited them inside. The first thing they noticed was that the lock on the door was broken. When they walked inside, they saw that the house had been completely trashed and was littered with debris. Their computer, TV, and other appliances had been stolen, and no room was left unscathed, including Diana's. Her favorite necklace, which her grandmother had given her, was missing, and her belongings were strewn all over the floor. It has been two months since the robbery, and Diana continues to feel unsafe in her own home. She refuses to play outside, will not sleep alone in her bedroom, cries often, and tells her parents she wants to move and might not ever want to go on a trip again for fear of bad things happening. Diana feels completely violated.

When we think of helping children cope with grief and loss, we often mistakenly focus on the most obvious presenting loss. For example, if a person dies, we help the child cope with the feelings directly related to the death of that person. We look for and expect to find certain emotions and behaviors, such as sadness, crying, and with-drawal. In our experience, however, the intangible losses that often surround the primary loss are both most crucial to treat and most diffi-cult to discover, unless you know what to look for. Such intangible losses might include the loss of a sense of safety after a child's home has been robbed, as in the opening case study, or the sense of betrayal felt after your trust has been violated.

In Part II of this book, we provide case examples that will help counselors and parents identify and treat the intangible losses that inevitably accompany larger loss experiences. Case studies provide examples of grief and loss experiences encountered by children and adolescents. Each case study will be accompanied by (a) an assessment of the primary, secondary, and intangible losses experienced by the clients; (b) a discussion of their cognitive, behavioral, and emotional responses to the situation; and (c) a sample clinical intervention, described in the words of someone involved in treating the child or adolescent. The intangible losses we describe include loss of innocence, safety and security, trust, power, control, stability, and faith and/or hope. We also discuss preexisting losses.

Case 1: Innocence—"Racism Rears Its Ugly Head"

Wanda, a 16-year-old African American, has lived in her predomi-nantly white small town since her family moved there when she was in first grade. She has many friends, is a class officer, and is on the high honor roll at her high school. Several months ago, Wanda began dating a young man, Dan, who is of Polish descent and who is a junior in high school. Dan and Wanda have liked one another for some time, but Dan never took the step to ask her out. Finally, Wanda took the lead and suggested that they start dating. Everything ran smoothly until Wanda noticed that Dan never wanted to hang around his friends when he was with her. In fact, he would completely ignore her when he was with his friends at school. She also thought it was odd that Dan never introduced her to his family, even though he had met her family and been at her house many times. When confronted, Dan would say that he "liked keeping Wanda as his own little secret."

Recently, Wanda decided to surprise Dan by bringing him a bouquet of balloons and a gift for his birthday. She arrived at his house to deliver the gifts. After she rang the doorbell, she stood waiting for what seemed to her to be an enormous amount of time. She heard an adult's voice yell out that there was some n***** on the porch. At the sound of the racial slur, Wanda felt as though she had been punched in the stomach. Soon after, Dan came to the door with his father immediately behind him and addressed her as though she were a stranger delivering flowers. He wouldn't make eye contact with her, then turned to his father and said, "No card, must be from my secret admirer," and closed the door. Wanda stood looking at the closed door for several minutes in a state of utter shock. After a few minutes, she saw the curtain move and Dan peek his head around it, winking and mouthing, "Thank you."

Dan has tried to talk to Wanda repeatedly since this episode, but she refuses to return his calls. Wanda's mother is very concerned about her. She doesn't know what went on between her daughter and Dan, but she has noticed that Wanda is acting very differently since coming home in tears after she delivered the gift. When she tries to talk to Wanda about what happened, Wanda says that she and Dan broke up. Wanda's mother suspects there is much more to the story because she has noticed significant changes in Wanda's behaviors. She has quit many of the clubs that she was involved in, has uncharacteristically missed several days of school, and has begun to distance herself from even longtime friends. Her grooming has also changed for the worse, and she has begun to refer to herself as ugly. Wanda's mother has called to ask you, the counselor, to see her daughter.

Case Analysis

Identifying the Primary Loss

Wanda's primary loss is the loss of her innocence.

Identifying Secondary and Intangible Losses

The loss of the relationship with Dan can be characterized as a secondary loss because the impact of losing the relationship is not as profound as Wanda's loss of innocence and feelings of betrayal. Wanda also has many other secondary losses. They include loss of trust, dignity, safety, her worldview, identity, and community. "Are my other friends and their families thinking of me in that way, too?" she wonders.

Identifying the Client's Responses to the Loss Situation

Cognitive. Although no specific cognitive losses are documented in this case study, the counselor should be wary of all-or-nothing thinking, egocentrism, and suicidal ideation—cognitive responses that are characteristic of both loss and adolescent thinking. Wanda's current view of herself as ugly may be a sign of internalized racism.

Behavioral. Wanda is isolating herself from her community, school, friends, and family. She is also not maintaining good hygiene, which in all likelihood is a behavioral manifestation of her emotional state and, at a primitive level, keeps people away.

Emotional. Wanda's poor hygiene, a behavioral response, could be indicative of her current affective state. In essence, she is saying, "I am not worth basic caretaking," a belief consistent with her referring to herself as ugly. She feels ugly. She also feels alone, hurt, angry, scared, and worthless. In addition, she may have fear of ever initiating a relationship again. Look what happened when she did.

Discussion Questions

1. How would you help Wanda cope with this racist encounter?
2. Do you think Wanda was adequately prepared for the realities of racism in our society?
3. How would you help Wanda recover her feelings of self-worth?
4. In what ways could Wanda's mother help her?

The Counselor's Response

It is imperative that I earn Wanda's trust, but establishing rapport and a trusting relationship will be quite a challenge. Wanda has been betrayed by her boyfriend and may be suspicious of pending betrayals. She may also feel betrayed by her family or friends for not preparing her for the pain that she is experiencing. Last, but maybe most important, I am white. Why would she trust me?

I would go about establishing a warm, safe, trusting relationship with Wanda by acknowledging the obvious. I would share with her that her mother told me what had happened with Dan. I would invite questions and corrections from Wanda repeatedly so that she could feel that her view and words mattered. I would use reflective listening if she offered any verbal reactions. In addition, I would make sure that I was keenly aware of any body language—facial expressions and so forth—and respond to those with reflection as well. I would immediately put Wanda in the role of the expert, framing my reflections as guesses and hunches. I would overtly state, "Although I do have a clue what it is like to be a teenage girl, I have no idea what it is like to be African American." It is my intention that this would bring the issue of race into the session in a concrete and overt way and demonstrate to Wanda that in this place we can talk about race and racism out in the open.

In the very first session, I want to assess Wanda for depression, suicidal ideation, and self-injury. I am concerned that she is overwhelmed with anger and pain. This would be an ongoing assessment.

When trust has been established, our sessions would include a variety of interventions to help Wanda express her pain. I would not limit our sessions to verbal exchange but would invite Wanda to participate in sand-play therapy, narrative assignments, and role plays. Any play-therapy interventions would be altered to reflect the developmental considerations of a 16-year-old. The intention is to afford Wanda multiple ways to tell her story, to experience her pain without being overwhelmed, and to gain insight. The primary goal is to help Wanda express her feelings, not to debunk her perceptions. I am aware that as a result of a counselor's own feelings of guilt, if the counselor is white, a counselor may mistakenly try to tell her "not all white people are that way" or attempt to turn the counseling session into a social lesson instead of focusing on Wanda's feelings. If the counselor were a person of color, it might be helpful to provide therapeutic self-disclosure and share examples of how the counselor has developed strategies to combat racism in his or her life.

I would also try to connect Wanda with a support network of individuals who can help her in her quest for racial identity in a predominantly white school. Other students of color or recent graduates may be positive role models for her. I would suggest that Wanda engage in bibliotherapy. Books like Toni Morrison's *The Bluest Eye* (2000) would be helpful; so would books on race relations that might help to normalize her situation and help her find her place in the broader social context. *The Skin I'm In: A First Look at Racism*, by Pat Thomas (2003), is a great resource for younger children. Last, I would try to facilitate communication between mother and daughter. Each has experienced deep pain as a result of this incident. Wanda's mother probably feels that she let her child down by being unable to protect her from the realities of racism. Wanda may feel angry that Mom sheltered her too much and did not prepare her for the prejudice she might face in the "real world." This incident, although incredibly painful, can serve as a catalyst for mother and daughter to open up dialogue that may have been too uncomfortable to approach in the past. As the counselor, I can help facilitate this dialogue. Together, Wanda and her mother can examine the impact of racism on their lives and become a support system for each other—and perhaps for others in their community.

Case 2: Safety and Security—"The Big Teddy Bear"

Nick is a 13-year-old who has always enjoyed being in school. He is a rather large kid, not overweight, but taller and bigger than most of his peers. Some of his classmates call him the "gentle giant." His mother says he is her "big teddy bear." He grew up with an alcoholic father who abused Nick, his younger siblings, and his mother until his parents divorced when he was in fourth grade. Nick is a gentle soul, but he hates his father and refuses to see him. Nick has always held a protective role in his family and describes how he used to "take on" his father to distract abuse away from his mother and siblings. After his father left the house, Nick swore he would never raise his fist to anyone again. He was determined never to become like his father.

For Nick, school always represented a safe haven. It was his sanctuary; he would stay after to help the teachers, talk to the janitorial staff, or work on the stage crew for drama and musical productions. Nick regularly stopped by the guidance office to check in and say hi. Two things have recently happened in Nick's life that have shaken his predictable world. First, his mother started dating a new man and spontaneously married him after a weekend trip to Las Vegas. Although he has been nothing but kind, this man reminds Nick of his father to a remarkable degree. They look very much alike and have similar mannerisms. Although the man has never acted aggressively toward Nick, Nick feels himself cowering, flinching, and becoming defensive each time his new stepfather approaches him or even touches him affectionately on the shoulder.

Worst of all, since school began this fall, Nick has become the target of a bully, Chuck, who moved into the district over the summer. When Chuck arrived at the school, he noticed Nick and mentioned to a friend that he looked like a tough kid. The kid explained that although Nick was a big kid, he was "kind of a wimp." After that, Chuck began to taunt Nick in the hallways, in gym, and, worst of all, after school. One day after school, Nick arrived at the guidance office shaking and breathing hard. The school counselor led him to her office and tried to calm him through what appeared to be a severe panic attack. "I'm not going to let him do this to me again," he said with clenched fists. The counselor was not sure to whom he was referring.

Case Analysis

Identifying the Primary Loss

Nick's primary loss is the loss of knowing what to expect.

Identifying Secondary and Intangible Losses

The other losses Nick is experiencing include a loss of stability, consistency, power, and control. He may also be feeling identity confusion as a result of his own angry reaction. He may be asking himself, "Am I really a nice person, or is it a facade? Am I really my father?"

Identifying the Client's Responses to the Loss Situation

Cognitive. Cognitively, Nick has regressed to a time when he felt it was his job to protect his mother from his father. His thinking is markedly confused. He may also wonder, "What is wrong with me?" He has exhibited symptoms of a panic attack and may fear having more.

Behavioral. Like his cognitive response, Nick's behavioral response is characterized by regression. Nick's behavior is characteristic of previous developmental periods and his past relationships. He currently behaves in ways that resemble his responses in his past relationship with his father years ago—trembling, hiding, and withdrawing.

Emotional. Nick is overwhelmed by fear and anxiety. He is scared, confused, and alarmed.

Discussion Questions

1. How would you help Nick identify what is going on in his life?
2. How does Nick's past history play into his current struggles?
3. What suggestions do you have for Nick's mom in helping her to help Nick?

The Counselor's Response

My first task is to get Nick through his panic attack. I will ask Nick to tell me what time it is and then suggest that he will be feeling calmer in about 10 minutes. (A panic attack rarely lasts longer than 10 minutes; Maxmen & Ward, 1995.) In addition, I hope that my suggestion will become internalized.

In order to invite Nick to share what is going on with him, I would tell him that I am confused about who and what he is talking about. If I have an established relationship and am aware of Nick's past, I would use this opportunity to help Nick make some connections regarding how overwhelmed he is presently. I would be careful not to use words to describe him like *fear, frightened,* or *afraid.* These could be "button-pushing" words that would immediately require him to defend himself. If I can keep his defensiveness to a minimum, then I can insert gentle confrontations and hunches into our conversation. For instance, I might say, "I wonder if I was confused as to who you were talking about because I was thinking Chuck reminded you of your dad."

I would continue to meet with Nick to check in regularly for the next few weeks. If there are additional panic attacks or an escalation in his anxiety or aggression, I would refer him to a counselor or therapist outside of school. At that time, I would encourage his mom to do some work with Nick. I would suggest that family counseling might be a good intervention because they all have some major adjusting to do. On the other hand, if Nick demonstrates an ability to contain his anxiety and function without impairment in school, I would reinforce the notion that he can visit me and let me know how things are going on his own terms.

Case 3: Trust—"You Promised Not to Tell!"

Thirteen-year old Carynn made her best friend, Reilly, promise. She had no reason to believe that Reilly would not keep the secret. The two had been best friends for the past two years (since fifth grade) and knew many private things about each other. Carynn knew when Reilly had her first period, that Reilly's brother got caught stealing from school, and that Reilly's mom and dad did not get married until after Reilly's brother was born. Carynn did not think twice about telling Reilly what had happened while she was at basketball camp.

Carynn loved basketball, and from all reports she had some talent. With help from a local charity, Carynn was able to attend a special basketball camp. Carynn was very excited and a little nervous because the camp was two hours from her hometown. She had a great time, worked hard, and made a lot of new friends. One of her friends was actually more like a boyfriend, according to Carynn. Andy, 18, was an assistant coach-counselor. Carynn told Reilly about how nice and cute he was. The big secret was that Carynn, as she put it, "let Andy do stuff to her." Reilly was not sure if Carynn meant sex, so she asked. Carynn made Reilly swear not to tell anyone because Andy had made Carynn swear and said he would say she was lying if she ever told.

Reilly was upset that her friend had had sex. It seemed exciting, but she knew she was not ready and was worried about Carynn.

Reilly talked about it with her mom. After the shock, Reilly's mom, a caseworker and therefore someone mandated to report child abuse, did so. Later that week, Andy was arrested, and his mug shot was shown on the news. Carynn was horrified, scared, and mostly ticked off. How could Reilly have done this to her?

Case Analysis

Identifying the Primary Loss

Carynn's primary loss is the loss of being able to trust her friend.

Identifying Secondary and Intangible Losses

Carynn is likely experiencing several secondary losses as well. Her image of friendship is shattered, and she is no longer able to interact with Reilly's mother. She has also been stigmatized by the arrest of her "boyfriend." Also, she does not appear to recognize it yet, but she has been victimized by an 18-year-old man who should have been looking out for her; thus she has experienced a loss of trust. She has lost her innocence to this person, and she was threatened about disclosing the abusive relationship.

Identifying the Client's Responses to the Loss Situation

Cognitive. At this point, Carynn can think only in concrete, black-and-white terms. She thinks her friend has betrayed her, and she feels violated.

Behavioral. Carynn has responded to Reilly by becoming angry. She might be expected to cry, yell, or ignore her friend. She might also act angrily with other friends and family. Another possibility is that she may try to get in contact with her "boyfriend."

Emotional. By far, Carynn is most likely to be emotionally affected by this experience. She will probably feel angry, betrayed, hurt, confused, and embarrassed. She may begin to doubt all of her relationships and lack a sense of trust.

Discussion Questions

1. How do you begin your intervention with Carynn?
2. What personal feelings emerge from you as you review the case?
3. How do you describe confidentiality and being a mandated reporter to Carynn?
4. How do you earn Carynn's trust?

The Counselor's Response

It is always difficult to establish a relationship with a client whose trust has been violated. For this reason, I would take great care in establishing rapport with Carynn. Our first instinct is to protect children, so it would not be surprising for a counselor to have a strong negative reaction to Carynn's camp counselor. He preyed on this young, inexperienced girl, used her for sex, and then made her swear to keep it all a secret. These are the classic hallmarks of a sexual predator. It would be very easy, then, to launch into a lecture about how Carynn needs to protect herself from "boys like this." I would avoid doing so; rather, I would listen sympathetically to Carynn's story and her feelings, and keep my own values at bay.

One problem is that the client is a 13-year-old girl. From her perspective, she was in a relationship with this man and may even think she is in love. Denigrating him to her would therefore be counterproductive to the counseling relationship and might result in her aligning herself more strongly with him. It would be wiser to build a trusting relationship with Carynn, educate her about healthy relationships, and help her eventually to examine whether the experience she had with her coach-counselor qualifies as a relationship. I could then provide information for Carynn about protecting herself physically, emotionally, and sexually. On the other hand, Carynn might also now feel that sex and sex acts are dirty because the camp counselor was arrested. There may be a lot of confusion about her sexual identity: Is she "dirty" or "bad" because of what she did? These and other issues are important to explore.

It would be crucial also to explore Carynn's feelings about Reilly and to acknowledge her feelings of mistrust and betrayal, maybe by encouraging her to write a letter about how she feels. After Carynn has had an opportunity to have her voice heard, she and I can break down what happened into smaller parts and examine each. Carynn could put herself in Reilly's shoes and imagine how she might have been feeling. An empty-chair technique might be useful in this situation. Carynn can explore Reilly's motivations for talking with her mother and examine why Reilly may have been concerned about her. It would be important not to push her into reconciling with Reilly, while at the same time allowing her to examine what real friendship means. In time, if Carynn is in a place where she would like to resume her friendship with Reilly, I might recommend one or more joint sessions to facilitate the reconciliation.

Case 4: Power and Control—"Why Is He Acting This Way?"

Alexandros has just entered prekindergarten, and his parents are very concerned. Alex had always been a very happy child. He was the only child of professional parents. His maternal grandparents lived two doors down and provided a great deal of the child care since Alexandros had been born.

The concern is that Alex is refusing to participate in any activities at school. He has been behaving aggressively and has been biting other children. Although Alex is bilingual, at school he refuses to speak English and will converse only in Greek. Alexandros's parents are beside themselves. They feel guilty about not beginning his socialization process earlier. They are worried that he is truly spoiled.

Alex's father thinks that perhaps Alex's grandmother has been overindulgent and that Alexandros is used to always having his way. This has been an ongoing issue with his mother-in-law, but they cannot beat the price and comfort of having someone in the family care for him. He doesn't want to say this in front of his wife, but he calls you to tell you his feelings.

Case Analysis

Identifying the Primary Loss

Alex's primary loss is the loss of the one-on-one attention he is used to receiving from his nana.

Identifying Secondary and Intangible Losses

In transitioning to prekindergarten, Alex is experiencing several secondary and intangible losses. He has lost his routine and sense of stability. He is no longer receiving the unconditional love he is used to receiving from his grandmother. He has to share and learn to interact with complete strangers, and he doesn't like that. He has lost power and control over his situation.

Identifying the Client's Responses to the Loss Situation

Cognitive. Alex may think that if he is "bad," he will be able to go back to staying with Nana. He may think that he is being punished by being sent to prekindergarten.

Behavioral. Behaviorally, Alex is acting out aggressively with the other children and refusing to participate at school. He also refuses to speak English at school, which may signify an attempt to gain control where he has none—through regression.

Emotional. Alex is very angry. He is confused and does not understand why he is being ripped away from his familiar routine with his grandmother and being forced to share and interact with these other children. He may feel abandoned by Nana.

Discussion Questions

1. What is your strategy for working with Alexandros?
2. What if he won't speak to you in English, and you do not speak Greek?
3. How would you handle Alex's dad's secret phone call?

The Counselor's Response

Alex's life has been thrown into chaos, and he is seeking to regain power and control over it the only way he can. Ironically, adults think that most children will be excited to go to school and interact with other children. Imagine what a frightening proposition this is, though, to a child who has spent the majority of time at home without much social interaction with peers. Picture the seeming chaos of entering a room with 15 to 20 strange children, several unrecognizable adults, and a variety of routines, sights, and sounds that are unfamiliar to you. You are used to having your toys all to yourself, but here children grab things from you and tell the teacher if you grab them back or want to keep playing with your toys. You have no idea why Mommy and Nana have left you here. You think they might be mad at you and punishing you for being bad, but you can't remember doing anything wrong. You think that maybe they will forget you, and you will have to stay here with these people forever. When looking at the situation from a child's perspective, then, Alex's behaviors make perfect sense.

Before counseling Alex, I would inform his father that I intended to share the information about the close relationship with Nana with Alex's mother so that everyone would be on the same page. I would avoid laying blame and using words like *spoiled* and simply work with Alex's parents to help them understand why Alex might be acting this way. In counseling Alex, it would be important to allow him to have freedom and control in the counseling sessions to avoid replicating the very problems he is experiencing at school. This would mean allowing him to speak Greek, even if I have no idea what he is saying. I would use a play-therapy approach with Alex, allowing him to tell his story and express his feelings and needs through his play. By allowing Alex a safe place to express himself, he will be less likely to feel the need to express his anger through aggression in school. Most of all, I would reassure Alex's parents that children need time to adjust and that Alex's problems are understandable and likely to remit once he realizes that Mommy and Nana will come back.

Case 5: Stability—"A Life of Chaos"

Luanne loves her mommy and misses her greatly. She is quick to inform you, her counselor, that she will be seeing her mom now on Tuesdays and Thursdays. Eight years old, Luanne has had a rough life by any definition. You have been working as her counselor over the past year. Referred for acting-out behaviors, Luanne has been provocative with other children and adults. She says and does many inappropriate things that are often linked to sexual knowledge and are always "adult." She cries easily and has difficulty paying attention, and her hygiene is poor.

Her case history reads like a nightmare, but familiar story lines and themes persist throughout. At age three, Luanne disclosed being sexually abused by her mother's boyfriend. Quite bright and verbal, Luanne's allegation was founded, and she was removed from the care of her mother until other arrangements could be made regarding the perpetrator. Luanne lived in foster care for nine months. She reunited with her mother in a new apartment in a new town. Her mother also had a new boyfriend. Luanne began Head Start that year.

As Luanne turned four, her mother informed her that her current boyfriend was leaving and that they would be moving in with Luanne's maternal grandparents because "Mommy was going to have a baby." Luanne wanted to know if the baby would have a daddy because she did not. Indeed, the baby's father was Luanne's mom's former boyfriend and Luanne's abuser.

Living with her parents did not work out for Luanne's mom, so three months after Luanne's brother, Jeff, was born, they moved out. Luanne was still involved in the Head Start program, but now she was changing locations.

Fast-forward three years, when you begin your work with Luanne. She is now in her third elementary school because she, Jeff, and her mom have moved several times. Five months ago, Luanne's mom was scared about her own mental condition and voluntarily put both Luanne and Jeff in foster care. Sister and brother were separated in the process, but last week they were reunited in a single foster care home. They are scheduled to return to the care of their mother in eight weeks.

Case Analysis

Identifying the Primary Loss

Luanne's primary loss is the loss of her sense of safety and stability.

Identifying Secondary and Intangible Losses

Luanne has suffered many losses as a by-product of her frequent moves. She has had to continually readjust to new people, schools, and situations. Her needs have always taken a backseat to her mother's needs. She also suffered abuse and a loss of innocence at the hands of at least one of Mom's boyfriends.

Identifying the Client's Responses to the Loss Situation

Cognitive. Luanne is likely to be very confused and may view the world with a nomadic perception. She may have come to expect frequent changes and may be reluctant to become attached to anyone or anything. On the other hand, she may overidentify with others in an attempt to find a "home"—a stable environment.

Behavioral. Behaviorally, Luanne is acting out her confusion and sense of loss. She attempts to make connections the only way she knows how and is rebuffed. She acts out and is very "sensitive." This is a child in pain.

Emotional. Emotionally, Luanne is confused, sad, angry, hurt, and desperate to connect with others.

Discussion Questions

1. How have instability and insecurity played a part in forming Luanne's worldview?
2. What are the possible interventions that you would use?
3. How would you address issues like cancellations and termination with Luanne?

The Counselor's Response

Any counselor assigned to a child with an unstable history such as Luanne's has to be extremely cautious in providing her with a sense of normality and routine. A counselor who might be moving or going on maternity leave should not take a case with a child who needs consistency. It is important to note that the relationship with the counselor may represent the most consistent relationship Luanne has ever had. This relationship can become the model for how to develop and maintain a healthy relationship. Luanne needs care—she needs an advocate who will make sure that her hygiene needs are met. She needs to understand boundaries, personal space issues, and the difference between appropriate and inappropriate behaviors. She needs the basic knowledge about social skills that each of us takes for granted.

Luanne also needs a place where she can express herself freely. I would provide Luanne with opportunities to explore her strengths and find her voice so that she can ask for what she needs. Luanne also needs strategies to help her handle her emotions and not become overwhelmed by them. Self-regulating strategies, such as guided imagery or relaxation techniques, could prove to be very effective tools for her when she feels out of control. More than anything, Luanne needs consistency. I would strongly advocate that Luanne maintain a foster care placement for an extended period of time. If she is reunited with Mom, there needs to be a plan in place to allow Luanne to continue at her current school and to continue with counseling.

I would recommend that both the foster family and Luanne's family of origin receive specific parenting training to allow them to anticipate and deal with Luanne's needs. With any child who has suffered multiple losses, it is important to put a great deal of planning into the termination process. Luanne should have plenty of fore-warning when her case is about to close, as well as the opportunity to gradually reduce the treatment rather than receiving an abrupt goodbye. I could possibly involve Luanne in a going-away ceremony of some sort like the "Goodbye, Cookie Jar" activity (see chapter 11). Through the termination process, Luanne will be able to see that relationships can end in a positive way. This will serve as a model for her when future relationships come to a natural conclusion.

Case 6: Faith and Hope—"The Eternal Optimist"

Twelve-year-old Natalie has always been an optimist. She is a strong believer in free choice and a person's ability to change the world. This outlook has been nurtured and perpetuated by her grandfather, who has raised her since she was an infant. Her mother signed custody of Natalie over to Natalie's grandfather when she was born. Natalie's mother has been in and out of mental hospitals prior to and since

Natalie's birth. Natalie has a vague recollection of visiting her mother in a mental institution when she was much younger. It was a scary experience for her. Natalie's grandmother died several years ago. Natalie visited her in the hospital quite often throughout a prolonged illness. Since then, Natalie and Papa have lived together on their own. Natalie and Papa spend evenings reading together and discussing politics. At the encouragement of her grandfather, Natalie has written several letters to the editor to express her views on various subjects and has joined advocacy groups such as Amnesty International.

Of her own volition, Natalie recently began volunteering at a local nursing home. She visits elderly residents and reads to them on a regular basis after school. She has been appalled at the conditions at the home. Although no one is being overtly mistreated, the whole atmosphere seems sterile and cold to Natalie. She has become particularly close to one resident named Phyllis. When Phyllis and Natalie first met, Phyllis was a feisty woman of 89 who had just arrived at the facility. Over the months, Natalie has noted a change in Phyllis. She seems very sad, and all the life has gone out of her. At the same time, Natalie's grandfather has noted a sharp change in Natalie's usual optimistic personality. She does not seem interested in current events. Even when her grandfather reads specific news stories that he knows would normally get Natalie's ire up, she seems uninterested. When Papa asks, "Doesn't that just make you want to write a letter?" she responds, "Why bother?" "What's the point?" or "Nothing I can do will make a difference anyway." Papa is very concerned about Natalie's uncharacteristic lethargy and apathy. When he confronts Natalie, she cries, "Oh, Papa, Phyllis doesn't want to live anymore. She wants me to help her kill herself. Nothing I say helps. I'm useless!"

Case Analysis

Identifying the Primary Loss

Natalie's primary loss is the loss of her sense that the world is fair.

Identifying Secondary and Intangible Losses

Natalie is also experiencing the loss of her own sense of power and control and learning once again that people she cares about die and then leave her.

Identifying the Client's Responses to the Loss Situation

Cognitive. Natalie was raised to be thoughtful, but her cognitive style is not working now. She cannot write a letter or deal practically with an experience that is emotionally based. Natalie is also realizing that Papa does not have all the answers and is not always right.

Behavioral. Natalie is less energetic and engaged in things that were once important to her.

Emotional. Apathy, guilt, fear, and despair characterize Natalie's current emotional response.

Discussion Questions

1. What is contributing to Natalie's sense of hopelessness?
2. How do Natalie's past losses contribute to her current pain?
3. How would you involve Natalie's grandfather in the counseling process?
4. How would you counsel Natalie to help her work through her losses?

The Counselor's Response

Natalie has experienced major losses in her life connected to her mother and grandmother. How those losses were handled and experienced will affect her current and future experiences of loss (James & Friedman, 2001). The loss of Natalie's mother and grandmother were both connected to an institution—a mental hospital and a hospital, respectively. Now Natalie is again close to an institutionalized woman. She fears a goodbye. It's as if her loss antennae are up.

Getting historical information from Natalie would be helpful in terms of case formulation, but I want to use it here to get a sense of Natalie's world through Natalie's eyes. It is my hunch that Natalie has yet to deal with her historical losses. Together, we can learn what worked, what did not, and what she needs. This information will dictate the course of her counseling intervention.

Additionally, it is critical that grandfather be involved. He is her primary support, and without his input it is likely that gains in counseling will be short-lived or never truly obtained. I would have at least one meeting with Natalie's grandfather alone to get a sense of where he is in the grieving process and what he thinks Natalie needs. It is my feeling that caregivers often have incredible insight into children but doubt themselves and defer to the counseling professional. I do not want to set up that dynamic here. What I want to do is use a positive asset search (Ivey & Ivey, 2003) to help Natalie and her grandfather see their strengths and then use those skills they already have. It would also be helpful to use bibliotherapy to help Natalie learn about the death of loved ones. *The Fall of Freddie the Leaf* (Buscaglia, 1982) would be particularly useful. *When Dinosaurs Die: A Guide to Understanding Death* (Brown & Brown, 1996) is an excellent resource for younger children.

Case 7: Preexisting Loss—"I Miss Nana"

Leah's paternal grandmother died five years before she was born. When Leah was three years old, precocious and quite verbal, she wanted to know how people in her family were connected. For example, she understood that Grandma Hot was "Mama's mommy," Tia was "Mama's sister," and Aunt Kitten was "Dadden's sister." Following this reasoning and questioning, Leah became confused. "Who's Dadden's mommy?" she asked. "How come Papa doesn't have a wife?"

Leah's parents struggled to give Leah developmentally appropriate answers. They supplied her with pictures of Nana. They talked with Leah about what Nana was like. Over the past two years, Leah has not only regularly asked more about Nana but also has expressed that she misses her.

Her parents have grown more concerned about Leah lately. She asks for Nana several times a week. During these requests, she cries and exhibits regressive behavior. Her parents are not sure whether these behaviors are connected, but Leah has trouble sleeping and, at five years old, rarely makes it through the night without needing to be reassured. She wants to make and buy presents for Nana.

Case Analysis

Identifying the Primary Loss

Leah's primary loss is the loss of a relationship with a grandmother she never knew.

Identifying Secondary and Intangible Losses

Leah has lost her sense that the world is equal and fair. There is a piece missing in her life that she cannot explain.

Identifying the Client's Responses to the Loss Situation

Cognitive. Leah has missed out on a relationship that she feels entitled to. She sees the connection that should exist between people—Dadden should have a mommy—and for her the picture is incomplete.

Behavioral. Leah has reacted to her loss by crying and exhibiting regressive behaviors. She needs reassurance and has trouble sleeping through the night. She expresses the desire to buy Nana gifts.

Emotional. Leah is confused and afraid. Her sense of balance and justice has been upset. She misses the opportunity to connect with a loved one who was taken from her without her knowledge, control, or understanding.

Discussion Questions

1. Should Leah's parents be concerned?
2. What are your feelings about preexisting loss?
3. How does spirituality play a role here?

The Counselor's Response

A bright, precocious child, Leah may have stumbled into a situation that many of her age-mates have not even contemplated. Leah needs to make sense of her world. She has been able to make sense of her surroundings until this discovery. Everything has been congruent to her thus far. At some level, she is frightened because she has lost understanding of what is around her. Confusion from this may cause some of the fear she experiences at night.

She is surrounded by people who love her, and each has a mate or partner. She is confused as to why Papa has no wife and Dadden has no mommy. After all, in Leah's eyes, grandfathers are supposed to have wives. When she discovers that Papa did indeed have a wife but that she is no longer with him, she sees imbalance. To a five-year-old, this situation does not compute. She discovers that she was supposed to have another grandmother, Nana, but was denied the opportunity to know her. This is unjust and very confusing. Leah is trying desperately to find a way to connect with a person she never knew.

Her parents have done all the right things in introducing Nana to Leah through pictures and stories. This has likely led to Nana's taking on a living persona in Leah's mind. Leah can picture her—what she looks and smells like, how she would treat Leah. In essence, Leah has created a perfect grandmother with no faults or foibles who gives only unconditional love. Nana may be quite real to her; why isn't she around? There may be perceived rejection. Leah may feel that she is being denied the presence of Nana. Looking at it from this perspective, it makes sense that when Leah is insecure or upset, she would call to mind her grandmother and ask for her ideal Nana to help and comfort her. To Leah, Nana is a real person in the same way that other children have imaginary friends.

It is also important to note that Leah's missing grandmother may represent the inconceivable thought that Leah herself could lose a parent. If it happened to Dadden, it could happen to her. At five, she may not be able to put words to those fears. From this point of view, her regressive behaviors and need for reassurance in the night make sense.

I would help Leah and her parents work through Leah's anxieties. I would reassure her parents that, from a developmental perspective, Leah's behaviors make sense, and I would encourage them to view Nana as a real person in Leah's life. As Leah ages, she will be able to come to a more realistic understanding of death and may develop a more mature relationship with her late grandmother. I would hope, however, that she will hold onto many of the childhood memories she created of Nana.

Case Study for Reader Analysis

Last week, 14-year-old Larry tried out for the football team. He was so excited. Football was his favorite sport. He had been playing with his buddies every weekend and after school all last year. That was how he made friends when he moved into this new community. Tryouts were hard, but he was feeling confident and looking forward to being part of the team. He was sure that would help him make even more friends at his new school—a new school that he did not want to go to anyway, a new school that had many kids who were a different color, a new school that was in a community far from where he had lived before his parents were divorced.

The list of players was posted, and Larry did not make the team. He immediately called his mother at work. He was sobbing so hard, she thought it was something serious (she did not think that not making the football team was serious). She could not leave work early, so Larry would have to wait two hours until she returned, and then she promised they would talk about it.

When Larry's mom arrived home, Larry looked awful. She realized something was dreadfully wrong and called 911. In fact, Larry had taken what was left in the bottle of his allergy medication. This was indeed a suicide attempt. Larry has been released from the county mental health clinic and referred to you.

Discussion Questions

1. How will you go about forming a relationship with Larry?
2. What losses is he suffering from?
3. Would you include Mom as part of the counseling process? Why and in what way, or why not?
4. How will you continue to assess for suicide?
5. How would you gauge Larry's progress?

SUMMARY

In this chapter, we have shared a variety of cases and counseling interventions that illustrate intangible losses experienced by children and adolescents who have experienced a significant primary loss. These intangible losses, such as the loss of a sense of safety or a loss of hope, are often overlooked by adults attempting to help children and adolescents who are grieving, but these losses may have the most significant and long-lasting effects on children and adolescents. Therefore, it is imperative that clinicians and parents become adept at exploring the secondary losses that accompany any loss experience.

CHAPTER 5

Losses through Death

Tom, a 17-year-old high school junior, has been thinking a lot about death lately. Many of the books that he has been assigned to read in school, and many of the song lyrics he has been listening to, deal with death in one way or another. When he broaches the subject with his family, he is met with looks of concern, and his father thinks he needs to go out and have some fun rather than brooding about such deep issues all the time. Tom has convinced his parents that he is not obsessed with death or contemplating suicide. Instead, he is merely curious and is trying to understand the spiritual side of life. As a result of this conversation, Tom and his mother have decided to do some reading together and attend some church services in the area to allow Tom to find a place to explore the issues of death, life after death, and spirituality that interest him so much.

Whenever the topic of grief and loss in children is mentioned, the picture immediately comes to mind of a child coping with a death-related loss. Because death is an inevitable part of the life cycle, it is very likely that a person will experience a death-related loss in childhood or adolescent years. As a society, however, we tend to be inept at helping children through the grieving process. We abide by the myths presented in previous chapters. We try to hide death and grief from our children in an effort to protect them, and in the process deprive them of the opportunity to experience, learn about, and work through grief-related processes (McGlauflin, 1999; Rando, 1984; Wolfelt, 1991).

This chapter is designed to help practitioners determine appropriate counseling interventions for children and adolescents who have experienced death-related losses. This chapter and the other chapters in Part II of this book are laid out in case-study format. Several cases will be presented, followed by an assessment and a first-person sample response for each case. Topics discussed in this chapter include (a) explaining death, (b) death of a family member, (c) death of a friend, (d) death of a teacher, (e) attending the funeral, and (f) the death of a pet.

Case 1: Explaining Death—"What Happens When You Die?"

Laura is seven years old. Her best friend is her next-door neighbor, Hailey, who is one year older. Three years ago, Hailey was diagnosed with leukemia, and she has been receiving chemotherapy and radiation treatments much of the time since then. Several months ago, Hailey went into remission, and the doctors were hopeful that she would stay cancer-free. Recently, however, her cancer has returned and has spread quickly. Hailey's health is fading fast, and she is now receiving hospice care and is not expected to live longer than three months.

Laura and Hailey have been through a lot together. Laura has been there when Hailey's bones were too weak from radiation to swing or roughhouse. She helped Hailey pick out hats and wigs when she lost her hair and helped her decorate her IV pole when she was in the hospital. As part of her therapy, Hailey has decided to write a will, and she is leaving all of her toys and dolls to Laura. Because Laura has been through so much with Hailey, both sets of parents were under the impression that Laura knew that Hailey was going to die. It wasn't until Hailey spoke to Laura about the will, however, that Laura began to grasp the gravity of the situation. That night, Laura came to her parents and asked what was going to happen to Hailey when she died. After some squirming, her parents told her not to think about that until the time came and just to enjoy the time she had with her friend. Laura was not pacified, however, and insisted that she needed to understand death. Laura's parents are committed to helping Laura, but are unsure where to begin.

Case Analysis

Identifying the Primary Loss

There are two primary losses for Laura. One is pending—that is, the physical loss of her friend. The other, the loss of innocence, is the primary loss she is presently experiencing.

Identifying Secondary and Intangible Losses

Although Hailey still has several months to live, those around her, including Laura, are already experiencing a variety of losses. Laura has lost a way of life with her friend. She has lost a sense of fairness about the world. Laura is in the process of losing the false but common impression that children do not get ill and die.

Identifying the Client's Responses to the Loss Situation

Cognitive. Laura is responding to the pending loss of Hailey with concrete thinking, confusion, and "a need to know why."

Behavioral. There are no clear behavioral manifestations connected to loss at this time in Laura. However, if Laura's parents and counselor are able to collaborate to assist Laura, she will likely experience natural behavioral manifestations of loss in the forms of aggression, expression of feelings, and perhaps regression.

Emotional. When dealing with death-related losses, it is important to anticipate the types of feelings the child might be experiencing in the given circumstances. In Laura's case, it would be likely that she is experiencing a fear of the unknown regarding Hailey's impending death. She is also likely to experience a wide range of emotions both now and after the death of her friend, including anger, betrayal, abandonment, guilt, sadness, lack of control, loneliness, confusion, and disenchantment.

Discussion Questions

1. Why is it so difficult for adults to discuss the concept of death with children?
2. How would you assist Laura's parents in helping Laura make sense of her friend's death?

The Counselor's Response

The death of a loved one is a difficult thing for anyone to experience. Many adults do not talk to children about death because they feel it is important for them to have the "correct answers." With death, as with so many other subjects, the truth is that the answers are complex and rarely fall easily into correct or incorrect schema. It is also likely that the adults in children's lives are also experiencing loss and therefore may not be emotionally available to their children. In addition, adults often look to the way adults dealt with them when they were children. They feel dissatisfied with the way losses and deaths were handled by adults in their pasts but have no other examples to pull from. Finally, fear is at the core for many adults when discussing death or loss with children. They are afraid about their own feelings and how the child will react. What if they say or do the wrong thing? What if they say too much or too little? They may be afraid of death themselves. The result is often that the adult says or does nothing. This approach leaves the child alone emotionally, without the support of caring and well-intentioned adults.

Hailey's illness and inescapable death are serious issues for Laura and her parents. I want to see them in counseling together for a variety of reasons. I would like to model open, age-appropriate communication between Laura and me for the benefit of the family. I also want her parents to witness and then practice identifying Laura's feelings about Hailey and her illness. It is important for Laura to witness her parents' experience as well. She learns, as she observes their grief, that grief is acceptable, human, and shared by adults and children. Having the family in session together also lets the natural supports that are part of this family emerge. Initially, the family might not easily be able to identify their strengths. As their counselor, I would bring these strengths out and note them overtly. When they feel more confident, they can begin to use their resources to discover ways to talk to their child.

Working with Laura and Hailey together would be a wonderful opportunity. This time-limited part of our intervention would probably take place outside of my office. It seems that someone has been thoughtful in preparing Hailey for her own death. I would use Hailey as a resource to help Laura uncover and discover her feelings about Hailey and how much she will miss her friend. Hailey would serve as a role model for Laura to be emotionally connected, thoughtful, and curious. I would encourage the girls to take some photographs, write stories, sing songs about their friendship and each other, and perhaps create a scrapbook about their friendship.

My work with Laura would continue through the physical loss of her friend. I would help her complete any unfinished projects if she chooses to do so. Of course, I would allow her the opportunity to talk or play out her feelings and thoughts. It will also be important for me to give Laura the chance to decide when and how her relationship with me will end. This decision will ground Laura in reality and confirm that she does have control of some things in her life, including the way in which our relationship will end.

Finally, I would have made referrals at the beginning of our intervention to increase Laura's experience of support. Hospice, funeral homes, and the school counselor can all be resources for Laura and her parents.

Case 2: Death of a Family Member—"Do You Know My Baby Cousin Died?"

Connor is described by most people as a warm, intelligent, outgoing, thoughtful little boy. His parents divorced when he was four years old. Connor has adjusted well to the inevitable changes that accompanied their divorce. He lives with his mother and visits with his father for two months during the summer (his father lives 2,000 miles away).

Connor spends a great deal of time with his auntie and her boyfriend, James, who live in the next town. He was very excited to learn that his auntie was pregnant, and he had been very active in the conversations about her pregnancy, the planning that was taking place, and the celebration of her pregnancy. He joined his auntie, mother, and grandmother at his auntie's sonogram appointment. He even got his own "picture" of his baby cousin.

Connor was with his auntie and James at the park last month when his auntie collapsed. Connor rode in the car with James (who was frantic) behind the ambulance to the hospital. Connor's mother was already at the hospital when they arrived. She wanted to take Connor home, but he refused. He was too concerned about his auntie and his baby cousin. Connor's auntie suffered a late-term miscarriage. The entire family was devastated and struggled "just to keep it together."

For the next month, Connor said to everyone he encountered, "Do you know my baby cousin died?" His mother and family were incredibly worried. He wasn't sleeping well and no longer seemed like himself. In addition, he was protesting his departure to visit his father, which was two weeks away. He had never done this before.

Case Analysis

Identifying the Primary Loss

For Connor, the primary loss is the unexpected death of his yet-to-be-born cousin.

Identifying Secondary and Intangible Losses

Connor is experiencing several secondary losses, including missing out on the joyous, long-anticipated experience of his cousin's birth.

Keep in mind that the months that had elapsed during his aunt's pregnancy would seem long indeed to Connor. He also is mourning the loss of what might have been. He was expecting to have a new baby cousin to play with and look out for, and he was unexpectedly denied that opportunity.

Identifying the Client's Responses to the Loss Situation

Cognitive. Connor is giving clues to his thought process when he utters the words "Do you know my baby cousin died?" He seems to be trying to communicate about his loss and may be trying to make sense of what happened.

Behavioral. Connor's behaviors include an inability to sleep, a desire to talk about his cousin's death, and a strong need to stay close to his mother and her family.

Emotional. Connor is likely to be experiencing a number of emotions, some conflicting. He appears to be sad, but his overarching emotions are probably fear and confusion. "How did this happen?" he might wonder. He probably has some feelings of anger as well.

Discussion Questions

1. Does Connor's loss history play into your clinical formulation of Connor? How?

2. What is your counseling plan?

3. What feelings emerge for you as you listen to what is going on with Connor?

The Counselor's Response

It is likely that the death of Connor's cousin has triggered memories and feelings of other losses he has experienced, including the loss of his father's proximity after the divorce. His change in personality and inability to sleep indicate that he is suffering symptoms of depression. As with any depressed child, I would monitor him closely for other symptoms of depression typical in children—such as irritability, acting out, withdrawal from friends and favorite activities, change in eating habits, and suicidal thinking or behaviors *(DSM-IV TR;* American Psychiatric Association, 2000). Connor has had his dreams and hopes dashed, and his cognitive level of development makes it very difficult for him to fully comprehend the complexities of this loss.

It appears that Connor has a desire to speak about his loss. Very often, when family members have experienced a loss themselves, they are reluctant to talk about it with their children. If the emotions are too raw for family members to discuss, counseling provides the perfect opportunity for Connor to talk about his feelings and thoughts related to his cousin's death. I would allow Connor to express himself freely through speech, art, and play to work through his conflicting thoughts and emotions. I might assist Connor in creating a way for him to say goodbye to the baby. Some kind of memorial, like releasing a helium balloon into the air, would be helpful because so much time has been spent preparing for the "big day" when the baby would have been born. This activity might give Connor a sense of closure and add to the lesson that death is a part of life.

I would also suggest that Connor's trip to his father be postponed until Connor has achieved a sense of safety. Very often after a death, young children will become preoccupied with thoughts of their own death or the death of those close to them (Fitzgerald, 1992). Connor might be expected to become clingy toward his mother and auntie and be afraid to leave their sides. The thought of traveling 2,000 miles away would likely be overwhelming to Connor, and I would expect his acting-out behaviors to increase as the time to leave for his father's drew nearer. I would contact Connor's father and try to work with him and the mother to ease Connor's fears and increase his sense of safety. When Connor does leave for his father's house, I would suggest frequent contact with his mom and auntie through phone calls and letters, and I would also set up a referral for Connor to continue with counseling after he arrives at his father's home.

Case 3: Death of a Friend (Child)—"I Still Talk to Cara"

At eight years old, Billy and Cara had already been friends for five years. They had met in Head Start, a preschool program designed to prepare children with the skills to successfully enter kindergarten. Billy and Cara had been telling people that they were going to get married for years now. To their parents, it did not seem very farfetched.

Cara had been getting sick a lot over the last few months. It seemed as though she caught everything that was going around at school but could not recover in a reasonable time. Cara's pediatrician was concerned. Cara had always been healthy; perhaps, the pediatrician thought, she wasn't getting enough sleep, proper nutrition, or exercise. Cara's parents had a difficult time advocating for further testing for their daughter but desperately wanted it. In March, on their way to their seventh trip to the pediatrician in less than two months, Cara's mother decided she would make it a point to stand up for what she believed was needed.

The pediatrician totally concurred, as she, too, was beginning to become very concerned. After a battery of tests, it was discovered that Cara had a malignant tumor in her pancreas. The cancer was spreading aggressively. Of course, Cara's family and friends were devastated and frightened. Billy was not. He wanted to read her books and tell her knock-knock jokes.

She was hospitalized by the end of March to receive treatment. When Billy saw that Cara had lost almost all her hair, he asked his parents if he could get his head shaved so Cara would not feel silly. He visited her every three or four days until the day she died. She died three hours after one of Billy's visits. During that visit, she told him that he was the best husband she ever had.

The loss hit the community hard. However, Billy did not cry or seem sad. He talked about Cara every day and even said he had seen her during the night. He asked his mother if regular boys like him could be married to angels like Cara. It seemed that every day Billy asked his teacher or parents another one of these types of questions. The adults in his life were quite concerned about this fantasy world he was living in. Yesterday, Billy got in a fight with another boy on the bus. Evidently, Billy was telling the other kids that he still talks to Cara and she talks to him. The other child called Billy a liar, and the situation escalated from there.

Case Analysis

Identifying the Primary Loss

Billy's primary loss was the death of his very best friend.

Identifying Secondary and Intangible Losses

In this case, Billy's secondary losses consist of the exasperation he feels when his family and friends refuse to believe that he is still in contact with Cara.

Identifying the Client's Responses to the Loss Situation

Cognitive. Billy's cognitive response seems to indicate that he denies the reality and finality of his friend's death.

Behavioral. Behaviorally, Billy is asking questions about the nature of life after death and is acting out when his ability to communicate with Cara is questioned.

Emotional. Emotionally, Billy is struggling with feelings of confusion and anger regarding the death of his friend.

Discussion Questions

1. What are your major concerns about Billy?
2. How does spirituality factor in?
3. What if Billy is indeed "speaking" with Cara?
4. Are you concerned that Billy has not cried or seemed sad about Cara's death? Why or why not?

The Counselor's Response

Billy's case is a very familiar one to clinicians who work with children coping with loss. Adults often panic when they hear about children "seeing" or "talking to" a dead person. In fact, these reactions are very common and should be expected even in adults after the experience of the death of a close loved one (Schoen, Burgoyne, & Schoen, 2004). Seeing or speaking with the lost person should not be considered pathological. Billy's mind simply cannot comprehend that his dear friend is gone. He needs to maintain contact with her, and he does so. This can be considered a defense mechanism that prevents Billy from having to experience the trauma and pain associated with his friend's death. Another way to view this, however, is from a spiritual perspective. We know very little about what happens after death. Many cultures believe that people can maintain contact with the dead after they die. Some believe that children are open to paranormal experiences because they are open-minded. Although I am not advocating the existence of paranormal phenomena, it will be necessary to evaluate Billy's family's cultural and spiritual beliefs about life after death in order to help Billy work through his experience.

As a counselor, I would work with Billy to translate his thoughts and feelings about Cara into a more tangible format, such as music or a scrapbook. I would encourage him to maintain contact with the real world, but I would not force him to give up his communications with Cara. I would encourage Billy's parents to discuss Billy's questions about angels and life after death. I might suggest they enlist the aid of local clergy and read books together on the subject. Most important,

I would urge Billy's parents not to panic and to allow him the time and space to work through his loss. Adults can take a lesson from children in how to commemorate and maintain relationships with the dead. Last, I would prepare Billy's parents to expect that there might come a time when the reality of the loss of his friend will come crashing down on Billy. When he is developmentally capable of processing his friend's death, Billy might begin to express the more classic symptoms of grief and mourning.

Case 4: Death of a Friend (Adolescent)—"Teenagers Aren't Supposed to Die"

Debbie was making her way through adolescence relatively unscathed. She was dealing well with school and developmental transitions. Her mother and stepfather attributed this to their ability to maintain constancy over the years. They had lived in the same town and house since Debbie was three years old. Their routine, including their expectations of Debbie and her siblings, dinner times and bedtimes, house rules, and traditions, were adjusted, not abandoned, as the children grew up.

Debbie was a decent athlete and student. She was on the yearbook staff and worked on the school newspaper. She was thoughtful, fun, attractive, and popular. Debbie had an interesting variety of friends. Her parents approved of Kevin, her boyfriend for the past year and seven months. Over the last month, however, this picture of Debbie has changed dramatically.

Debbie's friend Ray received a call from Debbie that scared him. She said that she was sure no one cared about her. At a party later that night, he noticed raised red "scratches" on Debbie's arm. He said something to Kevin, and Kevin was also concerned. He added that she had been smoking a lot more pot lately, sometimes even during school hours. Kevin said he would talk to her. After the party, Kevin tried to talk to Debbie about the scratches as they drove home. She answered him with tears and said, "So you are dumping me? Well, then, f*** off!" Kevin wasn't sure how it happened, but he had managed to break up with Debbie rather than express his concern.

At home, Debbie's parents had also noticed some changes. Debbie was frantic one morning because none of her clothes fit. Her mother had noticed that she had put on some weight but wasn't worried because Debbie still had a cute figure. Her stepfather swore he smelled alcohol on her breath after she attended a football game, but he shrugged it off. She was 18.

Kevin stopped coming around the house and calling. Debbie told her parents that it was because Kevin's friend Sean had died. Debbie's parents had heard about Sean's death. Sean was on his way to pick up his little sister from dancing school when a drunk driver ran a red light and plowed through Sean's car. The entire school and community were devastated. Debbie attended Sean's funeral mostly because everyone else did, but also because Sean was Kevin's good friend. Actually, Debbie could not stand Sean and often vied for Kevin's attention when Sean was around. Her parents thought it was peculiar when Debbie smiled as she told them about Sean's funeral.

Debbie's parents want you to work with their daughter because they are afraid she is using drugs and alcohol.

Case Analysis

Identifying the Primary Loss

It is particularly difficult to pinpoint a particular loss in this case. However, Debbie's primary loss is most likely the loss of her sense of predictability, order, and immortality.

Identifying Secondary and Intangible Losses

Debbie is changing drastically. She does not seem to recognize herself physically or emotionally any longer. She has lost her sense of identity. She has lost the security and continuity of a long-term relationship with her boyfriend.

Identifying the Client's Responses to the Loss Situation

Cognitive. Debbie thinks that no one cares about her. It appears that her thinking is somewhat confused, given her life circumstances as presented in this case. She also seems to lack trust in people she once turned to for advice and consolation.

Behavioral. Debbie's primary behaviors are predominantly self-destructive. They include self-injury and self-medication with drugs and alcohol. She is also pushing away people who care about her.

Emotional. Debbie is filled with self-loathing. She appears to lack self-esteem in all areas of her life. She feels angry, scared, lonely, and desperate to escape her pain. She may feel guilty about Sean's death because she did not like Sean.

Discussion Questions

1. How do you assess Debbie's alcohol and substance abuse? How do you report your findings to Debbie's parents?

2. How do you account for Debbie's behavior?

3. How do you engage Debbie in the process of counseling?

The Counselor's Response

Working with Debbie would require, first and foremost, establishing a good deal of trust. I assume that Debbie experienced a very traumatic, hurtful experience. Whenever an adolescent presents with a rapid change in personality, change in behavior, and self-destructive tendencies, I immediately look for precipitating traumas like rape, sexual abuse, or some other violation. With Debbie and clients like her, it is crucial to perform a lethality assessment and depression screening to ensure that she is not a danger to herself. I would also want to explore Debbie's feelings of rage, mistrust, and self-loathing, as well as investigate her need to push those closest to her away. My guess would be that she is trying to defend herself against abandonment. I would also want to explore the role of Sean's death in contributing to Debbie's current behaviors. She is incongruent when she smiles through her description of the funeral. The death appears to have hit her very hard, although not in the way you might generally expect. I believe that Sean's death made Debbie aware of her own mortality and pointed out the randomness and chaotic nature of life. Here is a girl whose sense of order and predictability in the world has been shattered. A vital young man her age is inexplicably dead. Debbie now feels lost and scared. Will she be next? She may even feel guilty because she doesn't feel sad about his death. These are all issues to be explored with Debbie in counseling.

It would also be prudent to address Debbie's cutting behaviors. Eventually, after building rapport, I would bring these behaviors into the open by looking at the scratches together and writing a "do-no-harm" contract. I would suggest that Debbie's parents have her evaluated and treated for alcohol and substance abuse before the problem escalates further. I would also explain to them that Debbie's drinking behavior is likely a coping response to enable her to deal with her sense of loss and despair. I would help facilitate communication between Debbie and her parents because this would be the key to helping them understand Debbie's issues and helping her cope.

Case 5: Death of a Teacher—"What Happened to Mrs. Martinez?"

Mrs. Martinez was a much-loved kindergarten teacher at Justin's elementary school. Justin's mother read in the paper that Mrs. Martinez had died unexpectedly of a heart attack over the weekend. After reading that the school planned to address the death with the children, Justin's mom breathed a sigh of relief. She would not discuss the death with Justin but would let the school take care of it. She did not relish the idea of talking about death to her young son. It was a topic that had been very much avoided in her household when she was growing up.

On Monday, the children arrived to find that they were to report to the auditorium for a special announcement by the principal. At the assembly, the principal announced the "passing" of Mrs. Martinez, discussed the details of a planned memorial service, and told the children they could speak to a counselor if they were sad or upset. Justin wasn't really paying attention while the adults were talking. He was paying attention to the people around him; then he noticed that some of the people from his class were crying, but he didn't know why. He couldn't understand where Mrs. Martinez was. When the children returned to their classroom, there was a new teacher there and "some other lady" who turned out to be a counselor. The counselor gathered the children into a circle and asked if they had any questions to ask or anything they wanted to share. Justin raised his hand and asked where Mrs. Martinez was. After the counselor finished giving her statement about the teacher's death, Justin replied, "Oh, okay, well, when will she be back?" Several of the other children echoed his comment, and one little girl yelled, "She's not coming back, you dummy! She's dead!" At this point, Justin and some of the other children began to cry. Since then, Justin has been getting in trouble at school. According to his new teacher, he has been acting out, and when he is confronted he says that he wants Mrs. Martinez back because he misses the way she used to do things. Justin's mother has avoided the situation, saying it is a "school problem" and they need to take care of it.

Case Analysis

Identifying the Primary Loss

The death of his teacher is Justin's primary loss, although he does not grasp the finality of it. Many of the secondary and intangible losses he experiences are a result of the concrete primary loss of death, as well as his inability to process the finality of death.

Identifying Secondary and Intangible Losses

For Justin, the loss of his routine and the things that he can count on are at the core of his loss experience. He is experiencing losses connected to his worldview, classroom community, and support system.

Identifying the Client's Responses to the Loss Situation

Cognitive. As expected, Justin is responding concretely because of his age. He also seems preoccupied and distracted and is perhaps even ruminating on the loss of Mrs. Martinez.

Behavioral. According to Justin's teacher, he is "acting out." It would be wise to ask the teacher to provide an operational definition of these behaviors and identify baseline behaviors to review to see if there have been any behavioral changes.

Emotional. Emotionally, Justin is markedly confused and angry.

Discussion Questions

1. How might Justin's mother have handled the situation differently?
2. Was the school counselor's approach age-appropriate? What other interventions would you suggest?
3. How would you work with Justin to help him to adjust to the death of his teacher?

The Counselor's Response

The adults in Justin's life could have addressed the death of Mrs. Martinez differently. For whatever reasons, his mother, school counselor, and new teacher made some choices that do not demonstrate understanding of or empathy for Justin and the other children. I have been asked to act a consultant to Justin's mother, the school counselor, and the new teacher.

The most important people in children's lives are their parents. When Justin's mother decided not to discuss Mrs. Martinez's death with Justin, she was in essence saying, "I don't care about something and someone that is important to you" or "Get over it." Either way, her refusal to discuss the death of his teacher—how Justin was feeling about the many changes at school since Mrs. Martinez's death and even death itself—left Justin to deal with it alone. It set up a separation of school and home and sent a message that things that happen at school are not important at home. I doubt that is the message Justin's mother intended. I would talk to Justin's mother about providing support for Justin and would encourage her to speak about the ways that she *already* supports him and has supported him through other losses. She can still do this. I would also listen to her. It is my hunch that this death may be difficult for her for a number of reasons, particularly if Mrs. Martinez was her contemporary. I would provide support for her so that she can support her son.

The school counselor, although well intentioned, used an intervention with kindergartners that I would not advocate. First, she asked them a question, and then she asked them to verbalize their questions to her. Five-year-olds have difficulty answering questions with anything beyond "I don't know." Often they are trying to determine what the "right" answer is, and in this case there is no correct answer. This type of question requires cognition beyond that of the typical five-year-old (Fry, 1995; Metzgar, 2002). Second, she asks five-year-olds to verbalize their thoughts and feelings. This is not the way children naturally express themselves at this age (Axline, 1969; Landreth, 2002). It would have been better to provide the children with materials with which they can express their feelings—such as toys, paints, and crayons. Many adults, fortified with the tools of verbal communication, have difficulty expressing grief. The principal's use of the euphemism "passing" during the assembly is an example of adult language used to try to soften the impact of death. However, euphemisms only confuse children at an already confusing time. Although the counselor's expectation that the children will express themselves verbally is unfounded, she can still provide them with support in the context of a group as well as individually by incorporating play and art materials that will allow children to express themselves.

Finally, it will be imperative to work with the teacher who is replacing Mrs. Martinez. What a situation to walk into! I would want to discuss her experience in that classroom of hurting and confused little ones. I want to tease out the things that she has done well and help her identify some things she can do differently or improve upon, and I would prefer that she initiate this contact because she is the expert on her classroom. I am the mental health professional; she is the education professional.

If I had the opportunity to work individually with Justin, I would want to employ a play-therapy approach with him. Because the nature of his loss is clearly linked to the death of his teacher, I would be directive and focus on his experiences of loss. I might ask him to draw a picture of himself when Mrs. Martinez was the teacher and then draw a picture of what he looks (feels) like now. I would help him create a goodbye story, picture, or clay creation to acknowledge Mrs. Martinez's death. If Justin asked questions about death, I would try to answer them at an age-appropriate level, but I would also say, "I don't know," when that was indeed the case. It is important to recognize Justin's feelings, past and present, about Mrs. Martinez. I cannot assume that Justin did not experience this loss fully just because he is little. I want to honor the magnitude of his experience.

Case 6: The Funeral—"Saying Goodbye to Poppy"

Erin's parents contact you because they are not sure whether they should bring Erin to her great-grandfather's funeral. It seems that everyone in the family has a different opinion, and no one is afraid to offer it unsolicited. Several years ago, you worked with Erin after she had witnessed a child being struck by a car while riding her bicycle. The child was Erin's neighbor.

Erin is six years old and one of 10 great-grandchildren. She knows Poppy and feels connected to him. In fact, when Erin was two, Poppy even lived with her and her brothers for an entire year. In the three years he has been in the nursing home, she has visited him once a month. He died yesterday at age 97 of natural causes.

Erin's parents are convinced that they should bring her to the funeral but have a number of concerns. Because of their past positive experience with you, they seek your consultation.

Case Analysis

Identifying the Primary Loss

Erin's primary loss is the death of her great-grandfather.

Identifying Secondary and Intangible Losses

With regard to the funeral, Erin is faced with the possibility of never seeing Poppy again and not being able to say goodbye.

Cognitive. Cognitively, Erin may feel torn about whether she should attend the funeral. She may be confused by her parents' reluctance to have her attend and may interpret this reluctance to mean that funerals are awful and scary events.

Behavioral. Erin might act out or present as moody.

Emotional. Emotionally, Erin is likely to feel confused, angry, and sad and may feel that her parents are usurping her ability to choose whether to attend the funeral. She may feel powerless.

Discussion Questions

1. What are your personal beliefs about bringing children to a funeral?
2. What suggestions do you have for Erin's parents?
3. How can they prepare her for the funeral?

The Counselor's Response

Attendance at funerals is a common theme in counseling children and adolescents through death-related losses. Parents often question whether their children should be there. In some families, custom dictates that all children must attend; in others, children are not allowed at funerals in order to "protect" them. Fitzgerald (1992) has suggested that it is important that children be allowed to attend and take part in funeral rituals, visits to the grave, and memorial services to allow them to put the death in meaningful perspective, in keeping with the family's beliefs and experiences.

There is no right or wrong answer to this dilemma. My personal bias is that the child should be involved in the decision whether to attend. In this case, I would suggest that the parents discuss with Erin what a funeral, wake, or visitation means. What is it like? Who will be there? What is expected of children? These issues should all be addressed. Erin should be encouraged to ask questions, and it might be a good idea to have a brochure available with pictures of caskets and the like. Most funeral directors have pamphlets that are specifically geared toward children. Erin should not feel obliged either to attend or not attend the funeral. This conversation should give her parents an idea of how she feels about attending.

If Erin does not choose to attend the funeral, it is still important for her to be allowed to take part in memorializing the loved one. For example, she may want to visit a special place, frame a picture, or create a special keepsake commemorating the life of their special someone. If Erin does choose to attend, it is very important that the experience be very structured so she knows what to expect. Sometimes it is possible for families to view the body and say goodbye privately before or after the formal wake. This alternative might better suit some children (Shaw, 1999; Webb, 2002). No child should be forced to kiss or touch the body. (Some adult clients have never gotten over the trauma of being forced to kiss a dead relative's body.) Erin's parents should allow her to say goodbye in whatever way she chooses and be prepared for a variety of emotions and questions well after the funeral takes place (Goldman, 2004; Shaw, 1999; Silverman & Worden, 1992).

Case 7: Death of a Pet—"How Could You?"

Janet, age 10, returned home from school last week to find her mother crying. Janet's mother, Liz, told Janet to sit down because she had something important to tell her. Liz explained that she and Janet's father had put their 14-year-old German shepherd, Brandy, to sleep after a long conversation with the veterinarian about Brandy's deteriorating health. Brandy had been having difficulty eating and keeping her food down, and the doctor had found some tumors in Brandy's stomach. Janet's parents had decided that it would be easier on Janet if they "put Brandy to sleep" without Janet's knowledge. At this point, Janet fled the room, sobbing, and has since refused to speak to either of her parents. Janet's father does not understand what all the "hubbub" is about. After all, it was just a dumb dog and Janet hardly paid attention to her anymore anyway. His answer to the problem was to offer to buy Janet a new puppy. Janet responded to this by screaming at her father and calling him a murderer.

Janet is distraught for several reasons. She feels guilty about not having paid more attention to Brandy. She misses having Brandy around to act as her confidant. To her, Brandy was a nonjudgmental listener who loved her unconditionally. She used to confide her hopes and dreams to her. Most of all, Janet is angry that she never had the opportunity to say goodbye to her beloved pet. Janet's mother realizes that in trying to protect her child, she may have made things worse. Liz is angry with herself because, in a similar experience in her childhood, her parents euthanized her pet cat without her knowledge. She had tried to put that experience behind her, but the current situation has brought out a number of feelings in Liz as well.

Case Analysis

Identifying the Primary Loss

Brandy was Janet's pet, family member, and friend. Her death is Janet's primary loss.

Identifying Secondary and Intangible Losses

The death of a pet during adolescence is often the first significant death experience in a person's life (Trozzi, 1999). Certain losses are directly associated with that loss, among them loss of innocence, friendship, stability and routine, a sense of fairness about the world, and a changed perspective of the parents.

Identifying the Client's Responses to the Loss Situation

Cognitive. Janet is shutting her parents out, which indicates that she may be having difficulty cognitively processing the magnitude of this loss.

Behavioral. Shutting her parents out is also a behavioral response. Angry outbursts, with or without aggression, are also behavioral indicators of her experience of loss.

Emotional. Some of the many feelings Janet is likely to be experiencing include anger, guilt, betrayal, fear, mistrust, disloyalty, resentment, and loneliness.

Discussion Questions

1. The death of an animal is often overlooked as a cause of grief in our society. Why do you think that is so?
2. How did Liz's childhood experience with the death of her cat predict her handling of Brandy's death?
3. How would you work with Janet and her parents to allow Janet to say goodbye to Brandy?

The Counselor's Response

In the United States, how much time off school or work is given when there is a death in the immediate family? Extended family? What about a close friend? In any of the aforementioned scenarios, a week seems to be at the more generous end of the scale. If you lose a pet to death, time off work or school is unheard of. The dominant culture in our country fears grief, loss, and death. In fact, Rando (1984) has referred to the United States as a grief-denying culture. It is no wonder that helping children and adolescents deal with the loss of a pet is over-looked and minimized, as are many other sources of pain in children and adolescents.

Because many people have experienced having the loss of a pet minimized or denied, when they encounter another person (a child, adolescent, or adult) who has lost a pet, they tend to treat that person as they have been treated, tending to react to that person without the respect and sympathy they would give a person who has experienced a different type of loss.

When my friend and her family lost their pet, I looked for a general sympathy card to send to acknowledge their loss. I found one that was specifically directed at the death of a pet. I share this example to illustrate that there are people who empathize and sympathize with the death of a pet. I would encourage parents and counselors to become familiar with the many suggestions in the literature on this topic. We recommend *I'll Always Love You,* by Hans Wilhelm (1989), for children and *Goodbye, Friend: Healing Wisdom for Anyone Who Has Ever Lost a Pet,* by Gary Kowalski (1997), for adolescents.

In Janet's case, ritual and past experience are important. How has Janet's family dealt with other losses? This may be the most signifi-cant loss that they have experienced as a family. When working with Janet, I will want to be very respectful of Brandy's memory, and that respect should be obvious to Janet. I would start my intervention by creating a genogram, with Janet's help (Goldenberg & Goldenberg, 1997). This would help me determine the nature of other losses, and it would give me the opportunity to acknowledge the place pets have in Janet's family. I would ask, "Was Brandy your first pet?" and "Do you have any other pets?" and then add, "I like to list them here as part of the family because, for many of us, they really are." (With children and adolescents, I list their friends as part of their genogram for the same reason.)

The counseling intervention I plan for Janet would look very similar to the one described in the analysis of Justin's case. Mrs. Martinez was an incredibly important *person* to Justin in the same way that Brandy was an incredibly important *friend* to Janet. Therefore, I would engage Janet in a series of activities designed to elicit her feel-ings and thoughts about Brandy's death and what has emerged in her family since then. In addition to some of the activities noted in Justin's case, I would also employ a sand-play therapy intervention. Many adolescents are attracted to the sand-play therapy tray and the figures and miniatures. I may ask Janet to "show me in the sand what it feels like without Brandy." As she creates her sand story, I would make few tracking and reflective responses. When she was satisfied with what she had created, I would simply ask her to tell me about it while listening intently for feelings and themes. If I could respond to her feelings and the themes, I believe she would be able to show me her pain, and I would be able to provide her with the opportunity to heal through being heard. I would also suggest that Janet develop a way to memorialize Brandy. This would allow her a way to say goodbye in an atmosphere of acceptance.

Case Study for Reader Analysis

Gabby is a huge fan of a local musical group called *Theo*. Last night, she received an instant message from her friend Tory. Tory was letting everyone know that Jake, *Theo*'s lead singer, had died yesterday in a boating accident. Tory knew, she explained in her message, because her father is a police officer and he was at the scene.

Gabby ran into her mother's room. She was crying and talking so quickly her mother could not make out what she was saying. After a few minutes, Gabby calmed down enough to relate the story to her mother. Her mother urged her to wait until the local news confirmed Tory's message. "This could all be a rumor or a gag," she said.

It was true. Jake had drowned. Gabby's parents tried to be respectful of Gabby's feelings. Gabby's mother remembered what it was like when John Lennon was murdered, so she thought she was being empathic. Gabby's parents even let her skip school to attend a memorial service.

In the month since Jake's tragic death, Gabby has been, in her mother's words, "foggy." Gabby told her parents that she wishes she were in heaven with Jake. When her older brother heard how Gabby was reacting, he called her pathetic. Later that day, Gabby keyed his car. For Gabby's parents, that was it—no more being understanding or taking this lightly.

Discussion Questions

1. What are Gabby's primary, secondary, and intangible losses?
2. How can you demonstrate empathy to Gabby?
3. What recommendations do you have for her parents?
4. What interventions would be part of your counseling plan?

SUMMARY

In this chapter, we have shared a variety of cases and counseling interventions describing death-related losses experienced by children and adolescents. In the chapters that follow, we will discuss losses that are not death related, many of which are overlooked in the traditional research on grief and loss in children and adolescents.

CHAPTER 6

Interpersonal Losses

Amy, Ellen, and Stephanie have been friends throughout elementary school. They ride the same bus and spend summers together talking and playing. Amy lives in a trailer park up the road from Ellen and Stephanie. Stephanie and Ellen's mothers sat their daughters down to discuss a "situation" with them. It seems that it was all right for the girls to associate with Amy when they were children, but now that they will be entering middle school, the mothers feel it is no longer appropriate for Ellen and Stephanie to be friends with Amy. The mothers explain that, although Amy seems like a very nice girl, she is bound to get into trouble with drugs and pregnancy like all the girls who live "over there." Amy cannot understand why her friends have suddenly abandoned her. Since school started, they refuse to sit with her on the bus and will no longer hang out with her at school or at home. She is feeling lonely, hurt, and confused.

This case study illustrates the pain that often accompanies changes in friendships. The previous chapter of this book discussed losses children and adolescents experience as a result of the death of a loved one. Children and adolescents experience interpersonal losses far more frequently than they do losing someone through death. An interpersonal loss, such as having a friend or family member move away, can have a profound impact on the life of a child or adolescent. Too often, these types of losses are overlooked or minimized by parents and professional helpers.

Social relationships are important both to children and to adolescents. For young children, family relationships are particularly meaningful. Although many children attend day care and nursery schools, members of the family are their primary source of social and emotional support. Peer relationships, although crucial for developing appropriate social skills and behaviors such as sharing, do not always hold the significance for young children that they do for older children and adolescents.

Although family relationships are particularly important to younger children, peer relationships are crucial to teens (Vernon & Al-Mabuk, 1995). Adolescents often define themselves and their moods on the basis of how well their friendships are going (Vernon, 1993). Any parent or professional who works with adolescents on a regular basis is aware that most adolescents' worlds consist of feelings and discussions about who is mad at whom, who is dating whom, and who isn't speaking to whom. In this developmental stage of an adolescent's life, a teen learns the nuances of relationships and how they work. It can be a wonderful time or a painful time in a teen's life, or more likely both a wonderful and painful time of growth and self-discovery. Often relationship losses that seem trivial to adults are absolutely devastating to children and teens.

This chapter will discuss in more detail an interpersonal loss that children and adolescents are likely to experience in three different contexts: loss of relationships in the form of loved ones moving away, lost friendships, and breakups with romantic partners. The loss experienced by children and adolescents who are in the foster care system will also be explored.

Case 1: When Loved Ones Move Away— "Losing Grandma"

Sarah, who is three, has recently been told by her father that her 80-year-old grandmother is moving to a retirement home an hour away. Sarah has been very close to her grandmother, who has lived next door to Sarah all of her life. Each day, Sarah visits Grandma for lunch after nursery school and stays with her until her mother comes home from her teaching job at 4:00 p.m. They have a steady routine that includes doing household chores together and watching Grandma's favorite game shows and soap operas. She also stops by each evening to watch "Wheel of Fortune" with Grandma and kiss her good night afterward.

Grandma is very excited about moving to this new adult facility, which will allow her to live in her own apartment without all of the maintenance issues she has in owning her own home. Sarah's parents and her grandmother assure Sarah that she will still see her grandmother often and will be able to stay over on weekends. Sarah's grandmother is scheduled to move out of her house in two weeks. Yesterday the "For Sale" sign went up in Grandma's yard. Sarah cried when she saw it and refused to go over to her grandmother's house that evening. Her teacher at nursery school reported to Sarah's mother that Sarah had been put in the time-out chair twice that day for hitting one child and calling another names. She was concerned because this kind of behavior is not typical of Sarah. She also stated that Sarah has seemed withdrawn over the past couple of weeks.

Case Analysis

Identifying the Primary Loss

Sarah's primary loss is the loss of her grandmother's company and proximity to her home.

Identifying Secondary and Intangible Losses

In this case, Sarah is faced with several secondary losses associated with the primary loss of her grandmother's presence. She is faced with the loss of access to the house next door, as well as loss of her familiar routine. Sarah's sense of stability is also threatened: She is also likely to feel a lack of trust in her ability to count on the people in her life to be there for her.

Identifying the Client's Responses to the Loss Situation

Cognitive. In the case presented, it is important to try to ascertain what kinds of thoughts and fears Sarah is experiencing. For example, she may be thinking, "Grandma doesn't love me anymore" or "People, even those close to you, can't be trusted." It is important with children this young to anticipate what kinds of thoughts they might be having because they are very often incapable of verbally explaining what is going through their minds.

Behavioral. In this case, Sarah may be expressing her underlying thoughts and feelings behaviorally, through hitting and acting out at school and by withdrawing from Grandma and refusing to participate in her normal routine. It would not be unusual if she also began to experience somatic symptoms, such as headaches or stomachaches.

Emotional. As is the case with cognitive responses, it is important to anticipate the types of feelings Sarah might be having. Sarah is likely experiencing a fear of the unknown regarding Grandma's impending move. She may be experiencing fears ranging from where she will sleep when she visits Grandma to what her routine will be like after

Grandma leaves and, ultimately, whether Grandma will still be her buddy if she doesn't live next door. Sarah is also likely to feel sadness, anger, and confusion with regard to her changing circumstances.

Discussion Questions

1. What methods could you use to discover what thoughts and feelings Sarah is experiencing?

2. What kinds of activities and conversations could you have with Sarah that might alleviate her fears about her grandmother's move?

3. Would it be wise for Sarah to be allowed to say goodbye to Grandma's house? How might this be facilitated?

4. What steps might be taken both before and after the move to facilitate a smoother transition for Sarah?

The Counselor's Response

It is critical for me, as Sarah's counselor, to approach Sarah at her own level. Sarah needs to feel safe, and by approaching her at her level physically, cognitively, and emotionally, I can begin to create an environment of safety. Sarah's age will dictate much of my counseling work with her.

Conceptualizations of her presenting problem, emotional, cognitive, and behavioral responses are all filtered through her most salient culture—her age. A play-therapy approach with 30-minute sessions would be most beneficial for Sarah. Using a play-therapy approach would allow Sarah to demonstrate what she is thinking and feeling through her play. I can reflect back to Sarah what she believes she is experiencing, thereby giving her a verbal means of expressing herself. It would be crucial to make time to meet with her parents and her grandmother regularly for consultation because they are the most important people in Sarah's life. I would encourage her parents and grandparents to use reflective listening responses with Sarah and would likely spend several consultation sessions practicing these skills with them. This experience would help them to pick up on and understand the multiple and varied feelings Sarah has about this transition.

I would also recommend that Sarah's parents and grandmother give Sarah the opportunity to say goodbye to her grandmother's house. They may even want to have an intimate ceremony or party that commemorates the times Grandma and Sarah have shared. As a caveat to this activity and to alleviate some of Sarah's fears, it would also be good for the family to include Sarah in the preparation for the move and in the move itself. For example, she could help pack and unpack boxes. A photo of Grandma and Sarah in Grandma's new residence for Sarah to take home with her might also elicit conversation or play pertaining to her perspective, and it would also make a nice keepsake.

After establishing a trusting relationship and rapport with Sarah, it would be imperative to define what losses Sarah is facing, not from our own perspective as adults, but from Sarah's. In this case, Sarah is faced with several secondary losses associated with the primary loss of her grandmother's presence. For example, Sarah is faced with the loss of access to the house next door. To her, each step, tree, and flower along the path between the two houses is a familiar friend. She will miss having access to the inside of Grandma's house, with all of its accompanying smells, sights, and sounds. Will she still be welcome when the "new people" move in? Will it look the same? In addition, her room in her grandmother's house, with her favorite comfy mattress and pillow, will be gone. Will she be able to sleep in Grandma's new place? Will her bed still be there? These are some of the many questions that may be whirling through Sarah's mind.

It is also important to note that Sarah's routine will be heavily impacted by her grandmother's departure. Children are creatures of habit who crave structure and consistency. For all Sarah's young life, her relationship with Grandma has been constant. Sarah may feel that she is losing her best buddy and her way of life.

As already mentioned, Sarah is losing her sense of stability. She is also likely to feel a lack of trust in her ability to count on the people in her life to be there for her. If Grandma is moving away, who will be next? What will keep Mommy or Daddy from leaving her as well? Sarah is also experiencing a lack of power and control over her life. She is helpless to change the situation that has been thrust upon her. Her acting-out behaviors in school and her refusal to visit Grandma may be Sarah's attempts to regain some control over her life.

Cases 2 and 3: When Friendships End—"I Miss My Friends"

Matthew is a nine-year-old who has lived in his inner-city neighborhood all his life. Matthew has a developmental disability that manifests itself in some behaviors and mannerisms that seem odd to people who are not familiar with him. For example, his speech is loud, his gait awkward, and he tends to chew on any object that is at hand. Matthew has attended the same elementary school since prekindergarten. He does not have many friends at school, but he and his older brother, Mitchell, who is 14, are very close to the children who live in the house next door. These neighbors—two girls, Erica, age 10, and Donna, age 13—have lived next door for five years. They know Matthew well and treat him like a little brother. They play together every day and walk to school together. Mitchell enjoys hanging out with the girls and appreciates that they give him some respite from watching his brother each day after school. It is also helpful for him to be able to talk to Donna about how Matthew's behaviors embarrass him sometimes. She understands and does not make him feel bad about his feelings.

The boys just found out that their next-door neighbors are moving to the suburbs a month after school lets out for the summer. Matthew does not seem to comprehend that the girls will no longer be living next door, even after having it explained to him. He still talks about walking to school together next year and playing kick ball and swimming together all summer. Mitchell's parents say that Mitchell has been "being mean" to his brother lately—yelling at him and telling him to grow up. He has also been picking fights with the girls next door and refuses to hang out with them anymore. His grades in school have declined. Matthew's maladaptive behaviors have increased as a result of his difficulties with Mitchell.

Case Analysis: Mitchell

Identifying the Primary Loss

It is not a simple matter to determine what loss is primary to Mitchell. It seems simplistic to label his loss merely as the loss of friendship because many layers appear inherent in this loss. Perhaps it would be better to categorize the primary loss as a loss of understanding and assistance in caring for his little brother.

Identifying Secondary and Intangible Losses

As mentioned previously, there are many secondary and intangible losses embedded in Mitchell's loss of his next-door neighbors. In addition to losing a playmate, Mitchell is losing a confidant in Donna. She has an understanding of his situation and empathy for his experience that never leaves him feeling judged. Donna and Erica also provide Mitchell with much-needed respite from the pressures involved in caring for a younger brother with a disability. With Donna and Erica, Matthew's behaviors do not seem strange; they seem normal and expected. Mitchell may also experience a loss of freedom without the support of Donna and Erica after school and during summers.

Identifying the Client's Responses to the Loss Situation

Cognitive. Mitchell may be experiencing a variety of cognitive reactions to the loss of his next-door neighbors. For example, he may have the sense that he is now alone in dealing with his brother. He may experience an increased sense of responsibility and think, "I'll have to handle this on my own from now on." He might also be thinking that his current situation is an unfair burden on him. Some of his behaviors toward his brother might also make sense if Mitchell believes that he needs to prepare Matthew for the teasing that may await him in school and on the way to and from school after the girls' departure. He may be thinking, "I'd better toughen him up, or they'll eat him alive."

Behavioral. Mitchell is withdrawing from his friends next door. This may be an attempt to withdraw physically and emotionally before they abandon him. His hitting and yelling behavior with his brother and his declining grades may signal that Mitchell is feeling overwhelmed by his thoughts and emotions related to losing the girls next door.

Emotional. Mitchell is likely experiencing many confusing emotions, including fear of what will happen after the girls leave; fear of abandonment; anger at Matthew, his parents, the girls, and even himself; shame at being embarrassed over his brother's condition; and loneliness and fear that no one will understand him the way Donna and Erica do.

Discussion Questions

1. What strategies might be helpful in getting Mitchell to recognize and share his thoughts and feelings about the girls' move?
2. How could Mitchell's sense of burden be eased?
3. Is there a way for Mitchell to maintain some contact with Donna so that he can still benefit from her friendship and understanding?
4. Would it be important to deal with Mitchell's conflicting feelings of love and shame regarding his brother?

The Counselor's Response: Mitchell

Clinical work with Mitchell must reflect an accurate empathic understanding of his world. His loss is complex. He is losing a friendship and the sense of stability, trust, and understanding that were part of that relationship. It will be important for me, as his counselor, to let him know that I recognize that this must be a very frightening time for him and communicate my understanding honestly and gently.

Meetings would be scheduled to reflect a respect for the adolescent lifestyle—in other words, to work around his school, social, and extracurricular commitments. I would also demonstrate respect for Mitchell by treating him, in some ways, as if he were an adult. Specifically, this means allowing him to be responsible for providing demographic or intake information and scheduling and acquiring his informed consent. I would discuss the limits of confidentiality with him and assure him that the content of sessions will not be shared with anyone else unless I believe he is a risk to himself or others, or if someone is harming him. I would explain the parameters of the counseling relationship with him and his parents to achieve a shared understanding. (This is crucial in work with any adolescent.)

A useful approach with Mitchell would begin as a verbally based intervention, with opportunities for alternative communicative media readily accessible, including art supplies, journal paper, and sand. I would encourage Mitchell to talk about his friends, especially Donna, and their pending move and to share stories about their friendship. In doing so, I will be careful not to be too directive or move to a problem-solving mode before Mitchell recognizes the complexity of the loss himself. Once that complexity is established, the therapeutic relationship itself can be used to highlight Mitchell's ability to express his feelings. In particular, the relationship can help him to acknowledge that Donna is not the only person he can talk to and demonstrate that if he can share with me, he can also share with others.

Although it is important for Mitchell to view me as a support person, it is also crucial to help him tap other potential resources for support. I would consider assigning Mitchell homework that requires him to find ways of maintaining his friendship with Donna. It will be helpful to encourage him to get suggestions from other friends, family, and even Donna.

Building a support system that will help lessen the burden of Donna's moving away may also be helpful in providing tools for Mitchell to deal with the conflicting feelings he has regarding his brother. Getting him in touch with other siblings of children with developmental disabilities could be extremely helpful in that it would allow him to share his experiences with others who understand his situation. He would likely learn valuable tips about how to deal effectively with his younger brother. One of my goals would be to help Mitchell locate peer support groups within his community or those that can be reached through the Internet.

Case Analysis: Matthew

Identifying the Primary Loss

For Matthew, the sense of loss seems to have been postponed because he does not appear to understand the ramifications surrounding his next-door neighbors' move. This may mean that Matthew will feel the impact of the loss of lifelong friendship and routine suddenly and strongly when the girls depart for their new home.

Identifying Secondary and Intangible Losses

Matthew is likely to experience several secondary and intangible losses in this situation. He will lose the immediate unconditional positive regard that he receives on a daily basis from Erica and Donna. He will lose peers who accepted him despite his disability. He will also lose a regular social outlet and source of support. Considering Mitchell's yelling and hitting behaviors, he may already be experiencing a sense of loss of relationship with his older brother. Also, he may have lost the safety and security he felt in walking to and from school with the girls and having them there to advocate for him when others tease him.

Identifying the Client's Responses to the Loss Situation

Cognitive. At the current time, Matthew seems to be experiencing either denial that the girls are really moving or the cognitive inability to fully comprehend the situation and the possible consequences.

Behavioral. Although Matthew does not seem to fully comprehend the details of the loss he is faced with, he is already exhibiting behaviors that are a direct result of the situation. These include crying, angry outbursts, and an increase in maladaptive behaviors.

Emotional. Emotions that Matthew is likely to experience regarding his next-door neighbors' move include confusion, anger, fear, and hurt about his brother's behaviors. He may also experience a sense of abandonment.

Discussion Questions

1. Is it possible to prepare Matthew adequately for his impending loss, given the circumstances?

2. Would it be advisable to facilitate a conversation between the brothers about what is happening? Why or why not?

3. What strategies might you use to assist Matthew in facing his fears and feelings of anger and hurt related to the girls' move?

The Counselor's Response: Matthew

Like all children, those with developmental disabilities experience a full range of feelings and all of the intensity of those feelings. As Matthew's counselor, I would want to start out with some information about the nature and manifestation of his disability. Conversations with parents and child care providers would likely suffice.

Matthew does not appear to grasp the finality of the girls' move. It seems, however, that, although he may not be able to verbally acknowledge that he understands what is about to happen, he does have a sense of the impending loss. His talk regarding what the children will do next year in all likelihood demonstrates a wish that things will not change. It is his attempt to gain some control over the situation.

As with any nine-year-old, goals for the intervention would begin with creating a sense of safety for the child. I would make sure that Matthew recognizes that I accept him, as Donna and Erica do. One way to communicate acceptance is by allowing him the freedom to express himself with minimal limitations. Certainly, it is important to set limits that have to do with his safety, my own safety, and the condition of the setting, but I would not place so many restrictions on Matthew that he is unable to express himself. For example, I would not restrict or redirect his speech and chewing behavior in the context of the counseling relationship.

I would also develop a sense of Matthew's perception of the impending move. I can then make decisions regarding the counseling intervention based on Matthew's individual experience. It will not be useful for me to push an agenda of loss if Matthew does not perceive his current situation this way. Furthermore, following an agenda that belongs to me, as Matthew's counselor; his parents; or his teachers would not be therapeutic. Matthew would likely feel frustrated, diminishing the likelihood that he would return to counseling at a later date. Initial counseling may consist of helping Matthew's parents prepare him for the move. For example, they may want to drive Matthew by the girls' new home and school so that the move becomes more tangible and real. The bulk of counseling, however, may need to wait until after the move has actually taken place so that Matthew's reactions and needs can be better assessed.

Case 4: Breakups—"Let's Just Be Friends!"

Joe and Karen, both 16, have been dating for the past nine months. They are both sophomores at the same high school. Joe is very much in love with Karen and contemplates having a future with her beyond high school. Just yesterday, he bought Karen a beautiful necklace for her upcoming birthday with the money he had saved from mowing lawns over the summer. Today, Karen told Joe during lunch that she no longer wants to date him, but she wishes to remain "good friends." She also disclosed that she and Joe's friend Mike really like each other and have decided to start dating. She said that she and Mike felt that they wanted to do the right thing by telling Joe rather than going out behind his back. Joe is a very quiet and introspective young man who tends to withdraw and blame himself when things go wrong. He feels numb and even suicidal at the thought of seeing Karen and Mike together.

Case Analysis

Identifying the Primary Loss

The primary loss in this situation is the loss of Joe's relationship with his girlfriend.

Identifying Secondary and Intangible Losses

In addition to the primary loss of his girlfriend's presence in his life, Joe is likely to be experiencing many different secondary and intangible losses. First, his routine and sense of habit have been interrupted. Those working with clients who have experienced a breakup often overlook this, but it is often the first direct consequence experienced by a person whose relationship has ended. Each day for Joe may have been defined in terms of when he saw or spoke to Karen. He no longer needs to wait by her locker during the day, pick her up after school, or call her each evening before he goes to bed. He may miss the companionship of Karen's family and friends as well. Joe has also had many dreams shattered. He may have expected to go with Karen to the prom or on the senior trip. He may have even seen the two of them getting married one day. Joe has experienced a violation of his trust. Not only has he lost his girlfriend, he has lost his best friend as well. This may leave him questioning whether love really exists. He may also be experiencing a sense of embarrassment or wounded pride because Karen chose someone else over him. Joe has also lost his sense of identity. He is no longer one part of a couple but must forge a new individual identity that doesn't include Karen. He may be experiencing a sense of helplessness and lack of power and control over the situation.

Identifying the Client's Responses to the Loss Situation

Cognitive. Because Joe is introspective and tends to be hard on himself, it is possible that he blames himself for the breakup with his girlfriend. He may be saying to himself, "I'm a loser" and "It's all my fault." It also seems apparent that he is experiencing some level of suicidal ideation.

Behavioral. Joe's behavioral symptoms may include any or all of the following: somatic symptoms, refusal to go to school, social isolation and withdrawal, crying, difficulty sleeping and/or eating, and other signs of depression. It is important to note that not all adolescents manifest symptoms of grief or loss the same way. Some may act out, self-medicate with drugs or alcohol, or act as though nothing is wrong at all.

Emotional. Joe is likely to be experiencing a number of conflicting emotions, including sadness, shock, numbness, confusion, depression, anger at himself or others, and embarrassment.

Discussion Questions

1. Why would it be important to perform a lethality assessment with Joe?
2. What mechanisms could you use to help Joe recognize and deal with his thoughts and feelings?
3. Why would it be important to explain the grieving process to Joe?
4. What strategies might you employ with Joe to help him go about his daily life in the face of his loss?

The Counselor's Response

Joe is in a great deal of pain. During the initial session, I will have a lot to accomplish. It would be imperative to create an atmosphere of safety and trust and perform a thorough intake that includes a lethality assessment. Assessing for suicidal and homicidal ideation, drug or alcohol use, and self-injury would all be standard practice. The intervention with Joe will be based on this assessment, his immediate safety being the primary concern. It is prudent to set up a safety plan with Joe and his caregivers as well. His safety should be assessed throughout the intervention.

The primary goal in working with Joe is to offer him something that he is not likely to experience with friends, peers, or other adults. He needs to feel understood and listened to. What I do *not* do will be of major importance in this case. I will not self-disclose, compare him and his recently terminated relationship to relationships of his peers and contemporaries, offer advice, or minimize his experience of loss and pain. These are typical nontherapeutic responses that Joe will already have received from well-meaning family and friends.

I will also take care to tailor the counseling experience to Joe's needs. Joe is an introspective person. The pace of counseling should be gradual and allow for his introspection. I might assign him homework (so he has time to think and feel) and give him space or time during the session where verbal exchange would be secondary to his processing.

One concern I have is that Joe may become overwhelmed with grief; therefore, it will be wise to provide psychoeducational information regarding the grief process. It would serve Joe well to have grief parameters. For example, Joe could pick a 30-minute block of time for grieving. During this time, he could work on counseling homework assignments, listen to music, look at pictures, or cry. Setting aside time parameters specifically for grief will allow him to continue his daily activities. The time allotted will gradually be diminished as Joe works through his pain. The parameters are set so that Joe does not spend his entire day grieving, although he does indeed grieve.

Introspective adolescents may find narrative and journaling assignments especially useful for accessing grief. I might suggest that Joe begin writing a journal so he can express his feelings on paper. I could also invite Joe to bring in music or lyrics to songs that he experiences as being connected with his internal experience. This would provide an additional opportunity to understand Joe's loss from his perspective.

Case 5: Transition to Foster Care—"It's Hard to Explain"

Stephanie is an eight-year-old African American. She has lived with her foster care family for the past two years. Her foster family is white. Many service providers are involved with Stephanie, her foster family, and her family of origin. According to the state, Stephanie's family of origin is scheduled to be reunified in one year.

Stephanie is an energetic, active child. She has performed well in school academically and socially. She participates in youth soccer and dance. She has visitations with her family of origin, which includes her mother and three older brothers. A month ago, Stephanie and her foster family were informed that there would be some changes in Stephanie's visitations to help all parties prepare for reunification. Since the meeting, Stephanie has refused to participate in "family time" with her foster family. She no longer is interested in their regular Saturday adventures. She threw a tantrum last Saturday and was restrained by her foster father after she began hitting her head against the floor. A note from Stephanie's teacher indicated that Stephanie has also started to use hate words to describe herself and her family of origin.

Case Analysis

Identifying the Primary Loss

Stephanie's primary loss can be viewed as the anticipated loss of her foster care family.

Identifying Secondary and Intangible Losses

Stephanie is facing multiple secondary and intangible losses. Assessing these losses from Stephanie's perspective is imperative to attaining an accurate empathic understanding of the significance and complexity of her experience of loss. Loss of stability, control, power, security, sense of cultural self, identity, and community are all part of the fabric of Stephanie's loss. Many of the losses she is experiencing are likely to be overlooked because they are intangible.

Identifying the Client's Responses to the Loss Situation

Cognitive. Stephanie is likely to be confused by the impending changes in her life. These changes are not in her control, nor is she privy to the specifics related to these changes. She may be experiencing intense fear, thinking, "I don't know my family." The impending losses for Stephanie are filtered through an egocentric lens: "My foster family does not care." She may blame herself and think that she has done something wrong or bad.

Behavioral. All children experience and therefore manifest loss differently. In Stephanie's case, aggression towards self, acting out, withdrawal, and somatic symptoms demonstrate the magnitude of her experience. It is also crucial to note that the change in Stephanie's behavior is a key factor: It is not just that she is behaving in the aforementioned ways, it is that these behaviors are out of character for Stephanie.

Emotional. Fear, confusion, apathy, loneliness, and feeling overwhelmed are likely components of Stephanie's emotional experience. Because she is overwhelmed affectively, her behavioral and cognitive responses are likely to be exacerbated.

Discussion Questions

1. How can you structure your helping relationship with Stephanie so that her eventual discharge from the counseling relationship will not compound the other losses she will face?
2. How does Stephanie's cultural identity play a part in her experience of loss?
3. What are some ways Stephanie can be supported by her foster care and biological families during the transition and beyond?
4. As her counselor, how can you help the families and service providers involved with Stephanie recognize the complexity of her loss experience?

The Counselor's Response

In a situation such as this, in which a child has already experienced many separations and losses and is now facing yet another painful loss, it is critical to begin the relationship with a clear communication of the length of time you will be meeting. This is imperative for many reasons. First, the client has a right to informed consent and to know what to expect from counseling. Second, a helping relationship is predicated on the development of trust. Last, a counselor's most important duty is to do no harm to a client. By becoming yet another person seen by the child to be abandoning her, the short-term counseling process may result in more harm than good. It may instill in the child a notion that counselors cannot be counted on, preventing a client like Stephanie from seeking help in the future.

The ideal situation would be to establish a longer term counseling relationship that would take place before, during, and after the reunification of Stephanie's family. In this way, Stephanie will be able to count on at least one constant in her life throughout the transition.

It is impossible to adequately address this case without taking Stephanie's cultural identity into account. The fact that Stephanie has been living with a white family during a crucial time in the formation of her racial identity may mean that she has adopted the values of the mainstream culture. Unfortunately, this may mean that Stephanie has introjected the prejudice of some mainstream Americans who still view white people as superior to black people. After living happily with her foster family, she may also equate happiness and opportunity with white culture. The fact that she has begun using hate words to describe herself and her family of origin may point to the fact that she has a negative attitude toward her own culture. As her counselor, I would work with Stephanie to develop a healthy, positive attitude towards herself and her family with regard to her cultural heritage and identity. To facilitate this attitude, I might use cultural genograms, bibliotherapy, and films, as well as introduce her to African American mentors and role models to increase her knowledge and pride in her own culture.

It is easy for the complexity of Stephanie's losses to be underestimated by both her foster family and her family of origin. As pointed out in the case analysis, Stephanie may be experiencing her family's reunification as a rejection by her foster family. At the same time, her foster family may not understand the sudden change in Stephanie's behaviors and attitudes. She has always been so happy and cooperative and such a vital part of the family. They may be perplexed as to why she no longer wants to take part in family activities. Without violating Stephanie's confidentiality, I would explain the thoughts and feelings that Stephanie is experiencing. I would also help Stephanie and her family to develop ways to communicate about the transition and its impact on Stephanie. Stephanie needs to be assured that her foster family is not abandoning her, that she has not been "bad" or is not being punished, and that she can continue to have a positive relationship with her foster family even after the reunification.

Simultaneously, Stephanie's family of origin may not understand Stephanie's behaviors. I would explain that Stephanie may feel that she has to choose between her foster family and her family of origin. She may feel disloyal and guilty for having ambivalent feelings about reuniting with her mother and brothers. I would also work with Stephanie's biological mother and brothers to help them understand the variety of feelings that Stephanie is experiencing.

It is absolutely crucial that I develop a dialogue with both families to help them work together to smooth Stephanie's transition. Both families should be sending the same message to Stephanie about what will happen before, during, and after the reunification, and both should work to reduce her feelings of guilt, fear, confusion, and disloyalty. It would be helpful for the families to participate in some activities together and attend family therapy sessions, if possible. It would also be helpful for there to be as much planning as feasible before the reunification takes place. Stephanie needs the comfort of structure. She needs to know what to expect and when to expect it. She needs to know what kind of relationship she will be able to maintain with her foster family. It would be my goal to help the families to anticipate and respond to these areas of concern for Stephanie.

Case Study for Reader Analysis

Renee is a 15-year-old Latina. She has been living with her white foster care family for the past year. Prior to this foster care placement, Renee lived with three other foster care families, but she always ran away after less than a month.

Renee's biological parents used cocaine and alcohol throughout her childhood. The youngest of six children and the only one who is not currently in an independent living situation, she is a survivor of years of sexual, physical, and emotional abuse.

Renee was referred to counseling by her caseworker, who is concerned because Renee has chosen not to be adopted by her foster care family. Her foster care family is terribly hurt by her choice but wants to respect Renee's wishes.

Discussion Questions

1. What are Renee's primary, secondary, and intangible losses?
2. What makes Renee's experience a loss?
3. What is it like for you, as Renee's counselor, to be present with her grief and loss?

SUMMARY

We have explored several types of interpersonal losses, aside from death-related losses, that children and adolescents might experience. These losses include the primary, secondary, and intangible losses that occur when loved ones move away, friendships change, romantic breakups occur, and children suffer loss as a result of being part of the foster care system. Typical reactions and case analyses were provided for each type of loss.

For the most part, younger children tend to rely on their family relationships as the most important social connections in their worlds. Although family relationships remain important, older children and adolescents value friendships and other peer relationships as most significant in their lives. Adults tend to minimize the impact of nondeath interpersonal losses. Doing so is a mistake because children and adolescents who lose significant friends and family members may experience strong physiological, emotional, cognitive, and behavioral reactions that, if unresolved, may have a profound and lasting impact on their lives.

CHAPTER 7

Transitional Losses

Sixteen-year-old Dustin's mother was always extremely healthy and vibrant. Over the past year, however, she has not been feeling good and has been diagnosed with multiple sclerosis. The course of the disease is unpredictable. Sometimes Dustin's mother is just fine and displays very few symptoms. Other times she needs to be hospitalized and requires the use of a wheelchair to get around. Dustin's mother's illness has caused a number of drastic changes in his household and lifestyle. Although he used to have a very active social life, Dustin now has to spend time caring for his mother and younger siblings. He also misses the time he and his mother spent talking together. In Dustin's opinion, lately she seems too tired and preoccupied even to notice he is alive. He feels incredibly guilty for feeling this way because he knows that she cannot help being sick, but he can't help feeling neglected and burdened. He is also extremely angry at his father, who has taken a second job to pay for his wife's medical bills and make up for her lost income. Dustin only knows that his father isn't around to help when he needs him most.

Life transitions, both expected and unexpected, are responsible for most of the issues that we as counselors explore with clients. Children and adolescents are not immune to transitional losses. On the contrary, childhood and adolescence, by their very nature, are times of rapid growth and change. Children and adolescents need a great deal of support and encouragement in order to help them negotiate the transitions imposed upon them.

This chapter is designed to help practitioners determine appropriate counseling interventions for children and adolescents who have experienced transitional losses. Cases presented in this chapter will illustrate transitional losses related to moving, divorce, illness or disabling condition, substance abuse, parental job loss, and military deployment.

Case 1: Moving—"I Hate This Place!"

Eleven-year-old Emma loved living in the city. She liked having a real neighborhood, sidewalks, and streetlights. She loved having all the kids from the block (and there were many) congregate at her house after school, every weekend, and during the summers for impromptu games of kick ball and wall ball in the parking lot next door. She loved the sights and sounds of the city; somehow, the sounds of traffic and sirens were comforting to her. She also loved her school. She knew all kinds of kids and considered herself friends with everybody. Although she is white, she had friends who were Native American, Hispanic-Latino, African American, Asian American—and from many countries around the world. She took African dance lessons and participated in drama and sports. In short, she "had a life."

Emma's parents, on the other hand, grew up under very different circumstances. Mom was from the country, and Dad grew up in suburbia. They have wrestled with the idea of leaving the city for years due to increasing crime rates and decreasing housing values in their neighborhood. Although they loved their home and neighbors, a story in the newspaper about gangs at the middle school their daughter was scheduled to attend the following year scared them into deciding to move to the small town where Emma's mother works. To them, the move was exciting. They were able to afford a nicer home in a suburban neighborhood. Emma felt she was being sent to Siberia. She hated each new house to which she was dragged. She hated the town, the school, and all the "hicks" who lived there. Emma's parents tried to bribe her with the promise of a new puppy when they moved. They allowed her to pick her own room in the new house before her sister chose. They even let her finish out the school year at her old school in order to appease her.

Now that they have moved into their beautiful new suburban home, Emma is miserable. She mopes around the house, cries often, and tells her parents that she hates them for taking her life away from her.

Case Analysis

Identifying the Primary Loss

Emma's losses are multiple and complex. Loss of community captures the magnitude of her primary loss.

Identifying Secondary and Intangible Losses

There are many intangible and secondary losses for Emma. She has lost friends in moving to a new school and community. She has lost the familiarity with the school she attended, including the people, stability, and opportunities that setting provided. For example, she knew that Mr. Weinstein had been the junior varsity soccer coach for the past 10 years, and she could expect that he would be her coach if she made the team. She did not know who the coach was at her new school because it was a physical education teacher from the elementary school, and she hadn't been at the school the previous season. She lost the richness that her experience in a city school and neighborhood provided her. She was no longer part of a block or a neighborhood. She may have even lost some of her self-esteem. As an adolescent, she was forming her identity. She was already accepted and popular in her present community. Now she would have to start all over again in trying to gain acceptance. Moving may have her questioning, once again, who she is and how she feels about herself in relation to her surroundings.

Identifying the Client's Responses to the Loss Situation

Cognitive. Because adolescents tend to be egocentric, Emma may believe that her parents moved because of her. For instance, she may view this move as a punishment because they hate her. Also, she may be getting the message that "This is who we *really* are"—suburban, upper middle class, and so forth—and that is *better* than the way they were defined in the city.

Behavioral. Emma is currently demonstrating her grief through crying, moping, and lashing out at her parents.

Emotional. The complexity of the losses for Emma is taking an emotional toll. She is demonstrating some signs of mild depression and anger. She also seems to exhibit a sense of apathy.

Discussion Questions

1. How would you work with Emma to help her cope with this new situation?

2. What might Emma's parents have done to ease the transition before it happened?

3. Was it a good idea to move Emma during the summer rather than have her start earlier at her new school?

4. Now that the move has already taken place, what strategies might Emma's parents use to help her adjust to her new home and surroundings?

5. What steps can be taken so that Emma does not lose touch with her old friends?

The Counselor's Response

Emma sounds like a potentially articulate and willing participant in counseling. Her attitude depends largely on whether it was her decision or her parents' idea to participate in the counseling intervention. In establishing rapport with Emma, I would let her know immediately that participation in counseling is her choice. Making this plain is imperative because moving was *not* Emma's choice. She may be resistant to my involvement or to participation in counseling if it is her parents' idea. It is especially crucial to clarify this point because she doesn't seem to have had any say in all the changes she must confront. A lethality assessment and an assessment for substance use and self-injury are standard for a person her age. It will be a good idea to talk briefly about termination and discharge in the rapport-building phase and intermittently throughout the counseling intervention so that the multiple losses that occur with termination from counseling can openly be discussed and experienced. I would include discussion of termination as part of the process in order to lessen the potential for Emma to view the counseling relationship, once ended, as yet another loss.

After establishing rapport, I would take a history from Emma. This would allow her to share her story from her perspective. As part of the history taking, I would construct with Emma a genogram of her family (Goldenberg & Goldenberg, 1997). Separately, I would co-construct a diagram of her friendships. The genograms will give Emma the opportunity for direction and choice throughout the counseling intervention.

Once history taking is complete, I hope to engage Emma in focusing on the multiple losses she has experienced. If she is armed with insight, as many adolescents are, I would introduce the idea of multiple losses and help her to identify them. One by one, we would address her losses and grief. Emma's parents did include her in looking at houses, promised her a puppy, let her choose her room, and allow her to finish out the school year in the city. It seems that they anticipated that this move would be tough for Emma and tried to be thoughtful. Allowing Emma to finish out the school year has the benefit of giving her a scheduled and shared loss experience; however, the anticipation of the move and the multiple losses that came at the end of the school year could have been an enormous burden for her. I would determine how to involve Emma's parents by giving Emma the opportunity to make decisions regarding their participation. I would tell them this from the inception. I would also discuss with them the multiple and complex losses that their daughter is experiencing and encourage them to address their own losses connected to the move with their children, providing role-modeling of expression of feeling and a forum for Emma and her sister to do the same. Emma may be able to keep in contact with some of her friends through mail, phone calls, and the Internet if the technology is available. It is important that her parents allow her to keep in contact at her own discretion.

Finally, the move and its associated losses may have been mitigated by some additional planning. I would have encouraged Emma's parents to expose the potential losses and address them as they emerged for Emma. Promising her a puppy was a way of denying her an opportunity to grieve. My guess is that Emma's anticipatory grief also stirred up some difficult and unpleasant emotions for her parents. A going-away party that included a scrapbook of the people, places, and things that were meaningful to Emma may have given her some closure and would at least have been a tangible connection to her past community.

Case 2: Divorce—"Losing a Family"

Morgan is a 14-year-old girl whose parents have decided that she needs some help from a counselor. Morgan is the oldest of four children, her siblings being Alicia, 11; Amanda, 9; and Bonnie, 4. Three years ago, Morgan's parents decided after 15 years of marriage that they no longer loved each other and agreed to divorce. Morgan's parents were thoughtful about how and what they shared with the children. They overtly stated that it was not the fault of any of the children and that each parent loved each child unconditionally; that would not change.

It seemed that Morgan adapted well. Her father reported that she was sad and angry at first. Even after Morgan, her sisters, and her mom moved into a smaller house in a different community, she excelled socially and academically. Morgan's mother shared her former husband's perception and added that, over the last three months,

Morgan's grades have dropped a level (in some cases two), she has been keeping to herself, and she was caught smoking cigarettes. When Morgan's parents addressed her behavior together, in the spirit of co-parenting, Morgan screamed and sobbed for over three hours. Her parents reported that she said her life was not worth living and it was their fault for getting divorced. She hated them.

Morgan sat in silence with her head down while her parents reported this. After her parents were excused from the counseling office and it was only Morgan and me, Morgan said, "I'm not going to kill myself. Can I go now?"

Case Analysis

Identifying the Primary Loss

Morgan's primary loss is the breakup of her parents' marriage.

Identifying Secondary and Intangible Losses

Morgan has experienced many secondary and intangible losses as a result of her parents' divorce. She has lost her sense of stability. She has lost the familiarity and comforts of her family home. Most of all, she has lost the constant presence of her father in her life. Her notion of family has been shattered.

Identifying the Client's Responses to the Loss Situation

Cognitive. It is likely that Morgan has been doing a great deal of thinking since her parents' divorce. For example, she may be contriving ways of getting her parents back together.

Behavioral. Morgan has demonstrated somewhat erratic behavior. She has appeared, from all accounts, to adjust well to the divorce but has recently engaged in some rebellious behaviors.

Emotional. Morgan is very likely to be experiencing a great deal of pain, hurt, confusion, frustration, and anger regarding her parents' divorce.

Discussion Questions

1. If you were Morgan's counselor, how could you engage Morgan?
2. What are some of the intangible losses associated with Morgan's parents' divorce?
3. What is the potential impact of Morgan's developmental stage on her experience of the divorce?

4. In your role as the counselor, what advice would you give Morgan's parents?

The Counselor's Response

Morgan's response to her parents' divorce is not an uncommon one. Although from the outside it may seem that her behavior is contradictory, Morgan's responses are very appropriate to her age and developmental level. When first confronted with the divorce, Morgan went on autopilot. She continued her normal behaviors and did as she was expected to do while, at the same time, she was trying to sort things out in her mind. It is extremely common for children to harbor hopes of reuniting their parents. In fact, it is not uncommon for children of divorced parents to fantasize that if they behave well enough, their parents may reunite (Mack & Smith, 1991). Perhaps, initially, Morgan was experiencing a state of denial or false hope that her parents would simply come to their senses and reunite. From her perspective, if she was a "good girl," then she would be rewarded for her behavior, and her parents would see how happy the family was and get back together. Morgan is extremely angry and hurt. She is also very intelligent; after a few months, she realized that her parents were no closer to reconciling. Morgan then tried another strategy. She decided to engage in rebellious behaviors in an attempt to reunite her parents. Morgan's case is a classic illustration of triangulation. In triangulation, two family members become closer either in opposition against a third family member or, as in Morgan's case, in a combined effort to "save" the third party. Triangulation is a very effective strategy, and it did not take Morgan long to realize that each rebellious act resulted in her parents' joining forces, communicating more, and, ultimately, paying more attention to Morgan (Goldenberg & Goldenberg, 1997). Children and adolescents, who are so often voiceless, must somehow find a way to communicate their feelings of anger and frustration. Very often, counselors and parents fail to look beyond the presenting behaviors to examine the purpose and inherent message underlying the behaviors. Morgan has found a way to regain a sense of power and control over her chaotic existence. She has found a way to express herself and get her parents' attention.

In working with Morgan, it will be important for me as Morgan's counselor to realize that she is not likely to embrace counseling. The fact that her whole demeanor changes after her parents leave the room shows that Morgan is putting on an act in their presence. Morgan is likely to see me, the counselor, as infringing on her plans to reunite the family. Traditional counselors might approach Morgan by trying to get her to express her thoughts and feelings about the divorce. It is important to note that in Morgan's eyes the divorce is the unreality. Her family, as she always knew it, is her reality. She is therefore unlikely to engage in counseling that demands that she face the reality of her parents' divorce. In order to effectively counsel Morgan and establish a therapeutic relationship, I will need to meet her where she is. It is better to approach her with "You really want your parents to get back together" or "It must feel really good to see your parents working together like that." I will encourage Morgan to talk about her family, including what she loved about her family life before the divorce. After rapport is established, I can begin to confront Morgan gently about her hopes for her parents' reunification and about the ways she is using her rebellious behaviors to facilitate this. Most important, Morgan needs to gain a voice and find a healthy way to gain power and control in her life.

After meeting individually for a few sessions and establishing trust, I would suggest family therapy for Morgan and her parents. Morgan's parents need to understand the purpose behind her behaviors, and the entire family needs to learn to engage in more direct communication and express their feelings in an open, healthy way. This also means that Morgan's parents need to be ready and willing to hear and experience the full brunt of Morgan's anger and resentment toward them and their divorce. Ultimately, Morgan needs an opportunity to mourn her loss. She has a right to feel angry, hurt, and disappointed and will need time to work through all of her feelings.

Case 3: Coping with a Disability—"I'm a Freak!"

Eight-year-old Ian was recently diagnosed with a learning disability. He has always had trouble reading and identifying his letters, even before he attended school. For years, his teachers have called him "lazy" and "inattentive," and his classmates have called him "stupid" and "dummy." Even Ian's father sees Ian's learning difficulties as Ian's fault and says he just needs to buckle down. He often takes away privileges from Ian and punishes him for his bad grades. Ian's mother, however, has always suspected that Ian has an underlying learning disability. She has noticed her energetic, happy son becoming sad and talking about himself in negative terms. He calls himself a "loser" and a "freak."

When Ian was diagnosed with a learning disability, Ian's mother expected an abrupt change in her son's self-esteem. After all, now Ian knows he is not "dumb." In Ian's mind, however, the new label is only a nice way of proving that he is indeed a dummy. Now he knows he is not normal. Now that he has special attention in class and has to take his tests in a different room, it is even more obvious to his classmates that he is a freak. In addition, Ian's dad, whom he idolizes, seems not to agree with the notion that he has a learning disability. He believes that Ian is still just not trying hard enough. Ian dreads going to school each day. He complains of headaches and stomachaches and is constantly tired. When given the option, he prefers to play his Game Boy for hours on end and is becoming ever more sullen and irritable.

Case Analysis

Identifying the Primary Loss

Ian's primary loss is his identity. He had accepted his father's and peers' image of himself before he was diagnosed with a learning disability. Now that he has been diagnosed, he is having trouble integrating that definition into his current perception of self.

Identifying Secondary and Intangible Losses

There are several secondary and intangible losses in this situation. In addition to his loss of sense of self, Ian has had losses of self-esteem, status, and pride. Being labeled learning disabled does not bring Ian to a level of self-acceptance but confirms his negative value of self. Therefore, the diagnosis compounds losses that already existed and exacerbates others. These losses are, for the most part, relational in nature.

Identifying the Client's Responses to the Loss Situation

Cognitive. Ian is experiencing difficulty concentrating on school-related tasks and is engaging in negative thinking about himself.

Behavioral. Ian is experiencing a number of somatic responses in the form of headaches, stomachaches, and a lack of energy.

Emotional. Ian is experiencing a variety of emotional responses, including self-doubt, anger, fear, confusion, sadness, irritability, and apathy. Of all the emotional responses expressed, the most salient seems to be shame.

Discussion Questions

1. Do you think Ian's learning disability was adequately explained to him? How would you help Ian to understand his disability?
2. How does Dad's denial of Ian's learning disability affect Ian?
3. How would you work with Ian's parents to help them to help Ian?
4. How would you work with Ian to try to enhance his self-esteem?

The Counselor's Response

I would begin my work with Ian by focusing on Ian. The connection to his learning disability would eventually be made; however, I would start by getting to know him. I want to be thoughtful of Ian's age and provide opportunities for verbal and other forms of communication. This consideration will facilitate a positive counseling experience for this child.

I want to meet with Ian's parents separately from Ian, although I would provide them with additional and appropriate resources for support. I also would want to make sure I discuss with them their own perceived loss: having a child with a disability. I may need to refer them to counseling outside of my meetings with them because Ian is my focus.

Several components of my intervention with Ian are integral. First, I want to provide him with toys, art supplies, and other creative media so that he has multiple ways of sharing his experience with me. He will also have tangible successes as he creates. A positive asset search (Ivey & Ivey, 2003) will be an ongoing part of the counseling intervention. It is my job to help Ian identify the positive aspects of himself and his learning style. I will be very careful not to praise him. It is likely that Ian will reject my praise, and ultimately that could ruin our rapport. In addition, praising him could foster dependency.

When I have observed both behaviorally and emotionally that Ian has increased self-esteem, I would use a brief portion of the session for psychoeducational purposes. During the first or last five minutes of the session (I would leave it up to Ian), I would focus on what it means to have a learning disability from the perspective of the person with the disability. I may decide to use books written for children and about children with learning disabilities. (For a list of recommended books for children with disabilities and their caregivers, see www.ldonline.org.) Finally, I would consider group counseling for Ian. Many children struggle with learning disabilities. The social support and connection provided by a group could only be an additional benefit.

Case 4: Coping With Mental Illness—"Riding the Roller Coaster"

Three weeks ago, Roman, a Latino adolescent, was referred to counseling services again. Roman has received services intermittently since he was seven years old. At 14, Roman is again in trouble at school for acting out aggressively. Roman's behavior is rather inconsistent. Sometimes he is the picture of a good student: well behaved, interested, and engaged. However, he also has aggressive outbursts, seems to "check out," and can be negative toward even his best friends. Most recently, he was suspended from school for throwing a battery at a classmate on the school bus.

Roman is reluctant to meet with a counselor. The assistant principal reports that Roman is a troublemaker and that contact with home is sporadic at best. Ms. Hernandez, Roman's mother, is a frequent no-show at meetings regarding Roman. The last time she showed (a year ago) she was dressed inappropriately, wearing a see-through shirt, and made sexual advances to Roman's previous counselor. His mother monopolized the meeting, talking nonstop for 20 minutes. Hardly any of what she said made sense. "Off the record," the assistant principal said, "I hear she's a regular at County Mental Health." According to the bus driver, Roman threw the battery at a boy who had made fun of Roman's mother because she appeared to be drunk and was swearing at Roman as he boarded the bus.

Case Analysis

Identifying the Primary Loss

Roman's primary loss is having the normal mother he sees depicted in the media and in his friends' lives.

Identifying Secondary Intangible Losses

Children of parents with mental illness experience numerous losses. They are often "parentified," taking on adult responsibilities and losing the ability to be a child with someone who will parent them. They have no sense of stability because their parents' moods and periods of lucidity may fluctuate. Roman may also experience times when he feels that his personal safety is threatened.

Identifying the Client's Responses to the Loss Situation

Cognitive. Roman is likely to believe that no one understands his situation, which may indeed be true. He may also be afraid that he will become like his mother. It would be crucial to explore these thoughts in order to effectively counsel Roman.

Behavioral. Roman's behaviors fluctuate. Sometimes he is well-behaved in school, and other times he acts aggressively. In at least one instance, Roman acted aggressively as a response to an insult directed at his mother.

Emotional. Roman may feel embarrassment about his mother, isolation and alienation from others who have normal mothers, and anxiety about becoming mentally unstable himself.

Discussion Questions

1. How is Roman's experience of loss connected to his mother's illness?
2. How would you engage Roman in the counseling process?
3. Is it important that you verify that his mother is mentally ill? Why or why not?
4. How should you engage his mother in the counseling process?
5. As a mandated reporter, do you need to "hotline" Roman's mother?

The Counselor's Response

Roman's case presents the challenge to look at the issue from multiple perspectives. When working with a Latino youth, it is imperative that the counselor examine the part that Latino values—those relating to machismo and "la familia," for instance—play in the client's thoughts and behaviors (Robinson & Howard-Hamilton, 2000). As his counselor, I will examine the role that culture plays in Roman's behaviors. Young Latinos tend to value being strong and able to take care of the women in their lives. Family is the most crucial connection in life. As a result, Roman's mother's mental illness has probably forced Roman to care for his mother, as well as any siblings in the picture. He may feel frustrated in his inability to cure his mother or make things better.

It will be important for me to explore how Roman's mother's illness is affecting Roman's home life. Unless Roman is being neglected or abused, his mother's mental illness should not necessitate my making a report to authorities. However, I will equip Roman with resources to contact if his mother's illness reaches a point at which either she or Roman needs additional help and support. I will also work with Roman's mother and the county mental health agency to be sure that someone monitors Roman's household to make sure all parties are safe and that their needs are being met.

In understanding Roman, it is helpful to view his situation from the perspective of Maslow's hierarchy of needs (Maslow, 1987). When Roman's safety and family needs are being met, Roman functions well at school. He is able to concentrate on academic issues and can interact socially. When his mother's condition deteriorates and his life turns chaotic, it is not surprising that Roman reverts to survival mode and is unable to engage in task-oriented school behavior. The incident on the bus also indicates that Roman is acting aggressively in order to protect his mother. This is a very strong Latino value and must be understood from a cultural perspective.

As Roman's counselor, it is important for me to communicate my respect for him and his mother. I would share with him what individuals involved in the case, such as the bus driver and assistant principal have confided and allow Roman to express himself about the comments that have been made about his mother. I would probably disclose my own personal experience as the child of a parent with a mental illness and would ask him to share with me his feelings about his mother and their living situation. It wouldn't surprise me if Roman felt both proud and ashamed of his mother, and I would offer him a safe place to explore the conflicting and confusing emotions he is likely experiencing. Ultimately, I would work to help Roman feel that he is not alone in his struggle. I would engage him in bibliotherapy to help him understand his mother's illness and connect him with a support network of children in a similar position.

While I was working individually with Roman, I would also take steps to advocate on his behalf within the school district. With Roman's permission, I would meet with the principal and teachers who have labeled Roman a troublemaker to give them some information that would make them more empathic and less punitive with regard to Roman's plight. I would also make sure that Roman has an ally within the school whom he can turn to when he is feeling frustrated. This person could be a counselor, psychologist, teacher, or coach—someone Roman trusts and feels connected to within the building.

Case 5: Substance Abuse in the Family—"Somebody Notice Me!"

Austin is a six-year-old white male. He lives with his mother, father, and maternal grandmother. His parents are not married. Austin has been referred for counseling services for a variety of reasons. He has been bullying other children, especially girls, on the school bus. Austin regularly soils himself during the school day. Academic and social struggles are also present.

Austin's father and maternal grandmother are his primary caretakers. His mother works nights and does not get up until after Austin leaves for school. She returns after he has gone to sleep. In the last four years, Austin's mother has spent a lengthy amount of time away from home during three separate hospitalizations for recovery from alcohol dependence.

When Austin was four years old, he saw a counselor for seven sessions because he was reportedly suffering night terrors. The terrors subsided after a few visits. Austin and his family viewed the intervention as beneficial.

Case Analysis

Identifying the Primary Loss

Austin's primary loss is the loss of the presence of his mother in his life.

Identifying Secondary and Intangible Losses

Austin is likely to experience secondary losses such as a sense of instability and inconsistency. He also lacks the power to control his situation and his mother's behavior.

Identifying the Client's Responses to the Loss Situation

Cognitive. It is not immediately apparent what thoughts Austin may be having, but it is possible to surmise, given his age and circumstances, that he may think he is responsible for his mother's absence.

Behavioral. Austin appears to be engaging in attention-seeking behaviors, which is very understandable under the circumstances. His anger is directed primarily towards girls, which may be a misguided attempt to express his anger at his mother.

Emotional. Austin is angry, confused, and probably feeling guilty. He is trying his best to gain his mother's attention in the only way he knows.

Discussion Questions

1. How would you engage Austin in counseling?
2. How would you go about building alliances with his parents and caretakers?
3. What if Austin won't talk about his mother's alcohol dependence?

The Counselor's Response

Austin is very unlikely at his age to be able to directly express his thoughts and feelings about his mother's absence. First, from a developmental perspective, Austin is not likely to understand, let alone be able to articulate, his needs and emotions. Second, most families with an alcoholic member are pervaded by an aura of secrecy. In fact, many are known to be socially isolated from friends and neighbors (Carroll, 2000). Even if it has not been expressly stated that family business is supposed to stay within the family, Austin is likely to have incorporated this message. For this reason, it is crucial to work with Austin in indirect ways. It would be helpful to use creative techniques, such as art, play therapy, puppet shows, and stories, to help Austin gain a sense of control and have an opportunity to express his thoughts and feelings. This would allow him a place to act out, in play, his aggressive and angry feelings in a safe environment. In turn, he would have less need to act out inappropriately in school. Austin also needs information. He is likely to feel that his mother avoids him because he is "bad." He needs to understand, in developmentally appropriate terms, what alcoholism is and that he is not to blame for his mother's behaviors.

It is also necessary to build alliances with Austin's caretakers, including his mother. It would be important to assess the mother's ability to function with Austin in order to understand whether to encourage her to spend more time with him. If she is capable, it would be wise to work out ways in which Austin can spend more time with his mother. Austin's grandmother may be the best source of support for Austin. It would be helpful if she were able to answer Austin's questions, calm his fears, and engage in activities with him, such as going on walks, cooking, or engaging in other hobbies. Austin should be checked out by a physician to be sure that his encopresis is not medically based. This condition is likely to be a result of his emotional turmoil and symbolizes his lack of control, but it is best to be sure. This problem will probably spontaneously remit when Austin's emotional needs are met.

Case 6: Parental Job Loss—"Losing the Family Farm"

Sixteen-year-old John comes from a long line of proud farmers. He lives on a road that is named for his family, who founded his town in the 1800s. He belongs to the Future Farmers of America and the 4-H Club in his rural community. He is enrolled in the agricultural practices program at his local high school. He shows the goats he raises at the county fair each year and participates in local tractor pulls. Nearly all of his friends are from farming families as well. He is poised to attend Cornell University in their agriculture and life sciences program to prepare him to take over the family farm when his father retires in 10 years. In the meantime, his father has already deeded him a few acres of land, where John dreams of building his own house one day. He visits his land at least once every day and envisions exactly how his home will look.

John has seen many of his neighbors and family friends lose their farms over the years due to tax problems, drought conditions, and overextended credit, but he believed that such a thing could never happen in his family. Therefore, John is completely shocked when his father and mother arrange to talk with him and his sisters after dinner one night to explain that they have lost the family farm. His parents announce that they will be forced to move into an apartment in town and "watch their pennies" until his father can locate suitable work to make ends meet.

John is in disbelief as he watches his family's property auctioned off soon afterward. He finds it hard to look his friends in the eye and withdraws to his small room more and more often. His father seems to be drinking more and more. He doesn't get out and look for work, and John's mother, who has always been a stay-at-home mom, has taken a job as a clerk at the local grocery store. John's parents seem to be fighting a lot, and when they do, he goes to his room, slams the door, and turns his music up as loud as it will go. He finds himself feeling really angry with his father. He would like to hit him and scream at him. How could his father do this to him? How could he single-handedly lose the farm and the land that his family has held for generations? All of John's dreams have been shattered. He has started hanging out with a rougher crowd at school, smoking pot, and getting into fights. He is driving recklessly and taking part in drag races on a rural stretch of road. His parents are in so much pain themselves that they don't seem to notice John's anguish.

Case Analysis

Identifying the Primary Loss

John's primary loss is the loss of his family home.

Identifying Secondary and Intangible Losses

Secondary and intangible losses include John's dignity, dreams, security, and identity. John has lost his perception of his father and mother. There is also the loss that comes with financial hardship: moving to a different part of the community and smaller home. He has lost his connection to friends, family history, tradition, and ritual. Losses of connection to the past and future, to the land and his childhood home, and the farming lifestyle are also present and relevant.

Identifying the Client's Responses to the Loss Situation

Cognitive. Consistent with appropriate developmental egocentrism, John may believe he has a level of responsibility in losing the farm. It appears that negative self-talk and apathy are also present, as demonstrated by his behavioral responses.

Behavioral. John is using drugs (specifically, marijuana) and participating in other risky behaviors (for example, drag racing and fighting).

Emotional. John is likely to be experiencing a number of emotions, including anger, despair, fear, shame, worry, hurt, and loneliness.

Discussion Questions

1. What are the main issues John is facing in this scenario?
2. How would you work with John to help him cope with his loss and refocus on his goals?

The Counselor's Response

As John's counselor, I want to build rapport with him quickly by allowing him to tell his story while using reflective listening techniques to demonstrate accurate empathic understanding. It will be important to find themes and see the big picture in John's story because the multiple losses are overwhelming. Once themes are teased out, I would encourage John to begin to grieve.

The process and path John takes in grieving needs to be his own. Part of what is profound in the losses John has suffered is that he has had no power or control in the decision making that is connected to the losses. For example, John did not get to choose where the family would move after the farm was sold. This loss of choice is in direct contrast to the enormous self-determination John was prepared to achieve as the farm was passed to him. I would serve as a consultant to John, offering suggestions and providing support. Some suggestions for John would include carving out 5 to 15 minutes of each day to grieve. During this time, John could cry, scream, write, or stare into space. The goal is for him to feel the pain connected to the loss instead of trying to minimize, dismiss, or defend against it. John has been active in the farming community, and I would suggest that he continue in the same capacity if he felt he could, or perhaps become part of one of the organizations that works to prevent farm families from losing their land and livelihood.

Throughout the counseling intervention with John, I would assess his level of depression and risky behaviors. It is important to recognize that his risky behaviors may be veiled suicide attempts. His risk of suicide should be carefully monitored.

Case 7: Military Deployment—"How Dare You Leave Me!"

Amy is a happy and bright eight-year-old, the oldest child from an intact family. Both her parents are teachers. Her mother returned to work a few months ago after taking the past seven years off to care for Amy and her five-year-old sister, Kaela.

Amy has adjusted well to becoming an older sister, entering third grade, and having her mom return to work. Amy's father is in the Army reserves. Three months ago, he was deployed to a war zone. Amy's mother was concerned about how his deployment would affect her and the girls, and, of course, she was terrified for her husband's safety. Amy's mother found support for herself through family and friends.

It was clear that both girls were missing their father, but Kaela seemed to be able to talk about it and feel better. Amy reacted differently, and this concerned her mother. Amy refused to talk about her father at all. She would not speak to him on the phone, write him letters, or e-mail him. In school, Amy maintained her level of academic performance, but her teachers noticed that she was very sensitive. By sensitive, they meant that Amy fought a great deal with her friends and more often than not wound up in tears.

Case Analysis

Identifying the Primary Loss

Amy's primary loss is the loss of her father to military deployment.

Identifying Secondary and Intangible Losses

Amy is likely to experience several secondary losses, such as the loss of routine, loss of a sense of safety, and loss of special time with her dad.

Identifying the Client's Responses to the Loss Situation

Cognitive. Amy is likely to be having thoughts that her father has abandoned her. Although she does not express it outright, she is likely to be concerned for her father's safety as well.

Behavioral. Amy is punishing her father for leaving her. She avoids any contact with him, no matter how he tries to communicate. She also uncharacteristically reacts emotionally with peers and cries easily.

Emotional. Amy is feeling a variety of emotions. She is angry with Dad and Mom. She is scared that her father will be hurt. Most of all, she feels abandoned and lost.

Discussion Questions

1. How much information about the military and their role should Amy be exposed to?
2. How does your own view of the military affect your counseling?
3. What kind of outside support would be helpful to Amy?
4. How can you help Amy and her family handle media coverage of the war?

The Counselor's Response

Counselors need to assess many aspects of a military deployment. I would evaluate whether this is the family's first experience with military deployment, how the child typically has dealt with separation issues, the degree of anxiety in the family surrounding the deployment, the amount of change in routine expected within the household, and so forth. I would also determine what kind of military support services are available to Amy and her family. It would be helpful if there were a support group for children of deployed military personnel that Amy could join. The group would provide her with a space to share her feelings with other children who are going through the same experience. However, these services are often unavailable to reserve soldiers who do not live close to a military base.

Amy's response to her father's absence is not surprising. The only way she has to express her anger is by giving Dad the silent treatment. In counseling, I would help Amy get to a point where she could directly express her feelings of rage and abandonment with her father. She is in a difficult position, not wanting to add to her father's stress when he is in a dangerous situation but wanting to yell at him at the same time. Amy needs to know that it is okay to express her feelings. Amy's mother also needs to explore what nonverbal messages she is sending to her daughters. She may be saying, "It's okay to express yourself" or "Daddy's going to be okay," while at the same time covertly demonstrating her own fear and anger. Children, especially "sensitive" children, easily pick up on the emotions of the adults in their lives. Amy may actually be acting as the conduit for her mother's unspoken reactions to Dad's absence. Amy's fears are well-founded. Too often, adults dismiss the fears of children with minimizing words of reassurance, such as "Don't worry, it'll be okay." I would allow Amy a safe place to explore her fears and emotions. I would use art and narrative therapy to help her express her feelings and thoughts. I would validate her concerns and assist her in finding a way to reestablish a relationship with Dad.

Case Study for Reader Analysis

Evan is nine, the youngest of six children. He is developmentally delayed. All six children were placed in foster care two years ago, when their mother left them with a neighbor and never returned. The children's father is incarcerated and is scheduled to be released from prison in four years. He has voluntarily terminated his parental rights.

Evan misses his parents. He still pretends to call them each day. He makes up wonderful tales about why he is in foster care. He sometimes acts out aggressively when he gets mad, frustrated, and confused. The preadoptive foster care parents have recently decided that they are no longer interested in adopting six children, especially one with special needs. The case manager has just a few weeks to make a new placement, and it looks as though the children will be split up. Evan will most likely be moved out of the county.

Discussion Questions

1. How would you work with Evan to prepare him for his inevitable loss?

2. What suggestions would you give to Evan's caseworker with regard to placing Evan in a new foster care setting?

3. How do you help Evan cope with his preexisting losses?

SUMMARY

This chapter explored many examples of transitional losses experienced by children and adolescents. Topics covered included moving, divorce, illness or a disabling condition, parental job loss, and military deployment. Common reactions and case analyses were provided for each type of loss presented.

CHAPTER 8

Developmental Losses

Eddie is an eighth grader who is small for his age. He stands nearly a head shorter than most of his peers and is often picked on about his size. He is concerned that he will never grow, and his parents have noticed that his self-esteem has dropped drastically over the past two years. Eddie often refers to himself in derogatory terms, such as "loser," and has been picking fights with bigger boys to compensate for his short stature and to prove that he is not a pushover. Eddie's parents are concerned about him and the increasing number of behavioral referrals he is receiving in school.

In the previous chapter, losses related to transitions were examined. This chapter will discuss some of the developmental losses that children and adolescents are likely to experience. Childhood and adolescence constitute an unprecedented time of physical, cognitive, and emotional growth and change. Adults are familiar with the pain that often accompanies developmental changes such as the onset of puberty. Unfortunately, the unexamined pain some adults, including parents and counselors, experienced while growing up may prevent them from helping the children and adolescents in their lives. This chapter presents strategies for helping children and adolescents cope with developmental change. Topics include losses related to puberty and its accompanying physical changes, school transitions, and family life-cycle changes. In addition, we will explore the loss experienced by children who discover the truth about myths such as the one described in this first case example.

Case 1: Loss of Childhood—"Santa Doesn't Really Exist, Does He?"

It was a big day for 10-year-old Taylor. She was being allowed to sleep over at a friend's house for the first time ever. Taylor's parents are a bit on the overprotective side; Taylor is an only child. However, they have known the Breslaws for years, and Taylor and Arlene Breslaw have been friends since they were in diapers. Taylor's parents expected a good-night phone call from their 10-year-old around bedtime. Taylor did indeed call, and she was crying hysterically. Taylor's parents were, of course, alarmed. Arlene's mother said everything was fine, but Taylor started crying that she wanted to go home. It took Taylor's parents three minutes to get over to the Breslaw home to pick Taylor up. Arlene's parents shrugged and agreed to speak the following day.

Taylor was able to calm down relatively quickly. When she was able to speak clearly, she said, "You are both liars." Her parents were caught totally off guard. Taylor went on to say, "There no such thing as Santa. You are Santa, and you lied to me. It's not funny." Taylor's parents were speechless. They attempted to explain themselves to their daughter, but Taylor became upset again. They thought she was over-tired. That was three weeks ago. Since then, Taylor has been "mouthy" and disrespectful to her parents and her teachers. She refuses to do her chores and has even used foul language. Taylor's parents are worried that something more happened at the Breslaw house, and their relationship with the family has changed as a result.

Case Analysis

Identifying the Primary Loss

Taylor's primary loss is the loss of her trust in her parents. She always counted on them to tell her the truth.

Identifying Secondary and Intangible Losses

Taylor has also lost a sense of innocence and her ability to engage in holiday tradition that she loved in the way she had before.

Identifying the Client's Responses to the Loss Situation

Cognitive. Taylor appears to have extended the mistrust she experienced regarding her parents to everything her parents say and do. She feels that she has been duped and betrayed by them. How can she ever trust them again?

Behavioral. Taylor has reacted by becoming disrespectful to her parents and teachers, and she has begun refusing to do her chores.

Emotional. Taylor is very hurt and angry. She no longer feels safe in relying on her parents to be truthful with her. She may also feel somewhat embarrassed or ashamed, thinking, "Was I stupid to believe in Santa?"

Discussion Questions

1. Is there a way that Taylor's parents could have prepared her for this type of loss?
2. All children eventually find out about Santa. Make an argument that this is a significant loss for children.
3. How can you address Taylor's parents' notion that something else must have happened?

The Counselor's Response

This case pushes buttons for many people. Some parents struggle with the desire to engage in a widely accepted holiday tradition that forces them to be less than completely honest with their children. Others give no thought whatsoever to what will happen when a child finds out that Santa doesn't exist. Parents often minimize or dismiss the pain associated with losing such a well-ingrained belief. In any event, discovering that there is no Santa can be quite shocking and unsettling for some children, as it was in Taylor's case. It affects not only home rituals but how the children talk to each other about Christmas, their perceptions of the songs they sing, and their belief in the veracity of Christmas stories.

Taylor's parents are right when they suspect that there is more to the situation than meets the eye, but they are wrong in their suspicions that another event must have taken place to make Taylor this upset. Like many of us, they underestimate the impact of discovering a lie, no matter how well intentioned, in the family. To Taylor, this loss is significant not only because she has lost her sense of innocent wonder at a beloved holiday tradition, but also because she has lost her faith in her parents.

The case study mentions that Taylor is a somewhat sheltered only child, indicating that she has had to rely very heavily on her parents and has come to trust them implicitly. Taylor is on the cusp of puberty. At this stage in her life, relationships begin to take precedence over everything else. She needs to feel that she can trust her parents to tell her the truth. These very people have instilled in her a belief that honesty in relationships is absolutely crucial, and now she has discovered that they have been lying to her throughout her entire life. This awareness has caused Taylor a great deal of cognitive dissonance. She is not sure she even knows her parents anymore. What seems to her parents a little white lie signifies a complete breakdown in trust to Taylor. Also, it may be important to let Taylor express her anger with her parents without justifying her parents' actions by saying things that may trivialize her feelings, such as "They just wanted you to enjoy Christmas." It may be important for her to process and work through her anger before she can see the big picture. Also, Taylor may have feelings of shame, feel that she has been duped by her parents, and see herself as "stupid." It would be important to uncover and work through Taylor's feelings and thoughts.

In working with Taylor, I would provide her with a place where she could explore her feelings about what happened and her reaction to her parents' dishonesty. I might provide art supplies and have her draw her relationship before and after the incident to help her bring out the feelings she has. I would help her examine her parents' motives and facilitate communication between her and her parents about the underlying issue of trust and betrayal. I might suggest that she write a letter to loss. Such a letter might begin "Dear Santa, how could you have been a lie?" This activity might help her to explore her sense of loss in a nonblaming way.

Developmentally, Taylor has moved to a new stage of life, one that may have been thrust upon her prematurely before she had the proper defense mechanisms to cope. Had this situation occurred just a few years later, it is likely that Taylor would have already known and accepted that her parents are flawed, and she could have incorporated her shocking discovery more readily. It would be important, therefore, to help Taylor reconfigure a new relationship with her parents that incorporates the notion that they are imperfect human beings but that they still love her unconditionally.

Case 2: Puberty/Physical Changes—"I *Hate* the Way Boys Look at Me!"

Ellen is an 11-year-old who has always been a very active and social child until recently. Ellen began menstruating just before turning 11, and seemingly overnight her body began to change. She went from looking like a little girl, like all of her friends, to developing the body of a woman. The growth of her breasts is particularly noticeable; she went from a training bra (which she was not excited to buy and only wore at the insistence of her mother) to a D cup in a matter of months. To Ellen, these changes have made her feel as though she is inhabiting the body of a stranger. As an athlete, she has had to work hard to rediscover her center of gravity and balance, and her soccer coach recently approached her, suggesting that she purchase a sports bra with plenty of support. This exchange was entirely humiliating to her, and she realized that there is no way she can hide the changes in her body. Most troubling to Ellen is the way that her male peers have responded to the change in her appearance. Until recently, most of her friends were boys. She spent time with them playing kick ball and other games. Now she senses a change in their approach to her. They don't ask her to join them in games as often, and they make comments about her body that make her feel uncomfortable. Last week, Ellen came home extremely distraught. Through her sobbing, she told her mother that she would never show her face in school again. Apparently, the boys in her grade held an informal vote to decide who had the "biggest boobs in the school," and Ellen was chosen. She felt totally humiliated and, worst of all, her best friend was angry with Ellen, telling her that she "hogs all the boys' attention." Ellen's mother has brought her to counseling to work on issues related to her body image and self-esteem. She has noticed that Ellen's posture has changed. She tends to hunch and hide herself and wears the baggiest clothes she can find so her large breasts are not as obvious.

Case Analysis

Identifying the Primary Loss

Ellen's losses are many, and identifying her primary loss is difficult. However, Ellen's emotional manifestation of grief and behavioral changes suggests that loss of self or identity is her primary loss.

Identifying Secondary and Intangible Losses

Ellen is suffering from a multitude of losses. She has lost her perception of self. She has lost her anonymity and ability to blend in, as well as her childhood, friends, and relationships with peers and adults. She can no longer dress like all the other girls in her grade or on her team. She has losses associated with being objectified—losses of innocence, security, and safety. She has physical difficulties associated with the weight of supporting large breasts. Finally, she has the burden of being sexualized when she is too young to know what that means or how to respond.

Identifying the Client's Responses to the Loss Situation

Cognitive. Ellen's cognitive responses to her multiple losses are not obvious. However, feeling humiliated in school may indeed affect her level of concentration. She may also be distracted by her appearance. She may become preoccupied with how her clothes are—or are not—revealing her breasts.

Behavioral. Ellen has withdrawn and changed her style of dress and her posture. Although no other overt behavioral markers are indicated, there is research to suggest that early maturing females are more likely than their counterparts to engage in delinquent and sexual behavior and to use drugs. Early maturing females report more popularity with boys, which ironically is consistent with greater emotional upset (Steinberg, 1996).

Emotional. The same body of research that suggests early maturing females are more likely to use drugs and become involved in sexual and delinquent behavior also argues that these girls are more likely to suffer from depression (Steinberg, 1996). Some emotional cues suggest that Ellen is depressed. Her experience of humiliation and shame are significant in that they can be connected to the behavioral manifestations of her losses. She hunches over in an attempt to hide and make herself smaller (also potentially from the weight of her breasts)—a fitting posture for someone who is depressed, shamed, objectified, and humiliated.

Discussion Questions

1. How would you work with Ellen to develop a more positive body image?

2. What kinds of social stereotypes are projected onto girls who develop early, and what impact do these notions have on them?

3. What kinds of systemwide interventions would you suggest to school professionals to counteract some of the difficulties faced by girls like Ellen?

The Counselor's Response

I want to work very closely with Ellen's parents for a variety of reasons. First, I anticipate that Ellen's parents also hold stereotypes about buxom young women. Because I assume that Ellen is experiencing the loss of her childhood, even though she is still a child, I want to make sure that her parents do not fall into the trap of viewing her as an adult because she looks like one.

Second, because peers and adults alike, in the context of the school, are connected to Ellen's grief, I would want Ellen's parents' permission to speak with school personnel if appropriate and would absolutely obtain Ellen's permission as well. It might be helpful for me to advocate for Ellen with her soccer coach because Ellen's physical changes seem to be putting her at risk of losing her identity as an athlete. A systemwide intervention may also be necessary, but I want to be sensitive to Ellen's needs. Like many adolescents, her perception that everyone would know I was talking about her would likely get in the way of my addressing these issues directly.

My final reason for wanting to work closely with Ellen's parents is that they are suffering loss as well. The entire family is hurting. If I can serve as a consultant to Ellen's parents, perhaps they can be more emotionally available for her.

After establishing rapport and an atmosphere of safety with Ellen, I would state the obvious. Rather than hope that she initiates conversation about her breasts and the impact her physical development has had on her, I would put it right into the session. This is definitely a matter of style. My style would be to say something like "Ellen, you look so uncomfortable in your own body. I imagine your breasts have really caused some things to change for you." My intention is to give Ellen permission to talk about her body. In my experience, adolescent girls are often relieved that I am direct with them about physical appearance and its connection to their emotional state.

I also would consider sociocultural issues as I work with Ellen. As a counselor, I believe I have a responsibility to address the objectification and sexualization of girls and young women. It is necessary to address the mixed messages that adolescent girls receive about their bodies. Therefore, I would encourage Ellen to talk about her experience of mixed messages and listen carefully for Ellen's classification of self. I doubt that she refers to herself as a woman. If that is the case, I want to be cognizant of the need to match her perception and not refer to her as a woman. In this way, I am not another adult who is viewing her as older than she feels she is.

I am concerned about Ellen's self-esteem because I am familiar with the literature regarding early developing females and am now a witness to Ellen's behavioral and emotional responses to loss. I would use narrative assignments (many adolescent girls enjoy writing) and homework to help her recognize mixed messages and discover how, even with her physical changes, she can still be connected, confident, and athletic. Specifically, I would have her engage in a scavenger hunt (as described in chapter 11). In this hunt, she would have to support the argument that girls and women with large breasts can be smart, beautiful, cool, thoughtful, and athletic.

As always, I would see important indicators of growth (or lack of it) as "firsts" for Ellen. I would be particularly focused on firsts that are related to posture, the way she describes her body, how she views the bodies of other girls and women, and her sexual involvement with peers.

SCHOOL TRANSITIONS

Case 3: Entering Pre-K or Kindergarten—"I'm Not Going Back!"

It was the day they all had been waiting for. Andrea had been talking about going to kindergarten since she was three. Other children in her preschool had left her group for the wonderful world of kindergarten over the past two years. Now it was her turn, and she was so excited that her parents reported she had trouble falling asleep when she started fantasizing about it. Her parents were practically as excited as she was. They took her up to the school for a tour, talked about their experiences in kindergarten, and bought her new clothes and school supplies.

Andrea is the oldest of three, the only girl. Her parents report that she is bright, curious, and courteous. In fact, they have been very thoughtful about her education. They considered homeschooling her, sending her to a private school, or having her tested so that she could skip a year. Her mother said, "She has been able to count by 5s and 10s since she was four, and she was able to read at four years and eight months." When her parents made a commitment to public school, they got behind it 100 percent. Both parents had already met with the teacher to volunteer time in Andrea's classroom.

Imagine the surprise when Andrea returned home after her first day and said, "I hate school, and I miss my friends from preschool." Her parents had expected her to miss her friends at preschool because those children had been together since they were two. Andrea and her best friend, Ashley, were going to different kindergartens, so her parents anticipated the change would be scary and sad for Andrea, but they certainly did not anticipate that she would hate school.

Her parents tried talking with her, and Andrea said she did not want to return. She did not sleep well over the next few weeks and was increasingly irritable. She refused to use the toilet at school or join the other children. Her teacher and parents felt as though they had tried everything. That's when they consulted you.

Case Analysis

Identifying the Primary Loss

Andrea's primary loss is the loss of her routine and familiar surroundings.

Identifying Secondary and Intangible Losses

Andrea no longer feels as safe and secure as she once did. She feels a lack of control in her life.

Identifying the Client's Responses to the Loss Situation

Cognitive. Andrea may believe that there is a way for her to turn back the clock, that she can return to the safety of preschool.

Behavioral. Andrea is seeking control over her situation by refusing to participate in school and refusing to use the bathroom. She is also irritable at home and at school.

Emotional. Andrea is very angry. She is mad that she has been ripped away from her safety net without being consulted. She may feel that the exciting adventure she had been promised was a lie.

Discussion Questions

1. Is there a way that Andrea's parents could have prepared her for this type of loss?
2. What strategies would you give Andrea's parents?
3. What strategies would you give Andrea's teacher?
4. How would you collaborate with Andrea's parents and teacher beyond giving them strategies to help Andrea?

The Counselor's Response

The crux of this case study is that Andrea is desperately trying to regain control over her situation. Kindergarten was not what she had bargained for. She misses her friends and her routine, and she is hurt and angry that her parents are forcing her to endure this awful place. A smart little girl, Andrea is using every means at her disposal to express her anger and desire for control. She may not be able to prevent herself from being made to attend kindergarten, but she can control her reaction to it. She can withhold and refuse to participate to give voice to her displeasure. Andrea may have actually picked up on her parents' apprehensions about entering the public school system in the first place. She is likely to have overheard conversations about the pros and cons of public versus private versus homeschooling. This may have led her to conclude that other options are available. Despite all of her parents' rhetoric about the joys of kindergarten, previous conversations may have suggested that public schools are bad places. She may also be reacting to the pressure her parents have unwittingly put on her regarding kindergarten. They have thoroughly researched every aspect of kindergarten and have talked Andrea up to everyone in the education world, and Andrea may be having a difficult time dealing with their expectations. Also, her parents seem to have idealized kindergarten, and Andrea may be discovering it's a lot duller than it was presented to her. The end result is that she is incredibly unhappy.

Andrea's parents did their best to try to prepare her for her entrance to kindergarten. There is no way to predict which children will make a smooth transition to school and which ones won't. By all accounts, it looked as though Andrea would transition well. In advising Andrea's parents, I would suggest that she be given as many choices and options as possible under the circumstances. I would make it clear that at the present time there is no alternative to attending kindergarten. This in itself may show Andrea that her attempts to change that particular outcome are futile; she can then focus her energies elsewhere. I would help them to allow Andrea to express her feelings of anger and trepidation openly rather than resorting to covert means. When Andrea realizes that her voice is being heard, she may feel less of a need to act out.

Andrea's parents could also approach the teacher to see if Andrea has made any particular connections with any of the children at school. If so, those relationships could be fostered outside of school. I would also ask Andrea's teacher to track her behaviors. When is she most cooperative? What subjects does she love? When do her problem behaviors tend to escalate? What seems to trigger these reactions? Are some days better than others? In this way, the parents and teacher can better understand Andrea's experience and discover methods to reward her and give her a sense of control. For example, if Andrea likes to feel competent, the teacher might assign her a special task like erasing the board or reporting the weather. Most of all, I would suggest that Andrea's parents be patient with her and not show too much concern in her presence. Intuitive children often react to the anxieties of their parents, and Andrea is likely responding to her parents' fears and worries. I think they will find that the calmer they are about the situation, the more Andrea's anxiety and anger will diminish. This is much easier said than done, of course, because it is heartrending to see your child in pain, but Andrea's parents need to have faith in their child's resilience and capacity to grow.

Case 4: Elementary to Middle School—"This School Is Too Scary!"

John is a sixth grader who has Attention-Deficit/Hyperactivity Disorder (AD/HD). He began attending middle school a month ago. He has recently complained of stomachaches and comes up with a variety of excuses for not attending school. John's mother is concerned because up until this point John has always loved school. John has been reluctant to share his concerns with his mother. He just says that the school is so big that he gets lost and that his teachers then get angry with him for being late. None of his old friends are in his classes, so he has no one to ask for help, and the kids make fun of him for getting in trouble all the time. John feels completely over-whelmed by changing classes so often. The noise and the crush of people moving in different directions distracts and confuses him. He misses the structure of elementary school, where the children lined up and were led from one activity to another. Most of all, he misses having one teacher who really knows and understands him. Mrs. Jenkins, his fifth-grade teacher, always let him get up and move around the classroom when he was antsy, but in middle school, he is constantly reprimanded for his behaviors. He has tried to be "good," but he has recently given up trying and says he is hopeless. John's parents have sought counseling to help John deal with his school phobia.

Case Analysis

Identifying the Primary Loss

John's primary loss is the loss of the combination of structure and stability. In his elementary school, he knew what to expect and what was expected of him.

Identifying Secondary and Intangible Losses

John is experiencing a number of secondary and intangible losses, including the loss of his teacher, a sense of belonging, coping skills, friends, intimacy, and a familiar school building.

Identifying the Client's Responses to the Loss Situation

Cognitive. John was able to effectively cope and negotiate relationships in elementary school. His inability to employ formerly useful coping skills, along with negative self-talk and negative self-concept, are embedded in his cognitive responses to loss.

Behavioral. Somatic responses, such as stomachaches, are representative of John's behavioral responses to date. It is likely that additional behavioral responses will emerge as his anxiety and fear increase.

Emotional. John is feeling hopelessness, emotional loss, and fear. He is not in elementary school anymore, and he recognizes that the rules and culture are different. His emotional responses are linked to feelings of anxiety and confusion.

Discussion Questions

1. What kinds of interventions would you suggest for John?

2. How might John's problems have been prevented or alleviated even before school began?

3. How does John's disability play a part in his difficulties?

The Counselor's Response

I want to serve as a consultant to John. It seems to me that John was coping quite well with school prior to this recent transition to middle school. I want John to know from our first meeting that he already knows how to survive and succeed in middle school and that it is my job to help him make some minor changes and employ a few new strategies so he can feel good about himself and his experiences in school again. It is imperative that I overtly state that he will be able to be successful. Too many times, children with AD/HD and other disabilities are given negative messages.

The direction of our intervention will be on what worked in the past and whether it is working now. I will engage John in a coping skill inventory and assessment (as described in chapter 11). The goals of this intervention are multiple. First, I want to be clear that my role is that of an assistant, that John has the answers. Second, this intervention should help him feel more confident about his problem-solving abilities. In the future, he will not need to rely on me as his assistant or consultant because he will have recognized that the answers are within him. This intervention will tap his creativity, and it will demonstrate to John that there are many ways for him to solve problems.

I would be remiss, as John's counselor, not to recognize all the losses that are connected with his transition from elementary school to middle school. Opportunities to use reflective listening responses during the intervention will give John a space to share his experiences of loss and grief. As his assistant, I would have him dictate a goodbye letter to his elementary school and, if he chose, send it to his former teacher.

Finally, I would want to discuss with John's parents the importance of preparation for change. Transitions and change can be the most difficult aspects of life. They should be thoughtful and proactive about upcoming transitions for John and endeavor to prepare him as best they can. It would also be appropriate for them to act as advocates for John and be connected with someone at the school because such a partnership is essential. In fact, it is imperative that the parents of children with AD/HD and other documented disabilities meet with the school's child study team or committee on special education to develop an Individual Educational Program (IEP) or Section 504 plan so that the child has the tools he or she needs to succeed academically.

Case 5: Middle School to High School: "Stop Pressuring Me!"

Tammy is a ninth grader who has been struggling with transitioning to high school. Tammy's parents are both college professors and have high expectations that Tammy will excel academically in high school and attend an Ivy League school upon graduation. Tammy has always been a good student, but she has not been seen as a high achiever. She has always had much more interest in social activities and maintaining friendships. Tammy recently brought home her first-quarter report card. Although she was perfectly satisfied with her grades, which were in the mid- to upper 80s, Tammy's parents were absolutely livid and tried to impress upon her that "grades are everything in high school" and that now she is "playing for keeps." After expressing their profound disappointment, Tammy's parents forced her to quit all of her extracurricular activities and grounded her from the phone, computer, and going out with friends until she could demonstrate good grades during the next marking period, which is 13 weeks away. Tammy is devastated. Her friends have lost interest in being with her, and her boyfriend has broken up with her because she can't go out with him. Tammy cries often and has immense difficulty concentrating on her studies. She is worried that she will be unable to bring her grades up and feels doomed to a solitary existence. She barely speaks to her mom and dad.

Case Analysis

Identifying the Primary Loss

Tammy's primary loss is the loss of acceptance—acceptance by her parents, her friends and boyfriend, and herself.

Identifying Secondary and Intangible Losses

Not only has Tammy lost the experience and perception of acceptance, she is also experiencing a number of secondary and intangible losses. She has lost friendships; a way of life; relationships with her parents; self-esteem; her support systems; connection to her school, community, and peers through extracurricular activities; and her relationship with her boyfriend. These losses have secondary losses of their own. For example, her loss of relationships with her peers, friends, and boyfriend is also a loss of connection, support, status, and being part of a larger group.

Identifying the Client's Responses to the Loss Situation

Cognitive. Tammy's experience of loss is manifesting itself cognitively in her difficulty concentrating.

Behavioral. Tammy's behavioral response has been to isolate herself. She feels disconnected and is acting accordingly; however, this time she has decided how, when, and why to disconnect. Her parents initially chose to limit her connections, but now she's in charge.

Emotional. Tammy is fearful about her future. In addition, she is lonely, depressed, angry, and emotionally stymied.

Discussion Questions

1. How would you work with Tammy and her parents?
2. What potential consequences may evolve if the situation stays as it is for Tammy?

The Counselor's Response

It is my hunch that Tammy's parents will view me as their ally. I am also an adult and a professional. They will assume that I hold similar values about education. I want to use their perception of me to build trust with them. If they do not trust me, I will not be able to gain access to their daughter, and they will not be open to suggestions relating to their responsibility in the relationship.

It is also my hunch that counseling services have been initiated by Tammy's parents, not Tammy, because I do not see her as having the emotional energy to advocate for herself. I believe that Tammy's parents will probably want me to "fix" her and reiterate their message about the importance of grades and college.

When meeting with Tammy's parents, I would acknowledge that they want the best for their child and believe in her potential. I also want to plant some seeds. It is critical that I do not openly challenge the consequences they set up for Tammy; rather, I want to confront them gently. I would say something like "Tammy's academic success is so important to you both that you thought it was best to deny her all the things that she values." My goal here is to reframe their handling of the situation with their daughter so that they gain insight into her perspective. I would meet with them or at least confer over the phone regularly to continue to gently question their perspective and introduce them to their daughter's experience.

My individual work with Tammy would take on a much different style. I want to hear Tammy's story from her perspective, employing reflective listening skills to demonstrate to her that, although I am an adult and professional person, I have empathy for her. Because of her disconnection and isolation, she has not been able to share her story from her perspective. In listening and responding to her story, I do not want to be directive, nor do I want to work on problem-solving skills or study skills with her. There has been a major change in her life that is connected to a series of serious losses. I want to show her that I recognize these losses and respect her pain. In other words, I don't want her to see me as another adult who is trying to fit her into a metaphorical size 6 shoe, when she wears a size 10.

The relationship between Tammy and me is the key. Because Tammy has lost her relationships with all the significant people in her life, including herself, she needs help to begin to rebuild. I may invite her parents into a session, but only with Tammy's permission. The intent would be that when Tammy feels connected and supported again, perhaps she can share her perspective with her parents and advocate for herself. My role would be to support the entire system, model effective communication and empathy, and demonstrate negotiation skills. If her parents continue to insist that I help Tammy get it together academically, I would emphasize that my goal is to help Tammy begin to feel more emotionally healthy so that this will translate into more self-confidence and lead to enhanced academic performance.

Case 6: High School to College—"Freedom!"

Skyler was so excited. She had lived in a small town her entire life. Everyone knew everyone else, and that was not a good thing. She had applied to several four-year colleges, and she chose the schools she applied to on the basis of how close they were to her hometown. Her motto was "Nothing less than three hours away." She had received several acceptance letters and had decided on a school that offered her choice of majors six hours away from her hometown. None of her friends was going there. Her parents supported her decision. She had always been an independent child and adolescent. They also knew that high school had been tough for her socially. There was always some drama going on among Skyler and her girlfriends.

Skyler viewed prom and graduation as markers that she was getting closer to college. She started counting the days until she left for freshman orientation. Half her things were packed by July 4. Skyler's parents and paternal grandfather (who lived with them) were also excited for her until she began acting peculiar. Skyler stopped talking on the phone. She would let the answering machine pick up and not return calls, even from her best friends and two persistent boys her age who were calling for her. She slept late and did not leave the house except for work. Her parents swore they smelled cigarette smoke on her breath. Skyler had always been involved socially but had not gone out with her friends in weeks.

Two weeks before she needed to report to college, her grandfather found her crying desperately. She confided in him that she was too scared to go. "The school was too big, too far away, she did not know anyone," she explained. He asked Skyler if he could share how she was feeling with her parents. She was embarrassed but agreed. Skyler's parents thought that a brief counseling experience before leaving for college would benefit her.

Case Analysis

Identifying the Primary Loss

Skyler's primary loss is the loss of her vision of herself as an independent, carefree young woman with no ties.

Identifying Secondary and Intangible Losses

In going to college, Skyler is losing the safety and security of her home and family. Also, her sense of excitement about the future has been replaced by fear.

Identifying the Client's Responses to the Loss Situation

Cognitive. Skyler may be contemplating what might happen if she doesn't make it at college. She may be concerned that she is a failure or a fraud. What if she is not the independent free spirit she always claimed to be?

Behavioral. Skyler is showing her confusion and conflicted emotions by withdrawing from her friends and family. She has started smoking, perhaps in an effort to calm herself or to prepare herself for what she views as the "adult world."

Emotional. Emotionally, Skyler is full of conflicting feelings. She is excited to move on with her life, but she is also petrified. Her mind is filled with "what ifs," which only add to her confusion. She may be angry with herself for feeling a sense of loss over moving from the small town she always thought she hated.

Discussion Questions

1. How might Skyler's current state be linked to loss?
2. How could you structure an effective intervention if you only have about a month's time to work with Skyler?
3. What if Skyler does not want to go to college?

The Counselor's Response

When working with Skyler, it would be important for the counselor to empower her and allow her to explore all of her feelings and options. Skyler's choice of school is largely symbolic: "I want to prove to this town that I don't need them." Ironically, when the time arrives for Skyler to make the break, she is conflicted, which must come as a complete surprise to her. To us, her sense of fear and loss make sense. She is taking a drastic step: leaving the comfort and safety of the only world she has ever known. She is leaving her parents and grandfather and entering a new world all alone. From this perspective, all of her thoughts and feelings make sense, but to Skyler, these thoughts and feelings do not mesh at all with the person she always thought she was.

In working with Skyler, I would educate her about the transition from high school to college. I would try to normalize her fears and ambivalent feelings by encouraging her to imagine this situation as if it were happening to another person. If a friend were experiencing the same apprehensions about leaving home, how would she view her? How would she talk to her? I would use role playing to help Skyler become her own friend and confidant. I would also help Skyler examine who she really is and accept all sides of herself. It sounds as though she has a particular image of herself as strong and independent, but she may have more difficulty owning the parts of herself that are cautious and afraid of change. I would accompany her on her journey of self-discovery and help her find balance among all the parts of herself in a nonjudgmental way. Although it may seem incongruous, once rapport is established and Skyler has started to see herself more fully, I would use cognitive-behavioral strategies to confront some of the irrational thoughts and "musts" she is placing on herself. I would help her examine the underlying thoughts that are contributing to her anxiety. Such thoughts might include "If I don't fit in at this school, I am a failure" or "To have to come home would be the worst thing that ever happened to me." I would help her discover the covert messages she is sending herself so that she can confront and alter them as necessary. I would also encourage Skyler to develop a plan B and a plan C in case she is not happy at her college or decides not to attend at all. Allowing her to come up with alternative plans will give her a sense of power over her own situation. By brainstorming alternatives, she may decide to travel, join the Peace Corps or Americorps, attend community college, or work for a year. I would help her reframe her view of herself as a weak or dependent little girl to a thoughtful, mature young woman with lots of choices. In short, I would help her to eliminate the all-or-nothing thinking that is blocking her progress and help her to gain a more realistic sense of self.

FAMILY LIFE-CYCLE CHANGES

Case 7: A New Baby in the House—"I Don't Want to Be a Big Brother"

Evan was so proud to be a big brother. He wore his "I'm the Big Brother" T-shirt every day for a week after his baby brother was born. He brought pictures with him to school and showed them off to anyone in his first grade class or soccer team who would look at them. He was very proud. Evan's parents had expected the transition to be difficult. After all, Evan had been an only child for six years.

After six months, Evan's parents were still pleased with Evan's reaction to his baby brother. Evan's baby-sitter suggested that Evan might be jealous. When asked why she thought this, she replied, "I have seen Evan do sneaky things with the baby. Last time I watched them, I caught Evan trying to feed the baby cat food." Evan's parents were embarrassed, and they asked Evan why he would do such a thing. Evan cried hard and said that the baby-sitter was a liar. Not knowing what else to do, Evan's parents set up a video camera to record Evan and the baby. They were horrified. Evan was, in fact, trying to feed the baby cat food as well as "grown-up" foods that Evan's parents had told him were off limits to his brother and all babies. The videotape also showed Evan pinching his brother and then calling for his parent(s) or baby-sitter, saying, "The baby is crying." Evan's parents contact you because they are desperate about what to do.

Case Analysis

Identifying the Primary Loss

Evan has lost his place in the family as the only child.

Identifying Secondary and Intangible Losses

As a result of the birth of his baby brother, Evan has lost his status in the family. He no longer receives the undivided attention of his parents. In fact, some of his needs may go unmet for the first time in his life. He has also lost his status as a "good" big brother and may feel that he is viewed as a "bad" brother now because of what he has been caught doing.

Identifying the Client's Responses to the Loss Situation

Cognitive. Cognitively, Evan may feel that he has been replaced. He may think that his parents no longer love him. He likely resents his baby brother and sees him as the cause of his pain.

Behavioral. Behaviorally, Evan is seeking ways to punish this new interloper. He feeds him things that might make him sick and makes him cry. He may want his parents to view the baby as "bad" so that he can regain his status as the "good" son.

Emotional. Evan is angry. He is hurt and jealous over all of the attention this new baby is receiving, but he may be unable to verbalize these conflicted feelings. He probably engages in these behaviors covertly so there will be less likelihood that Evan himself could be viewed as "bad." He wants his parents to see the baby in the same way he does—as a pain in the butt!

Discussion Questions

1. What are your initial thoughts and feelings about Evan?
2. What strategies can you give his parents?
3. What losses might Evan be experiencing?
4. Is there reason for alarm?

The Counselor's Response

My response to Evan would be, "What a smart little boy you are to find a way to express the pain you are in!" Is there cause for alarm? Yes, but only if Evan's voice is not heard. If his pain continues to be ignored by his parents, it would not be surprising if his angry feelings toward the baby increased, and he began to hurt the baby more frequently or more severely. Evan is not a mean or bad child, although he may fear he will be seen that way because of what he has been caught doing. He is an angry, jealous child whose predictable lifestyle and place in the family have been usurped by an intruder. He just doesn't get it. How can his parents adore this little "blob" that can't even walk or talk and cries all the time? He is confused and feels abandoned.

Part of the problem for Evan's parents is that Evan did a fine job of pretending that everything was all right. He acted the way he was supposed to in his parents' presence and didn't show many signs of jealousy and discontent. This made it difficult for the parents to intervene because they didn't realize there was a problem. Now that the problem has been discovered, however, Evan's parents have an opportunity to intervene. I would assist Evan's parents in learning how to communicate with Evan on his level and help them understand the perspective of a six-year-old. It is important that they put things on the table with Evan, saying, "Evan, you have been pinching the baby when we are not around. I think you are angry about having this new baby in the house. You are mad at us but are taking it out on him." I would also set firm limits that it is not okay to hurt the baby. I would teach them how to use I-statements and reflective listening skills. I would also teach them to help Evan develop an emotions vocabulary so that he is able to communicate his thoughts and feelings. I would also suggest that the parents set aside special time just for themselves and Evan. For example, I would have them pay attention to consistency in bedtime routine so that he gets the one-on-one time he craves. Each parent might also have an "Evan's night out" with him during the week. I would also help Evan understand more about the baby's development process. I would help him to celebrate milestones, such as the baby's ability to sit up, crawl, walk, and so forth. Doing this will help Evan understand that the baby will not always be a little "blob" and that they will have more fun together as the baby grows and is capable of doing more things. Most of all, I would reassure Evan that he still holds a special and magical place in the family, no matter what happens. As he becomes more secure, the problematic behaviors will diminish.

Case 8: Older Sibling Moves Out—"Jim Doesn't Love Me Anymore!"

Eric is a seven-year-old whose older brother, Jim, recently left for college. Eric and Jim have always been close buddies and have spent a great deal of time together. Eric absolutely idolizes Jim and his friends. Although Jim and Eric never shared a room, Eric has had trouble sleeping since Jim has been gone. He says that Jim doesn't love him anymore since he rarely comes home, and when he does, he spends more time with his friends than he does with Eric. Eric's dad, who has custody of both kids, reports that Eric has been very irritable and acts out quite often both at home and at school. Dad does not seem to have made the connection between Jim's leaving home and Eric's recent behaviors. He is dumbfounded about what to do with Eric and seeks your help and advice.

Case Analysis

Identifying the Primary Loss

Eric's primary loss is the loss of his brother, Jim.

Identifying Secondary and Intangible Losses

For Eric, Jim's move out of the house and to college evokes many intangible and secondary losses. There is a physical and emotional loss of Jim. There is the loss of the support, companionship, and modeling that were all part of their relationship. Eric's family of three is now a family of two. It is possible that Jim also at times took care of Eric, so he may have also lost a caregiver and a routine. If Eric has had different child care arrangements since his brother left for college, there are likely losses connected to that transition. Finally, Eric has also lost connection with Jim's friends.

Identifying the Client's Responses to the Loss Situation

Cognitive. Eric is experiencing confusion, all-or-nothing thinking (for example, Jim doesn't love him anymore), and egocentric thinking.

Behavioral. Behaviorally, Eric is having difficulty sleeping and is exhibiting acting-out behaviors. (It will be important to have Dad define exactly what he means by "acting out.")

Emotional. Loss, grief, confusion, betrayal, distrust, abandonment, and irritability, often signs of depression in young children (Kauffman, 2001), are all consistent with Eric's clinical presentation. There are many emotional responses, and each may be overwhelming in its own right.

Discussion Questions

1. How might Eric have personalized Jim's leaving for college as abandonment?

2. What preventative steps might have been taken to prepare Eric for Jim's departure?

3. What strategies would you use to help Eric deal with the change in his relationship with his brother?

The Counselor's Response

It seems that the change in Eric's family has been minimized, or at least no one realized the potential impact one family member's moving out of the house would have on the entire system. Although I would have liked to work with Eric and his family before Jim left for college, some of that work can still prove beneficial.

In this section, I discuss the thrust of my intervention with Eric. Everything I discuss in this section is well suited for an intervention that is proactive rather than reactive with minor modifications.

First, I want to hear Eric's story. I will not limit him to verbal expression; these words may not convey the complexity of his experience. I will provide him with toys and art media to express his feelings. I will, however, ask him directly to tell me some stories about his brother. The connection between his current state and his brother's leaving for college is undeniable. By being direct, I am offering Eric an invitation to share his experience with me.

Although I am using a directive approach, I also want to demonstrate empathy. I would be diligent to respond to Eric with reflective listening. I will suggest that he bring in a photo of himself and his brother or a family picture. I would have him use toy figures to create a family sculpture—how it is and how he wishes it were, all the while providing reflections of his feelings. A letter to Jim may also be helpful—one that he may not send but that conveys his feelings.

This intervention with Eric need not be a lengthy one. Instead, I would conduct a variety of creative one-session activities that would allow him to share his experience, feelings, and thoughts. I would encourage Eric's father to take Eric for a visit to Jim at school (of course, with Jim's consent). If Eric's father has access to e-mail, that would be another way to stay connected. A Web camera would be even better. A T-shirt or memento with the name of the college that Jim is attending would also be a nice gesture. The rationale for all of these activities is to include Eric in this part of Jim's life. Giving Eric the opportunity to be connected to his brother, even though his brother has moved away, is the goal.

Case 9: Mom Goes to Work—"Don't Go!"

Christy and her mom were very close. In many ways, it was just the two of them. Christy had never met her father. Christy's maternal grandmother lived less than a mile a way. Her mother and grandmother are Christy's entire family.

At 11, Christy is a decent student and athlete. She has a few friends in school, but they are good friends. Actually, she prefers spending time with her mother than with her friends. Christy's mother, Joan, worked independently, cleaning houses during the day while Christy was at school. Joan's schedule was flexible (she worked for herself), and she was always able to make arrangements to be home with Christy during vacations and when Christy needed to stay home because she was sick. The advantages of Joan's working for herself were substantial, but the money was not. Joan was one of the millions of people in the United States who fell into the category of the working poor.

Then Joan got the offer of a lifetime: She was recruited by a cleaning agency to manage a staff of 25. She had applied for the job but never thought she would get the position. The job offered benefits, vacation and sick time, merit raises, and a salary. Joan had never had an inflow of money she could count on. In addition, she would be making at least three times more money working for this company than she was working for herself. No way was she turning it down.

Before accepting the job, she talked to Christy about it. Christy and Joan made lots of decisions together. The plan was that because Joan would have to leave for work when Christy left for school and not return until three hours after Christy had come home, Christy would go to her grandmother's.

The first month was great. Joan loved the extra money and bought Christy a new bicycle. They even went out for a fancy dinner to celebrate. Things were also working out well with their plan. Christy and her grandmother were doing just fine, and Christy was even learning a bit about cooking.

Christy announced that she was quitting the track team. Joan was surprised and asked if there was anything wrong. Christy said no. Two weeks later, when Christy's report card came, she had earned a failing grade (her first ever) in music. It wasn't long after that that Christy's grandmother said Christy was getting sassy. Joan tried to talk to Christy about these changes, but Christy shrugged her off. In desperation, Joan did something she was very ashamed of. She read Christy's diary. She found a series of pages in which Christy said that her mother didn't love her and that she was going to run away.

Case 9 Analysis

Identifying the Primary Loss

Christy's primary loss is the loss of the place she held in her mother's life as her top priority.

Identifying Secondary and Intangible Losses

Christy has lost her sense of routine and stability. Her identity within the family has been challenged.

Identifying the Client's Responses to the Loss Situation

Cognitive. Cognitively, Christy seems to believe that she is being punished and that her mother no longer loves her.

Behavioral. Christy is withdrawing from the activities she once loved. Her grades are dropping, and she is irritable.

Emotional. Emotionally, Christy is depressed. She is hurt, angry, and confused.

Discussion Questions

1. What are the losses for Christy that are connected to Joan's change in work?

2. What would be important to include in the counseling intervention with Christy?

3. What personal issues does Christy's experience bring up for you, the counselor?

The Counselor's Response

This case really strikes a chord for many counselors. As the mother of two teenage daughters, I wonder how they feel about the time and energy I spend with my clients. They must feel a good deal of confusion in that I can be warm and empathic on the job and then yell at them at home for not putting away the dishes.

Christy is really hurting. In her mind, she has lost her best friend. She had always seen her relationship with her mother as ideal and viewed herself as the most important thing in her mother's life. When discussing the job opportunity with her mother, the situation sounded great, but in reality it didn't work out that way. From Christy's perspective, her mom seems preoccupied when she gets home from work. Joan may have new friends and talk about her day with excitement and energy, or she may be tired and not as enthusiastic with Christy as she used to. Christy used to be the most fulfilling part of Joan's life, but now she has to compete with Joan's work for top honors. When Joan was there the moment Christy got home from school, Christy told her all the details of her day, shared her grades, and filled her in on the latest gossip at school. Now that Joan gets home three hours later, Christy has lost her enthusiasm for talking about her day. When Joan asks, she responds with "nothing much." I imagine that Joan is incredibly perplexed. She thought that her career change was a mutual decision between her and Christy.

However, Christy signed onto something that she didn't completely understand. Christy feels that Joan's work has taken the forefront as the most important thing in her mother's life. Christy is crushed, and she wants to run away. Also, Christy may feel that her mother is trying to appease her by buying her things with money from her new job (In some ways, this may be true!). In Christy's mind, the bike and other presents do not make up for lost time with her mother. Her sadness, lethargy, withdrawal from activities, and irritability all point to adolescent depression. It will be important to perform a lethality assessment with Christy to check for suicidal ideation.

In working with Christy, I would allow her an opportunity to express her feelings and frustration. Because she already keeps a diary, journaling might be an appropriate intervention with Christy. I might have her write her feelings about her mother's new job using a narrative approach. I might have her write a letter to her loss that starts out with "Dear New Job:" She might begin this letter "I hate you. You've taken my mom away from me." Journaling would give her an opportunity to get her feelings out on the table. I would also use cognitive-behavioral strategies to help Christy identify the negative messages she may be sending herself. For example, she appears to believe that her mother no longer loves her. I would help her examine the veracity of this statement and other self-statements she has been making. Then I would facilitate genuine communication and dialogue between Joan and Christy. With time and patience, I would help Christy express her needs and thoughts rather than turn them in on herself.

Case Study for Reader Analysis

"What the heck is this?" Jenn thought. She was very freaked out when she went to use the bathroom during art class and found "a mess" in her underwear. She thought she was dying. She headed straight for the nurse's office, even though her hall pass clearly stated that she was to go to the bathroom. The school nurse had handled this type of situation hundreds of times in her 24-year career. She was able to calm Jenn and explain to her that she was "a woman now." Jenn did not know a thing about menstruation or periods. The nurse assumed it was because Jenn had older brothers and was being raised by her father (her mother had skipped out on them when Jenn was five). The school nurse called Jenn's dad, and he came up to the school to get Jenn. He felt terrible that he had not prepared her, but she was only 10.

It was a slow change, but over the next year Jenn began to have some social difficulties in school. Her self-esteem plummeted, and she refused to participate in any kind of activity with her brothers. She started making little burn marks on her skin with pencil erasers. Jenn's dad was feeling ineffective and spent most of his time shouting at and grounding her. Yesterday he found a note in her things describing an encounter she was due to have with one of her brother's ninth-grade friends that included oral sex.

Discussion Questions

1. What are Jenn's primary, secondary, and intangible losses?
2. How does conceptualizing Jenn's experience through a lens of loss differ from conceptualizing the experience through a lens of development?
3. What personal issues are likely to emerge for you as Jenn's counselor?
4. What recommendations can you make to her father?

SUMMARY

This chapter has examined some of the normal, yet painful, developmental losses experienced by children and adolescents. Strategies were presented in an effort to help adults understand and intervene as they guide children and adolescents through their developmental journey. Specific case examples concerned losses related to puberty and physical changes, school transitions, and family life-cycle changes.

CHAPTER 9

Tragic and Stigmatizing Losses

Ten-year-old Gina's uncle is on trial for murdering his wife and children during a domestic dispute. Gina's mother is the defendant's brother. Gina's family lives down the street from her uncle's home, where the murders occurred. The two families were close, and Gina used to play each day after school with her cousins, who were killed. Gina's mother insists that her brother is innocent despite all of the available evidence and has been a constant presence on the local news proclaiming his innocence. Gina is not so sure. She feels that her uncle was responsible for the murders and is angry with him for taking her aunt and cousins away from her. When she has tried to express her feelings, her mother says she "will tolerate no such talk in her house." Worst of all, much of the town's wrath has been directed at Gina's family, and she has had to endure taunts, threats, and has even had people spit in her face and call her trash on the way home from school. She does not even want to show her face in public. Now that the trial has begun, community feelings have become more heated, and events have become even more hostile for Gina. She just wishes her mother would stop talking to the press and that life could go back to the way it was. She hates being blamed for something she had no part in.

Thus far in this book, we have discussed many different types of losses experienced by children and adolescents, including death-related losses, intangible losses, interpersonal losses, and transitional and developmental losses. Each type of loss brings with it varying degrees of accompanying pain and difficulty. In this chapter, we will discuss two particularly devastating types of losses—tragic losses and stigmatizing losses. Tragic losses, such as experiencing a sudden, unexpected death or coping with a natural disaster, are complicated to deal with and are especially traumatic to children and teens who experience them. Similarly, stigmatizing losses—such as losses related to murder, suicide, abuse or victimization, or parental incarceration—take a heavy toll on children and adolescents (Goldman, 2004). This chapter will present strategies and interventions to use with children and teens who experience tragic or stigmatizing losses.

TRAGIC LOSSES

Case 1: Sudden Death—"I Didn't Have a Chance to Say Goodbye"

John, 7, and Becky, 15, are a brother and sister who lost their mother in a car accident a few months ago. Their father, Joe, is in such a state of grief himself that he has dived into his work wholeheartedly. He is seldom home and has little emotional capacity to deal with his children's loss issues. Becky has been staying with various friends while John stays with his paternal grandparents most of the time. The grandparents are very worried about each of the children. They have noticed that Becky has developed friendships with a new group of teens who are reputed to engage in risky behaviors, such as drugs and sexual promiscuity. When they confront her, she screams, "You are not my mother! I don't have a mother!" and either retreats to her room or leaves the house to join her new friends. At one time, Becky confided to her grandfather that she felt terrible because the last time she had seen her mother before the accident, they had been fighting and she had said some awful things that she regretted. "I never got a chance to say I'm sorry, so now she'll never know!" she cried.

John, on the other hand, seems to have developed a clinging overdependence on his grandparents and literally will not leave their sides, even to sleep. He is desperately afraid that they will be killed, too, and leave him. He is extremely worried about his father at all times and misses him greatly. He feels that he is to blame for his mother's being killed because he didn't protect her well enough, and he also believes that is why his dad does not like to be around him anymore.

The grandparents have tried to speak to their son about the issues, but he does not seem to hear them and asks them to handle the situation. They have sought a counseling referral.

Case Analysis: John

Identifying the Primary Loss

The primary loss is the death of John's mother.

Identifying Secondary and Intangible Losses

John has lost a sense of safety, security, fairness, and innocence. He has lost his family (neither his father nor his sister is physically or emotionally available to him) and his routine. He has lost part of himself. There may be many other secondary and intangible losses relating to the preexisting relationship between this child and his mother.

Identifying the Client's Responses to the Loss Situation

Cognitive. John is experiencing egocentric and magical thinking. He believes he is responsible for his mother's death and his father's subsequent absence.

Behavioral. John is exhibiting regressive behaviors, such as clinging and difficulty sleeping.

Emotional. John is responding emotionally with fear, worry, guilt, and despair. He is also experiencing abandonment and isolation because Becky and Dad have essentially left him.

Case Analysis: Becky

Identifying the Primary Loss

The primary loss is the death of Becky's mother.

Identifying Secondary and Intangible Losses

Becky has lost a sense of safety, security, fairness, and innocence. She has lost her family and her father. She has lost her opportunities, the way she anticipated things would be, her sense of being like everyone else, and a connection to her family history. She has lost part of herself.

Identifying the Client's Responses to the Loss Situation

Cognitive. Statements like "You are not my mother" demonstrate concrete thinking on Becky's part.

Behavioral. Becky is also exhibiting regression behaviors as well as avoidance, potential self-medication, potential love and nurturance seeking, and possibly even promiscuity.

Emotional. Fear, guilt, and shame are characteristics of Becky's emotional response. Individually, each of these emotions can be debilitating; together, they can result in significant impairment.

Discussion Questions

1. What issues are inherent when dealing with a sudden, unexpected death?
2. What suggestions do you have for John and Becky's grandparents in dealing with this situation?
3. How would you work with John and Becky?
4. How would you involve Dad in the counseling process?

The Counselor's Response

In this case, I would take the referral from the grandparent, but depending on the setting that I am working in, I may not be able to see the minor children without parental consent. I would reach out to the father by telephone or e-mail (if it is an option). Again, depending on my work setting, I might even try to meet with him outside of my office—for example, at his workplace or at a public meeting place. I know that getting him to come in is my biggest hurdle. His loss has been traumatic. Discussing the impact on his children will, of course, deepen his pain and anguish, albeit temporarily. It would be helpful to let him talk about his feelings and be there for him because I may be the first person he has talked to about the loss. It is important to recognize that Dad is not just a parent, he is an "injured party," and explore to see if he is open to a referral to a counselor. I will need to be relentless in my efforts to contact, connect, and engage him in the process. Having a conversation with the grandparents would probably provide me with some information that would prove useful in contacting their son. I also may be able to provide them with some literature and useful Web sites so that they can continue to be supportive. I want to be cognizant and respectful that they have suffered a loss as well.

I am optimistic that I can, at the very least, get Dad's permission to work with his children. I would work with John and Becky independently because their age disparity means vast differences in terms of their cognitive, emotional, and behavioral development, as well as with the associated issues. I will discuss the nature of my intervention with John first and then follow up with my plan for Becky. Before I begin my work with either of them, I want to secure clinical supervision for myself. As a mother, I know that I will have a personal reaction in working with these children. It would be unethical and certainly unprofessional for me not to obtain support for myself during their course of therapy so that I can be fully available as a counselor to these children.

Considering John's age, the magnitude of the losses he has suffered, and his current condition, I would use a child-centered play-therapy approach. First of all, I recognize that his counseling will be a gradual process. Rushing John along by employing a different approach would be counterintuitive. Using a play-therapy approach would give John the opportunity to move at his own pace and in his own way. Taking a child-centered stance would allow John to do what he needs to do to begin healing. I believe that he has the power to solve his own problems. Therefore, I believe he will do what he needs to do, when and how he needs to do it, in the therapeutic play room, and he will grieve and heal in the way that best suits him.

This approach may seem simplistic, but as anyone who has been trained to use a child-centered play-therapy approach can share, it is not. I anticipate that John will show me his pain and demonstrate aggression, regression, and expression of feelings. As Webb (2003) notes, survivors have a strong wish for reunion if there are no opportunities for anticipatory grieving, such as that occurring in situations of terminal illness or disability preceding death. I will remain child-centered throughout the intervention, meaning that John will decide when he is ready for termination. This allows him the opportunity to be the expert on himself and to be in control of the loss of the therapeutic relationship.

As is the case with John, I want my work with Becky to be at her pace. I do not want to rush things, and I certainly do not want her to feel pressured by me. That said, I would let Becky employ her defenses. The defenses she is utilizing are keeping her from despair and allowing her to function. I will follow her lead if she is willing to talk. I want her to know that she can talk about anything and that I will not push her to talk about her mother or the loss she has suffered. Although I will not try to direct her talk, I would use sand-play therapy to engage her in alternative methods of sharing her perspective and experience in the context of counseling.

Being respectful is my main goal. I will rely on her to share her story from her perspective. I will overtly state that her family is worried that she is engaging in risky behaviors but also say that I will not share any discussion we might have about her behaviors with her family unless she is likely to harm herself or someone else, or if someone is harming her. This does not mean that I would not encourage her to share what is going on in her life with the people who care about her, but I would not intervene unless she gave me permission to or it fell under my responsibility as a mandated reporter.

Not unlike the termination process with her brother, I would allow Becky to give me clues or overtly state that she is ready to say goodbye. As with John, this gives her a chance to make decisions about loss that she can control. A goodbye ritual, such as creating a memory box or sending a balloon into the sky for Mom, may be fitting for either or both children (see chapter 11).

Case 2: Natural Disaster—"I'll Never Be Safe Again!"

Hogan is an eight-year-old only child whose house was recently destroyed in a fire. Immediately after the fire, he was in a state of shock. His greatest concern was that his cats were safe. Since then, the enormity of the loss has hit him. He now lives in temporary housing at the Residence Inn with his parents until the insurance money allows them to find or build more permanent housing. Hogan says he no longer feels safe. His after-school baby-sitter lives on the same street where he used to live, and each day he has to walk past the burned-out hulk that used to be his home. Last week, he began taking a longer, more roundabout route home so that he would not have to pass the house, but he can still see it from his baby-sitter's porch and windows. He keeps his eyes averted from the windows at all times and has become hypervigilant in checking all cords, appliances, and outlets in school, his apartment, and the baby-sitter's home because the fire in his house was suspected to be an electrical fire. He has frequent nightmares and checks on his parents in their bedroom several times each night. He will not let his cats out of his sight. He refuses to talk about the fire but has mentioned once or twice that he wishes he had saved his favorite teddy bear and the posters from his bedroom wall. He berates himself for not thinking more quickly and clearly and vows not to let that happen again. He also says that he no longer feels safe anywhere. His parents have decided that Hogan could benefit from counseling.

Case Analysis

Identifying the Primary Loss

Hogan's primary loss is the loss of his home and his belongings.

Identifying Secondary and Intangible Losses

Secondary losses include loss of a sense of safety and security and the comfort and familiarity of his home. Hogan also has losses associated with the knowledge that everything material and alive can be lost in a fire and in other catastrophes. Finally, he has lost memorabilia and memories.

Identifying the Client's Responses to the Loss Situation

Cognitive. Concrete and egocentric thinking are typical of children Hogan's age, and that type of thinking is also associated with his behavioral and emotional responses. His hypervigilence is a result of feeling unsafe and insecure. He has become hyperaware of his surroundings and is having trouble determining what is relevant perceptual information. His difficulty concentrating may appear to be an attention deficit problem if the experience of his trauma is overlooked.

Behavioral. Because he is obsessive about checking for safety, Hogan is having difficulty sleeping, nightmares, and difficulty concentrating.

Emotional. Fear is complex for Hogan. He is afraid of what happened and what might happen. He is also feeling guilty, overwhelmed, nervous, and anxious.

Discussion Questions

1. What makes losses related to natural disasters so unique and difficult?
2. How would you work with Hogan to help him cope with his loss and gain a sense of safety and control?
3. How can Hogan's parents help in the process?

The Counselor's Response

Hogan has a good prognosis connected to counseling for a variety of reasons. The trauma of being in a fire is recent, the loss is not associated with another individual, and he will receive counseling services (Maxmen & Ward, 1995). Counseling will give Hogan an opportunity to talk or play out his experience, take charge of the loss that he could not control, and provide stability. It is very important for Hogan to anticipate when, where, and how we will meet. This consistency will be the cornerstone of our work together. Without it, he will not feel safe enough to engage in the counseling process.

The aforementioned aspects of Hogan's loss are so important that I would be remiss not to share them with Hogan's parents. It is also important to remember that they have experienced losses related to the fire as well. Some family work seems appropriate, and I will plant the seed that, in addition to Hogan's individual sessions, there will probably be family sessions as well. This would be a good time to encourage the parents to get additional support for themselves in the form of individual counseling.

A play-therapy approach with Hogan would allow reality-based consistency and control. Hogan can anticipate that most things in the therapeutic play room will be the same for each session; however, there are toys that break and are occasionally put away in the wrong spot. He will, therefore, have experience feeling unstable and out of control in the play-therapy room itself. He will have the opportunity to try out a variety of ways he can respond to those difficult emotions without being overwhelmed. He will also have the opportunity to play. Hogan has taken on adult responsibilities and roles as a result of the trauma. In the playroom, he will be able to be a child and play out rather than talk out his experience.

As part of the counseling intervention, I would likely have Hogan (perhaps with his parents) take me on a pretend tour of their former residence in a pseudo-guided imagery technique. I would prompt for description that uses the senses, and Hogan would serve as the guide. After we tour each room, Hogan (or the family) could draw or create a picture of one in the sand to represent their memory. When we finish the tour of the house (see example interventions, chapter 11), Hogan could create a memory book to partially replace the memorabilia that were lost in the fire. This activity re-creates those memories and also provides new ones.

STIGMATIZING LOSSES

Case 3: Murder—"It's Worse Than Just Dying "

Gail is new to the community and school. She moved into the neighborhood the summer before fourth grade. She resides in a small town, and as her father notes, "It really does seem like everyone knows everyone else here." Gail's father is a single parent, and Gail has a twin sister, Linda. Linda has adjusted well to the move from a small, rural community. According to Gail's father, Gail has not.

Gail is a frail nine-year-old. She complains often of headaches and stomachaches. She has made no friends at her new school and has been fighting constantly with her sister. Gail's father reports that she has been "on a downward slide" since her mother's death two years ago. The family has attended counseling together, and they are in an ongoing healing process.

Gail's father also reports that, initially, the death was ruled an accident (Gail's mother was hit by a car while taking her morning walk), but it turned out that Gail's mother was actually murdered. The girls are aware that their mother, a defense attorney, was intentionally run down by a former client. In fact, part of the reason the family moved was to escape media coverage, which was interfering with their day-to-day lives.

Case Analysis

Identifying the Primary Loss

Gail's primary loss is the death of her mother under tragic circumstances.

Identifying Secondary and Intangible Losses

Gail has experienced several secondary and intangible losses surrounding the death of her mother. She has lost her home and sense of community. She has lost a sense of privacy. She has experienced a loss of safety and security with the accompanying sense of loss of power and control over her situation.

Identifying the Client's Responses to the Loss Situation

Cognitive. Gail is likely to have a variety of confusing thoughts. She may feel somewhat responsible for her mother's death because this is a typical reaction of children her age. She may think she is not safe and needs to remain home to feel comfortable.

Behavioral. Gail is fighting with her sister. She has frequent somatic complaints (headaches and stomachaches) and does not engage in social activities with peers.

Emotional. Gail is likely to be experiencing a number of emotions. She is probably very frightened. She is also likely to feel anger toward the perpetrator of her mother's murder and perhaps even toward her father for not protecting her mother. Gail seems very depressed.

Discussion Questions

1. How does the way Gail's mother died influence the counseling intervention?

2. How does the way Gail's mother died inform how you make sense of Gail?

3. How do you negotiate the feelings this child's situation raises for you?

The Counselor's Response

Dealing with a child who has experienced the loss of a parent through murder raises many serious issues. Because murder is always unexpected, the child is not prepared for the death, and this suddenness has implications for counseling. The child is likely to have unfinished business with the lost parent. Such a child did not have an opportunity to say goodbye and is likely to experience a great deal of shock and trauma. Also, a number of traumatic consequences exist in the case of murder, such as having to deal with the police and having the media camping out on your lawn or questioning people at school. A lot of whispering and gossip surrounds a murder, but not a great deal of direct communication. People feel uncomfortable addressing the topic with the victim's family and so may avoid them, which in turn increases the family's sense of isolation.

Gail has experienced several losses as a result of her mother's murder. She has had to move to a new town and school. She has lost her support network. Gail's father is likely very busy working through his own loss and the accompanying legal issues, providing for the family, and adjusting to his new role as single father. Gail is communicating through her somatic complaints that she does not feel safe. Somatizing is a typical aspect of posttraumatic stress disorder (PTSD; Maxmen & Ward, 1995; Worden, 1996), a condition that Gail might be suffering from. She is in a strange place with new people. She seems depressed, having little energy and no desire to engage in social relationships with peers. Her irritability is a common symptom of depression in children (Maxmen & Ward, 1995). In short, she needs help.

In working with Gail, as with any depressed child, it is important to perform a lethality assessment to be sure that no suicidal ideation is present. Dad is to be applauded for providing family therapy for himself and his children, but I would also recommend that Gail receive individual counseling to help her explore and express her conflicting emotions surrounding her mother's death. It might be helpful to provide Gail with an opportunity to say goodbye to her mother by writing a poem or letter or performing a ritual ceremony of some kind. I would also work with her to help her find a way to remember and commemorate her relationship with her mother, when she is ready. I might recommend creating a scrapbook of important mementos (see chapter 11). It is very important also to address Gail's need for a sense of safety. She is likely to feel a sense of danger or feel that she, too, might be murdered. Verbalizing these feelings would reduce their power over her. Gail needs a big dose of tender loving care and an opportunity to feel safe and secure.

Case 4: Suicide—"I Should Have Seen This Coming!"

Maria is a 16-year-old Latina female. Her good friend Tanya recently killed herself by taking an overdose of prescription drugs. Since then, Maria has been despondent. She blames herself for Tanya's death because she now notices several signs that foreshadowed Tanya's suicide. Also, Tanya's suicide note mentioned that she felt utterly alone. Maria believes that if she had been a better friend, Tanya would not have felt so alone. On the other hand, she feels angry at Tanya, even though she doesn't like to admit it. After all, only a bad person would be angry at her dead friend! She feels angry that Tanya did not confide in her and angry that Tanya implied to the world that Maria was not there for her when, in reality, Maria would have done anything in the world for her friend. She is also afraid for Tanya's soul. As a practicing Catholic, Maria believes that suicide is an unforgivable sin and that Tanya has doomed her soul to hell and eternal damnation. She has heard it mentioned in whispers at family and neighborhood gatherings and more overtly when her priest addressed the subject of suicide at mass. She does not like to think of her friend's being punished for being sad and hopeless, and the idea has made her doubt her faith in the church. Maybe if the church had been there for Tanya, she would not have felt so hopeless. Maria has no one to confide her feelings to, however, because she knows her views would be seen as blasphemous in her family. Lately, Maria has begun to feel sad and hopeless herself and often stays in her room listening to sad music for hours.

Case Analysis

Identifying the Primary Loss

Maria's primary loss is the death of her friend.

Identifying Secondary and Intangible Losses

In addition to her primary loss, Maria is also experiencing a loss of security and sense of power and control. Her faith, beliefs, connection to the church, connection to her religious beliefs, and connection to family and community have also been deeply affected by Tanya's suicide.

Identifying the Client's Responses to the Loss Situation

Cognitive. Cognitively, Maria is responding with egocentric thinking. She also may be questioning her current belief system and how it applies to "real life" and may be ruminating on faith, religion, and her friend's suicide. These symptoms provide evidence that Maria's experience has reached trauma level (Terr, 1995).

Behavioral. Maria is isolating herself and blaming herself for her friend's suicide. In connection with a cognitive response, she may believe that isolating herself will prevent her from causing any further deaths or grief.

Emotional. Maria feels guilty, angry, afraid, alone, sad, betrayed, scared (for Tanya's soul), and confused. Emotionally, she has been challenged to examine the belief system that is at the core of her identity.

Discussion Questions

1. What kinds of dangers and issues are inherent when dealing with grief from a teen suicide?
2. How do Maria's culture and religion play a role in her loss, and how would you work with her within her culture to address it?
3. As a counselor, how would you work with Maria?

The Counselor's Response

Relationship, relationship, relationship. Right now Maria does not feel connected to her family, community, or church. She even feels disconnected from herself because Tanya's suicide has been a catalyst for her to examine her belief system and, essentially, her identity. Building a relationship with Maria is key. I want to be thoughtful about our relationship because she already feels betrayed by Tanya, her family, and her religion. I will need to earn her trust. I would be remiss if I did not assess Maria for suicidal ideation. According to Sommers-Flanagan and Sommers-Flanagan (1995), Maria has a number of risk factors herself, including but not limited to her recent losses, among them the suicide of her friend, lack of social support, and her age.

I will use reflective listening skills to allow Maria to share her experience. Using these skills will also allow me to demonstrate empathy, positive regard, and acceptance. Although this philosophy will be embedded in the intervention, I will take a more directive stance and implement some specific interventions that I believe will be important for Maria in her healing process.

Maria and I share neither a religious nor an ethnic identity, so I will need to do my homework. I will consult the professional literature, but I will rely on Maria to teach me about herself. I do not assume that I share the same culture with any of my clients. I am always a learner in the counseling relationship. I might say, "We don't share the same cultural background, but I'll trust you to tell me all about Maria," to put the cultural issue on the table for discussion. It would also be important to address Maria's current confusion about her religion. Some counselors might try to tackle religious issues, telling Maria that Tanya won't go to hell. While comments like these may come from good intentions, they trivialize her strongly ingrained religious beliefs. I would help her to locate people within her community who may be able to give her information, solace, and comfort regarding her religious and spiritual questions. A local priest, church youth worker, or layperson may be able to provide her with the answers she is seeking. I would, however, allow her to explore her fears and questions about her religious beliefs within the context of counseling.

According to the case study, part of Maria's loss is her experience that she is in this alone. I would encourage her to bring family (however she defines it) and friends to sessions with her. Of course, if her friends are minors, I would need parental permission before engaging them in the process. My goal is multifaceted here. First, I want to challenge Maria's perception that she is physically alone. Second, I believe this particular counseling modality will demonstrate to Maria that she is emotionally supported. It will begin to reconnect her with the people who are important to her. Suicide is a loss that is stigmatized and still viewed as a taboo subject. Giving Maria and the important people in her life an opportunity to discuss suicide reduces the stigmatization. If the stigma associated with Tanya's death can be minimized by people to whom Maria is connected, then Maria can grieve her friend fully because she won't be limited to her perceptions of the way people are supposed to grieve those who die of suicide. It is my impression that this counseling modality will comprise most of my intervention with Maria.

Case 5: Abuse and Victimization—"You're Such a Prude"

Staci is a 13-year-old who has gotten into a great deal of trouble lately. Last week, she was suspended from school after being caught performing oral sex on a boy in the girls' bathroom. Staci's mother is beside herself when she calls to find out if Staci needs counseling. Her mother notes that she is so embarrassed, she is considering moving the family and homeschooling Staci. Staci's mother says she had a feeling her daughter was "promiscuous" because she had found a note from a boy in Staci's jeans the other day that alluded to a sexual encounter. Staci's mother tried to address her concerns with her daughter immediately, but Staci became aggressive and destroyed her room. Her mother backed off. In a small voice, Staci's mother said, "I should have protected her." She would not discuss what she had meant by that, but as a counselor, you recognize this statement as a code for past abuse.

Staci sees no problem here. She says she mostly enjoys performing oral sex, and it only hurts "a little" when the boys don't talk to her. She is really just interested in pleasing them. Staci admits that she has been "fooling around" with boys for over a year and even had a boyfriend who was a high school senior last month for a few days.

Case Analysis

Identifying the Primary Loss

Staci's primary loss is the loss of her sense of self and her ability to establish boundaries and have control over her own body.

Identifying Secondary and Intangible Losses

Staci's secondary and intangible losses are many. She has lost a sense of innocence and safety. She no longer feels that her mother can protect her. She has been treated as a sexual object and has internalized that image of herself.

Identifying the Client's Responses to the Loss Situation

Cognitive. Staci seems cognitively to be cut off from her feelings. She suggests that there is nothing wrong but then acts out aggressively and sexually. It appears that she may be repressing or denying her past sexual abuse.

Behavioral. Staci is seeking to give boys pleasure as though that is her only function and as though her own feelings, wants, and desires are unimportant. She says that everything is fine but then explodes when confronted about her behaviors.

Emotional. Staci is in pain. She is cut off from her deepest feelings and is going through the motions as she tries to make sense of her life. Underneath her numb exterior, there is likely to be anger, pain, hurt, and even despair over how she has been victimized. She may also blame herself for what has happened to her. She may be confused, not knowing how to relate to boys.

Discussion Questions

1. How do you negotiate your role as Staci's counselor when you think she is too young to be engaging in sexual behavior?
2. How can you address Staci's abuse history when neither Staci nor her mother has ever disclosed it?
3. What issues does Staci raise for you? How will you take care of yourself?

The Counselor's Response

As Staci's counselor, it is important that I not judge her or define her behaviors as wrong or promiscuous. Staci is trying to make sense of what has happened to her. The most crucial aspect of working with Staci, or any child who has been sexually abused, is to overcome her mistrust of others. Staci has been hurt deeply by someone who should have been protecting her, and it will be no small task to establish trust and rapport with her. I would not advise rushing into a discussion of her past experiences because she is well guarded, and I would not want to breach her defense mechanisms before she is emotionally ready to relive her pain. Instead, I would work with Staci on developing her own sense of self. I would explore with her all of her strengths and gifts and help her to rediscover the hopes and dreams that were derailed by her abuse. I would explore the notion of relationships and sex, discuss her views, and educate her about what healthy relationships really look like. I would help her reconnect with friends and her mother and try to facilitate communication between them. I might also suggest family therapy or at least joint sessions after some time working alone with Staci. Through the process of allowing

Staci to get to know herself, she would be in a position to examine her feelings about her abuse when she is ready. In short, I would allow her to have a safe place where she is not judged and where she was free to express herself without fear.

Case 6: Parental Incarceration—"I'm Not the Criminal"

Last month Jesse, a 10-year-old boy, found out that he would be living with his aunt for about a year. Jesse's mother had been found guilty of fraud and sentenced to a year in prison. Jesse has no idea what this means, except that he has to move into his aunt's house and share a room with his cousin Robert. He likes Robert; they're good friends.

Jesse came home to his aunt's from school last week complaining of a stomachache. He refused to go to school the following day, crying that he was still feeling sick. He attended the next day and was suspended. He had gotten into a physical altercation on the bus. He said the other kid had called his mother a "jailbird."

Jesse's aunt is at a loss. Jesse has always been such a joy. He is bright, thoughtful, and well mannered. She is not sure she can handle a troublemaker.

Case Analysis

Identifying the Primary Loss

Jesse's primary loss is the loss of his mother to incarceration.

Identifying Secondary and Intangible Losses

Jesse's secondary losses include his move from his own home, his feelings of confusion surrounding his mother's incarceration, and the lack of control he feels over his circumstances.

Identifying the Client's Responses to the Loss Situation

Cognitive. Cognitively, Jesse is confused. He is unsure exactly what is happening around him.

Behavioral. Jesse is responding to the taunting of his classmates with aggression. He is also responding to his anxiety by developing a somatic symptom, a stomachache.

Emotional. Emotionally, Jesse is feeling confused, hurt, angry, and anxious.

Discussion Questions

1. What can the counselor recommend Jesse's aunt do to be supportive?

2. How can the counseling intervention address the behavioral aspect of Jesse's situation?

3. How can Jesse's mother be involved?

The Counselor's Response

Jesse's case illustrates the harm that we can inadvertently cause children when we try to protect them. Jesse was ill-prepared for the incarceration of his mother. Not much information was offered to him about his mother's crime, arrest, and sentencing. Very often, families keep children in the dark about the details of a trial in order to protect them from being hurt. Most children, however, crave information. They need to understand what is happening in order to be able to predict what may happen next, especially when faced with monumental changes like moving in with relatives and losing Mom for a year. Jesse needs information. He needs to understand what is happening with his mother. He needs to maintain contact with his mother through letters, phone calls, and visits. Although he should have been prepared ahead of time, it is not too late to help him anticipate and deal with negative comments from classmates and others. Parental incarceration is stigmatizing to children, and Jesse's fighting behaviors and somatic complaints are to be expected.

In working with Jesse, it will be important to allow him to ask questions and talk about his mother's going to jail. Techniques such as having him draw or play out his feelings will be useful. There are also several good books geared toward child readers dealing with parental incarceration: *One Thing for Sure,* by David Gifaldi (2000), and *Let's Talk about When Your Parent Is In Jail,* by Maureen Wittbold (2003), are two good examples. Reading a book like this together would be an excellent way to facilitate discussion and generate feelings about the situation. What Jesse needs most is consistency and the knowledge that he has supportive people in his life who will be there for him in his mother's absence. I would work with Jesse's aunt to help her understand Jesse's mixed emotions and seemingly out-of-the-blue behaviors. By working together with Jesse and me, the family can devise strategies to help Jesse cope with his loss.

Case Study for Reader Analysis

Samantha does not want to go to school anymore. She complains of nausea every morning. Today, when her mother was again fighting with her about going to school, Samantha said, "If you make me go back to that school, I will get myself suspended and sent home!"

Sixth grade has been particularly difficult for Samantha. She began menstruating, her dog died, and her 16-year-old cousin Jeffery, who lived next door, committed suicide.

After her cousin's death, the community embraced Samantha and her extended family. However, a month after the suicide, it was rumored that a suicide note had been found and, in it, Jeffery had stated that he was homosexual. Since then, the teasing that Samantha has endured has been relentless. Samantha has begun to use hate words when referring to Jeffery, and this has caused some problems in the extended family. Jeffery's parents no longer want Samantha at their house. A rift between Samantha's parents and Jeffery's parents is widening, creating a great deal of tension for all involved.

Discussion Questions

1. What are Samantha's primary, secondary, and intangible losses?
2. How do you deal with Samantha's using hate language in session?
3. What personal issues are likely to emerge for you as Samantha's counselor?

SUMMARY

This chapter presented strategies designed to help children and adolescents cope with particularly traumatic and devastating losses. Case examples of tragic losses, including sudden death and death by natural disaster, were presented, as were cases of stigmatizing loss, such as murder, suicide, child abuse, and parental incarceration. Intervention strategies and sample responses were provided for each case presented.

PART III

Grief Lasts a Lifetime

CHAPTER 10

How Grief Manifests over Time

Grief does not simply disappear with time, as many people would like to believe. Grief changes—waxes and wanes—but losses always have a lasting impact on us. It is especially important when working with children and adolescents to recognize that as children's cognitive and emotional capacities develop over time, they will likely begin to understand old losses in new ways. Perhaps a child at the age of five had not fully understood the permanence of death, for example, when his grandfather died. As this child ages and begins to understand that Grandpa is never coming back, he may need to regrieve the loss in new ways. Parents and other caregivers do not always make the connection between an old loss and a child's current behaviors. Counselors, however, must be ever aware of this possibility. Throughout this chapter, we will discuss ways in which grief manifests over time and how loss experiences may resurface in parents and in counselors as a result of working with children who have experienced loss.

Case 1: The Impact of Multiple Losses—"The Final Straw"

David, age 16, moved to his current town nearly two years ago from a city in another state. He was not happy about the move, but his parents were quite pleased with how readily he adjusted to his new surroundings. He made several new friends and became active in sports and in the school band. One year ago, one of David's close friends was killed in an auto accident when his car skidded on a slippery road. Again, his parents were proud of how well he coped with the loss. He was a pallbearer, spoke at the funeral, and organized a memorial committee in school to plant a tree in his friend's honor. According to his parents, he seemed to get on with his life just fine. About two months ago, David's girlfriend, whom he had been dating for a year and a half, broke up with him and began seeing another boy. Again, he coped well. He and his girlfriend parted on good terms and were still friends. Three weeks ago, David was crushed when he was cut from the basketball team. He loved basketball, but rather than "let it get me down," David decided to join an intramural league, which he enjoyed very much. Two days ago, David's parents found him in the act of trying to commit suicide by hanging himself in his bedroom closet. His report card was attached to a suicide note that he had prepared and left on his bed. In the note, he said that he was distraught over a grade of 87 he had received in his technology class and apologized to his parents for letting them down. Every other grade was above a 95. David's parents were beside themselves. They had never been hard on David due to grades. What on earth could have possessed him to attempt such an act?

Discussion

David's case is an example of how losses pile up over time to have a cumulative effect on a person. David had experienced significant losses in a short period of time. He had moved, had a close friend die, experienced a breakup, and been cut from the basketball team, and yet he seemed just fine. Children and adolescents can be incredibly resilient in the face of adversity. David seemed to roll with the punches despite the blows that came his way. David's parents failed to realize, though, that David was just piling up his losses in the back of his mind, getting on with his life without ever really working through his grief. For this reason, the grade in technology was the final straw for David. To his parents, this was a seemingly unimportant event, especially when compared with all the tragedies he had lived through already. Therefore, they were not prepared when David's defenses came tumbling down.

A counselor must be aware of this possibility, however. That is why prevention is so important when working with children and adolescents who have experienced loss. A school counselor should have met with David after his friend's death. The counselor might have recommended to David's parents that David see a counselor outside of school to work through his grief. Counselors must also assess each new client for recent and past losses they may have experienced.

Creating a loss genogram with a client is especially useful for this purpose. In this way, the counselor can make note of any deaths, divorces, moves, or other events in the family. Constructing a timeline is also a helpful assessment tool. The counselor and client construct a timeline beginning on the date of the client's birth and continuing into the present, and they examine together all of the significant events that have taken place in the client's life. This tool allows for a great deal of exploration and may lead to significant self-discovery in the client.

Case 2: Grief Trigger Points—"I Deserve a Mom"

Amanda, age 15, had lost her mother to cancer when Amanda was 6. Since then, Amanda, her father, and her younger brother, age 12, had lived happily together. Amanda was invited to a sleepover at a friend's house. She and her friend Shelley were going to get ready for the semi-formal dance together and then come back to Shelley's to pig out on munchies and watch movies until dawn. When Amanda arrived at Shelley's, the house was full of joyful chaos. Shelley and her two sisters were sitting at the table, chatting and laughing, while their mother moved from one to the other arranging their hair in strange and wonderful ways. Shelley, who had a head full of curlers, directed Amanda to sit in the empty chair across from her. Not two minutes later, Shelley's mom was behind her, playing with her hair. She and the girls tossed around ideas of what style might look best on Amanda, and Shelley's mother finally decided on a French braid with a beautiful bow that matched her hot pink dress. Amanda sat there in ecstasy amidst the constant chatter and attention from Shelley's mother. When she was finally allowed to look in the mirror, Amanda concluded that she looked absolutely beautiful, like a princess. She and Shelley danced the night away and ate junk food until they were sick.

When Amanda returned home the next day, she was sullen and angry with her father and brother. Her father attributed her behavior to staying up too late and did not think too much about it until her rudeness had lasted a month, with no end in sight. When her father confronted her about her behavior and mood, Amanda said he was worthless and declared that she intended to go live with Shelley and her family. Amanda's father was completely flabbergasted and made an appointment for family counseling.

Discussion

Amanda's case illustrates how a current event can trigger emotions from a past loss. In this case, Amanda was mourning the loss of her mother. Her encounter with Shelley and her family represented to Amanda all that a mother-daughter relationship should be. Since she had no other experience to draw from, Amanda concluded that she was missing out, and she began to grieve the loss of the mother she had never had as an adolescent and would never have again. Amanda was angry over her loss. She felt that it was unfair that she could not experience the mother-daughter bonding that Shelley had with her mother. Amanda took out her feelings of anger and disappointment on those closest to her and even blamed her father for not being able to provide her with the motherly affection she craved.

A counselor should always be prepared to make connections between past losses and current behaviors and feelings. With a little digging, the counselor could discover the relationship between Amanda's idealization of Shelley's family and her feelings of loss over her mother's death. It would be important to help Amanda—and her father—make this connection and help the family to communicate openly about their feelings related to missing Amanda's mother. Together, the counselor and the family could devise ways for Amanda to work through her feelings of resentment and develop a healthy mentoring relationship with an adult woman, perhaps even Shelley's mother.

Case 3: Helping Parents Cope with Their Own Losses—"Stop Playing That Song"

Jimmy, age eight, had always wanted to play the piano. After Jimmy's grandfather died, his grandmother gave Jimmy his grandfather's piano. Jimmy was just three years old. Because her husband had been the consummate pianist, Jimmy's grandmother hoped that Jimmy had inherited some innate musical ability. She was right. Jimmy took to the piano right away. Jimmy's grandmother paid for private lessons, and Jimmy loved to play for her each Friday afternoon after school. On these occasions, Jimmy would play from a book of old standards that his grandmother adored. She was his biggest fan.

When his grandmother died suddenly, Jimmy took it very hard. Whenever he felt the loss of his grandmother very acutely, he would play his piano because it gave him comfort and solace. Unfortunately, it did not have the same effect on his mother. Each time he played the piano, it reminded her of her mother, and she would feel an over-whelming sense of grief. She soon forbade Jimmy from playing from the songbook her mother had loved so much because it "cut through her like a knife." Although she said it did not bother her, Jimmy could feel his mother's resentment, and one day he reported that he was giving up his lessons and would never play the piano again. His mother felt a huge sense of relief, which was obvious to Jimmy even through her protestations. Jimmy followed through on his promise to his mother but always felt a huge loss related to both his grandmother and his inability to play the piano. In his heart, he knew that his grandmother was disappointed in him.

Discussion

Jimmy's case illustrates how children are often affected by the unre-solved grief of their parents. It is not unusual for a parent to be so distraught with her own feelings of grief and loss that she is unable to be there for her children. As a result of Jimmy's mother's pain, Jimmy was forced to experience two profound losses: the death of his grandmother and the loss of his piano, which was such a comfort to him. In trying to accommodate his mother's needs, Jimmy also expe-rienced a sense of guilt and shame in feeling that he had let his grand-mother down by quitting the piano. It would be easy for Jimmy's mother to rationalize Jimmy's decision as a response to his own grief when in fact he was responding to hers.

This case illustrates that counselors must be aware of the impact of parental grief on the children and adolescents with whom they work. It is not unusual for a counselor to spend a good deal of time helping parents to see the connection between their own grief and their child's pain. For this reason, the counselor should be prepared to provide referrals for the parent to seek individual counseling.

HELPING HELPERS COPE WITH THEIR OWN LOSSES

Not surprisingly, counselors and other mental health professionals, who are skilled at recognizing symptoms of grief and loss in their clients, often overlook the effect that working with survivors of loss has on them emotionally. It has long been recognized that mental health professionals often suffer vicarious traumatization from working with victims of loss. Vicarious traumatization can be defined as the cumulative transformative effect on the helper from working with survivors of traumatic life events (James & Gilliland, 2005; Webb,

2002). Very often, this vicarious traumatization, or "compassion fatigue," comes about due to the surfacing of unresolved losses in the counselor's own life. As discussed earlier in this chapter, grief over early losses does not just disappear; it can be triggered by working with clients whose issues remind counselors of their own long-hidden feelings of loss. Also, since counselors are susceptible to the same myths that pervade our society about grief and children, those who work primarily with children may be even more susceptible to feeling traumatized by working with this population. An example from one of the author's own experiences helps to illustrate this concept.

When I (J. F.) worked as a school counselor for a residential home for children with developmental disabilities, I was assigned to work with a seven-year-old child who was a hospice patient. I was told that she had only a few months to live and that my task was to make her feel more comfortable with issues surrounding her own death. As a new counselor in my very first job, I quickly assembled a number of books and tools. We read *When Dinosaurs Die*, written by Laurie Krasny Brown and illustrated by Marc Brown (1996), and other books together. We talked about her feelings related to her own impending death. We discussed her beliefs about what happens when and after you die.

All the while we worked together, this child's health seemed to me to be improving. I secretly imagined that she was getting better because her complexion seemed less gray, her eyes were shinier, and so forth. I was therefore completely unprepared when I came to work one day to discover that my client had died during the night and that, as the only counselor, I needed to "be there" for the rest of the school. The remainder of the day remains a blur to me. I went to every class and made presentations to the students about this girl's death. I met with both the teaching and residential staff members and helped them through their grief. I did all of this as though I were on autopilot. At the end of the day, I came home completely numb. I could not move and was completely grief stricken. I went to work over the next couple of weeks and felt completely unconnected to the place. It was as though all the joy of my job was gone; it had been replaced by an over-whelming sadness. Soon after, I resigned and left my job at the school.

It wasn't until years later that I was able to examine and make sense of what happened to me during that experience. It became apparent when I was working as a doctoral intern in a college coun-seling center that I had unresolved feelings of grief and loss. During one semester, I was assigned almost a dozen clients who had issues surrounding death and grief. I couldn't understand why I was having trouble working with these students because I had never experienced the loss of a close loved one or friend. With the help of a supervisor, I was able to understand why I felt that I couldn't move on with these clients. Much of it related back to my experience with my seven-year-old client years earlier. My supervisor allowed me to explore my feelings surrounding the little girl's death, and three major themes emerged. One was my belief that children should not die. In my heart, I believed the myth that children should outlive their elders. The second discovery was that I felt helpless because I had not been able to keep her from dying (I guess we never outgrow magical thinking). Last, I was never able to process any of my own feelings because no one was there for me. The age-old question "Who helps the helper?" was answered in my case with a resounding "no one!" I had no support system to help me process my own feelings of loss.

I provide this example to illustrate how important it is for counselors to develop a support network of colleagues and friends to help them through the rough times and the absolute necessity of engaging in a process of professional and/or peer supervision. How does a counselor know when he or she is experiencing vicarious traumatization? James and Gilliland (2005) suggest that helpers look out for the following signs and symptoms of burnout and compassion fatigue:

Having no time or energy for yourself

Disconnection from loved ones

Social withdrawal

Increased sensitivity to violence and death

Cynicism

Generalized despair and hopelessness

Nightmares

Disrupted frame of reference

Changes in identity, worldview, and spirituality

Diminished self-capacities

Impaired ego resources

Disrupted psychological needs and cognitive schemas

Alterations in sensory experience

Intrusive imagery

Dissociation

Depersonalization

As already mentioned, mental health professionals who work with children and adolescents and who experience grief and loss are particularly susceptible to vicarious traumatization. Additional personal factors may also increase a helper's chance of experiencing compassion fatigue. These include a personal history of loss; personality and defensive style; coping style; current life context and stressors; training and professional history; availability of supervision; and willingness to engage in personal therapy (Greenstone & Leviton, 2002; James & Gilliland, 2005).

SUMMARY

In this chapter, we have discussed the ways that grief manifests itself over a period of time. People do not simply get over loss and move on, as many would like to believe. Losses in childhood and adolescence have a deep and profound impact on the lives of those who experience them, as well as on the caregivers who work with these individuals. It is common for the feelings associated with earlier losses to resurface later in life in times of joy, sadness, stress, or developmental change.

Further, current losses are compounded by previous and consequent losses. Each new loss is capable of triggering memories of past losses, and multiple losses build up over time to become more than the sum of their parts. This is why losses that seem minor may produce more severe reactions than are warranted by the circumstances.

This chapter also discussed how parents and caregivers must be willing to work through their own issues of loss in order to be able to help their child. Mental health professionals are not immune to the impact of working with children who have experienced loss. It is incumbent upon counselors to recognize and work through their own issues related to grief and loss and to be cognizant of the potential for compassion fatigue and burnout to occur. Counselors are encouraged to develop strong support networks and to seek supervision and personal therapy to help them cope with the vicarious traumatization that often accompanies working with children and adolescents who have experienced grief and loss.

PART IV

Interventions

CHAPTER 11

Selected Interventions

1. Goodbye, Cookie Jar
2. Paradoxical Scavenger Hunt
3. Pen Pal?
4. Stomp!
5. Remember Me
6. Loss Map
7. The Healing Heart
8. Doing Grief
9. Goodbyes and Hellos Book
10. Blanket of Love
11. Flannel Board and Pictures
12. Self-Esteem Game
13. Traveling Friends
14. All Mixed Up
15. The Storage Box
16. One Day in Time
17. When Doves Fly Away
18. This Is My Home
19. Making Music
20. Bubble Launch
21. Coping Skills Inventory
22. Goodbye Letter
23. Snapshot

INTERVENTION 1: GOODBYE, COOKIE JAR

Rationale

This activity-based intervention is intended to give children an opportunity to talk about the primary, secondary, and intangible losses consistent with the loss of a family member who is moving away.

Materials

An empty box or container that can be decorated (the cookie jar), paper, scissors, markers, crayons, stickers, and any other art materials you wish

Description

The counselor prepares the materials beforehand and sets the premise of the game, while allowing for flexibility.

Counselor: We are going to play a game today to help you say goodbye to your grandma because she's moving away. It's called the "Goodbye, Cookie Jar" game.

Child: Yum, cookies.

Counselor: These are not cookies for eating, but they are special cookies.

Child: But I'm hungry.

Counselor: You love cookies, and they would help fill up the emptiness inside. Do you want to see these special cookies?

Child: I guess.

Counselor: There are three kinds of cookies. There are memory cookies, feelings cookies, and wish cookies. On each cookie, write either a memory of your time with Grandma, a feeling you have about saying goodbye, or a wish you have. You know you can ask for help if you need it.

Child: I wish my grandma wouldn't move away.

Counselor: Let's write it down. It's so sad for you that your grandma is not going to live close by and you won't get to spend as much time with her. Maybe those could be feelings cookies.

Child: Oh, okay, two cookies—sad and mad. I'll make a memory cookie now. Remember when my grandma brought me here, and I showed her the playroom?

The counselor and child deposit cookies into a container that could have been decorated in a previous session as part of the intervention. The "Goodbye, Cookie Jar" game can be played in a final session or in a series of sessions. The child takes the "Goodbye, Cookie Jar" home when she has filled it.

INTERVENTION 2: PARADOXICAL SCAVENGER HUNT

Rationale

This activity-based intervention is intended to challenge children and adolescents with disabilities to examine their beliefs about their potential for a successful life.

Materials

Access to the Internet or library

Description

The counselor can use this intervention as part of the session or as homework. Used in the session, it allows client and counselor to collaborate on the task. This intervention can easily be adapted for use in groups.

Counselor: Remember last session, when you said that you are a loser and freak because you have a learning disability?

Child: Yep.

Counselor: I was thinking perhaps we could head over to the library [or computer] and do a search to find out if there are any famous people who have learning disabilities. And then we can decide if they are freaks or losers, too.

Child: Well, I don't think you can be famous and be LD.

Counselor: Let's find out.

At the library or computer.

Child: Cher. My mom thinks she's cool, but not me.

Counselor: You may not think she's cool, but would you agree that she is successful?

Child: I bet she's rich, too.

Counselor: And also a freak and loser, right?

Child: I don't know. Maybe.

The counselor and child continue to engage in their search. The counselor continues to gently challenge the child's perspective of self. The child serves as a witness that people with disabilities are smart, rich, successful, talented, athletic, and so forth.

INTERVENTION 3: PEN PAL?

Rationale

This intervention is intended to give adolescents an opportunity to experience the primary, secondary, and intangible losses associated with a close friend's moving away. These feelings occur as the activity progresses in the safety of a supportive relationship. The activity can be altered and used in interventions that focus on other losses.

Materials

Pencil, lined paper

Description

The counselor engages the adolescent by giving examples of some of the emotional responses he might be feeling in connection with his friend's moving away. The counselor suggests that the adolescent pretend or act as if moving has human qualities. Giving an example usually helps. For instance, "You might want to start off saying, 'Dear Moving: I am really annoyed that you are taking my friend away.' " The counselor prompts the adolescent by making suggestions based on the emotional responses that the adolescent has already discussed. When the adolescent is satisfied with the letter to "Moving," he can write an additional letter. In this case, the adolescent, again with prompts from the counselor (and based on the content of the first letter), acts as if he is "Moving" and responds to the original letter received. The letters should be read aloud. The reading of the letters makes the intervention more powerful—the words are not just written, but heard and shared.

INTERVENTION 4: STOMP!

Rationale

This activity-based intervention gives children and adolescents the opportunity to express their anger about a friend's move in a behavioral way, in an effort to prevent them from acting out their grief in a way that will cause them to experience other losses or stressors.

Materials

Empty cardboard egg cartons, markers or crayons, paper, tape

Description

The counselor invites the child to help write down "feelings words" to describe the emotions she has because her friend is moving away, each on a separate sheet of paper. The child tapes one feelings word to each egg carton. The counselor then tells the child that she can stomp or smash the carton if she can tell a story about how the feelings word tells how her friend's moving away makes her feel. With each stomp, the counselor reflects the child's feelings. The child is reminded that she can come back and stomp some more if she needs to because this is a special place (or time).

> **NOTE:** Counselors should share this activity with the child's caregivers. This activity could be used at home with paper only; stomping can safely occur outside and in some indoor areas. (Of course, limits with regard to safety and destruction of other property should be set.)

INTERVENTION 5: REMEMBER ME

Rationale

In this intervention, children and adolescents are given the opportunity to discover their feelings and thoughts about death. This intervention can be used to access and assess the youth's spirituality, religious beliefs, family dynamics, friendships, self-esteem, and perception of self. This intervention can easily be adapted for use in groups.

Materials

Paper and pencils

Description

The counselor engages the child or adolescent in writing a list. The counselor can decide whether or not to help the client with the writing, according to the client's lead.

Counselor: We have been talking and playing a lot about what it's like for you now that your grandpa has died after being sick for a while.

Child: Right.

Counselor: I was wondering if you would mind making a letter about you and the things and people that are important to you.

Child: No.

Counselor: It seems like you are not interested. Would you be interested if I worked on it with you, if maybe I did the writing?

Child: I don't know what to say.

Counselor: Let's start by making a list of people who are important to you.

Child: Okay. You write, though.

The counselor and child continue to engage in the task. To tease out a list of important people and things in the child's life, the counselor can ask questions, reflect feelings or content, and use other listening skills as the list emerges. Upon completion of the task, the counselor ends the session (or sessions) by suggesting that these are the things and meaningful people the child wants to remember about herself. The child thereby recognizes the important aspects of her current world, while simultaneously discovering losses and beliefs about the way the world works.

INTERVENTION 6: LOSS MAP

Rationale

This intervention focuses on the child's or adolescent's cognitive and emotional manifestations of grief. In this activity, multiple losses are identified. Identifying these losses gives the young person the opportunity to revisit past losses as well as discover past successful and unsuccessful coping strategies. The activity can be altered and used in interventions that focus on other losses, or it can be adapted for use in groups.

Materials

Paper and pencils, crayons or markers, stickers

Description

After establishing good rapport, the counselor directs the intervention by asking the child or adolescent to recall other losses besides the one that he is currently dealing with. The counselor may have to provide an example (certainly, there are many in this text). Examples of even seemingly minor losses, such as losing a tooth, a first haircut, or a baby-sitter's moving away are useful. The counselor uses symbols (created with the child or adolescent) to represent the loss. The symbols can be drawn, or stickers can be used. When it seems as though the losses have been documented, the counselor facilitates discussion of the child's phenomenological perspective of the loss, highlighting coping strategies and helping the child assess if the strategy worked and showing how he could apply it to the current loss situation. It is likely that this activity will occur over several sessions.

INTERVENTION 7: THE HEALING HEART

Rationale

This activity-based intervention is intended to allow children and adolescents to talk about the loss of a friendship and begin the process of healing.

Materials

Paper and pencils, scissors, adhesive bandages

Description

The counselor engages the child or adolescent regarding all the different feelings that can be experienced when a friendship ends. The adult employs active and reflective listening responses and invites the child or adolescent to participate in the activity.

The child or adolescent is instructed to cut out the shape of a heart and then cut the heart in half as a metaphor for the heartbreak that she is feeling because of the friendship loss. The counselor provides enough time (maybe more than one session or meeting) for the child or adolescent to share her emotional, behavioral, and cognitive reactions to the loss.

After the child or adolescent has shared about the loss, the counselor instructs her to use the bandages to begin to heal the heart. For each bandage that she applies, the child or adolescent is prompted to indicate a method of self-care. That method is written on the bandage. Some examples that children and adolescents have shared are listening to music, dancing, and playing video games.

INTERVENTION 8: DOING GRIEF

Rationale

The goal of this intervention is to provide permission for teens to grieve. The lives of teenagers are so often filled with doing that there is little time for feeling. This intervention can be used in the context of the counseling setting or as a homework assignment. The activity can be altered and used in interventions that focus on a variety of primary and intangible losses.

Materials

None

Description

After a solid counseling relationship has been established with the youth, the counselor reviews the client's daily schedule and asks, "When do you find time to grieve?" Typically, the youth will indicate that there is no time. The counselor works with the adolescent to find five minutes between this meeting and the next (assuming it will be about a week from the current session) to grieve, to spend that time thinking and feeling about the loss. The counselor may suggest a practice run in the session and should also discuss the parameters of choice to best allow for follow-through. (For instance, using study-hall time is not the best choice because there's no privacy and you have to go to math immediately afterward. Sundays might not be good because you go on visitation with your mom and you are never quite sure about the timing of your visit or if the visit will happen at all.) The intent is to give the youth the opportunity to be deliberate about self-care. A list of self-care activities should also be generated and recommended after the youth has experienced grief time.

INTERVENTION 9: GOODBYES AND HELLOS BOOK

Rationale

This activity-based intervention focuses on the grief and loss that children and adolescents experience with transitions. The activity can be altered and used in interventions that focus on many types of transitional losses and is well suited and easily adapted for children or adolescents, individually or in groups.

Materials

Throwaway camera(s), construction paper, pen or pencil, glue or tape; other materials can be added as the project goes on

Description

The counselor invites the child or adolescent to begin by taking pictures of people, places, and things he will have to say goodbye to, and people, places, and things that he is going to say hello to. The adults in the child's or adolescent's life are given an explanation and letter so that this activity can be worked on in and out of the counseling relationship. (See the following sample letter.)

The photos are developed, and the youth glues or tapes them to the paper. People may choose to write brief letters for the child or adolescent to include on the page with the picture. The counselor and client can then work inside the session to create narratives and captions for each picture page.

NOTE: The sample goodbye letter can be adapted for saying hello by replacing the "goodbye" references with "hello."

Sample Goodbye Letter

Dear Parent:

I will be embarking on a project with _____. My hope is that this project will help _____ through the grief process connected with transition. I will be sending _____ home with a camera. Please help _____ to take pictures of the important people, places, and things he or she will need to say goodbye to (or already has said goodbye to). Some examples are family, friends, every room in the house, pets, school, classroom, teacher(s), soccer fields, and so forth. Do not worry if he or she uses all of the photos—I will supply another camera. As the pictures are developed, I hope that you will continue to work on this project with _____ by helping to write stories and captions about the pictures he or she has taken and placed in the book.

Please call me if you need further clarification, want more information, or would just like to talk about this transition.

Thank you,

Counselor

INTERVENTION 10: BLANKET OF LOVE

Rationale

Loss is difficult for anyone, regardless of the type of loss or the age of the person. The experience of loss can take many forms, but often it results in an emptiness or void in a person's life. Something the person once had—whether it was a person, an object, or a feeling— is no longer present. Because the lost person, object, or feeling is no longer present, children and adolescents may fear that they will slowly begin to forget what they have lost, thereby compounding their loss. This activity is intended to be used with children of any age who have experienced any type of loss. It can be used for the loss of a pet, parent, or sibling—even adapted for a child who is moving away from familiar surroundings. This particular scenario is based on loss of a parent: It allows the client to remember and honor the loved one in a positive, interactive manner while sharing feelings with the counselor.

Materials

Sewing machine and thread, markers or fabric paint, muslin cloth, scissors, and other decorative materials as desired. (The amount of help the child needs should be adapted to accommodate the age of the child. The child can determine fabric colors for the quilt, possibly the child's or deceased parent's favorites.)

Description

In this activity, the child or adolescent expresses her feelings through drawings and then creates a quilt—a "Blanket of Love" that she will always be able to keep. The primary goal is to allow the child to create something unique to the relationship that she will be able to hold and snuggle with whenever she feels lonely for the parent.

Children of all ages are capable of drawing and, when asked, can usually tell you what the picture is about. After drawing as many pictures as the child likes, the pictures are sewn into a quilt (with or without the assistance of the counselor, depending on the age of the child) so the child can then snuggle and cover up with it.

The counselor creates the setting by explaining to the child what they are going to do, allowing for flexibility:

Counselor: We are going to draw pictures today that we can sew into a special blanket for you to keep.

Child: What do you mean, special blanket?

Counselor: In our time together, you have told me wonderful things about your dad and how much you miss him. It sounds to me like you and your dad did a lot of great things together and had many special times.

Child: We did, and I am really sad that we will never be able to do those things again.

Counselor: It is sad to think that you will never be able to do special things with your dad. Let's draw some pictures of some of the special things and times that you remember about your dad. Then we can sew them into a blanket that you can wrap yourself up in whenever you want to be close to him. It will be your Blanket of Love.

Child: Dad would like that. We always used to snuggle up in a blanket and read together. Maybe I can draw a picture of that.

Counselor: That sounds like a great picture for your blanket. Here are the crayons.

The child draws as many pictures as she wants. The drawing of pictures may go on for several sessions and should continue until the child feels she is finished. The pictures are then sewn into a quilt for the child to keep.

Applications

This technique is designed for children the counselor expects to be seeing for several sessions. It can be adapted to fit the situation (for example, a child could draw pictures of a pet, grandparent, or sibling). In addition, it could be adapted to a child who is moving or has moved by having the child draw pictures about fond memories they have of the place the family moved from or the place they live now. Friends and family could be included by having them draw pictures that can also be sewn into the blanket. Using fabric paints is an alternative for those who prefer not to sew. The options are limited only by your imagination and time. If the blanket is in memory of a person, such as a grandparent or mother, it could be sprayed with the favorite perfume of that person to give it the special smell that person always had.

INTERVENTION 11: FLANNEL BOARD AND PICTURES

Rationale

For children or adolescents, the process of reviewing their relationship with the deceased will take time, as will their ability to imagine life without that person. Through this activity, the child will be able to work on his relationship with the deceased by telling life stories through pictures. The child may then be able to expand verbally on his feelings. By using a flannel board, children can pictorially express their relationship with the deceased, portray memories, and look into the future.

Materials

Along with a flannel board, pictures of objects, magazines from which to cut pictures, paper, and crayons or markers

Description

This activity will take place over multiple sessions and will progress at different rates, depending on the child. The child's personal pictures can also be used at the appropriate time if the child is willing and able to bring them in. It's a good idea to let the child take the lead when deciding the pictures or topic for each session. The child will be telling a lot about the person who died and his relationship with that person. Information on the child's current life will also be shared. As time goes on, conversations about the pictures will take place. The child will have gained trust in the counselor, will be able to verbally relay information about the pictures, and will be ready to discuss what he is feeling. Again, the amount and depth of discussion will depend upon the age of the child.

> **NOTE:** If the flannel board is being used with more than one child, it is important for the counselor to take down the pictures with the child after each session and put them away in a special place (a folder, for example). Otherwise, the child may expect them to still be on the board when he returns for the next session.

Applications

This intervention can be used with all children and teens. The amount and depth of discussion will vary, but a good sense of the child's world—past and present—will be revealed.

INTERVENTION 12: SELF-ESTEEM GAME

Rationale

Sometimes grief or loss contributes to a child's loss of self-esteem. Children in therapy may have difficulty identifying feelings of self-worth. This game can be used to get children of any age to talk about themselves and identify strengths within themselves and their families. It can be helpful for building rapport with children, learning family history, building trust, and opening up lines of communication. Most important, it pulls out individual and family strengths and helps family members understand the severity of the loss. Playing this game with siblings or peers allows them to identify positive characteristics and feelings in one another, of which they would otherwise have been unaware.

Materials

A large square piece of corrugated cardboard, crayons or markers, coins of various denominations, dice

Description

With a marker, the counselor divides the cardboard into 20 smaller squares (similar to a checkerboard), designating a starting and ending point on the board. Each square includes a question or activity relating to self-esteem. Different coins may serve as markers to distinguish the players.

As the children and counselor roll the die and land on a square, they answer the question or do the activity and discuss the issue further, if the children wish.

Counselor: Would you both like to play a game I made called the "Self-Esteem Game"?

Child 1: That sounds like fun!

Child 2: Okay. *(Child rolls the die, gets a two, and moves his designated coin to the second square)*

Counselor: The question asks you to name two feelings that come to mind when thinking about one of the other players.

Child 2: Hmm. I guess I think she is very smart, and sometimes she's fun to be around.

Child 1: *(Smiles.)* Thank you. My turn! *(Child rolls a six and moves her designated coin to the sixth square)*

Counselor: "Name one thing you enjoy doing with the player sitting to your left."

Child 1: I like it when we have family barbecues and we help set the picnic table together. It's your turn. *(Counselor rolls a three and moves her designated coin to the third square)*

Counselor: I landed on an activity: "Everyone hug the person sitting to your right." *(Children hug each other and the counselor)*

Applications

This technique is helpful for all children who have little opportunity to listen to positive discussion about themselves due to loss or to a chaotic family environment. This type of play will heighten their sense of self and understanding of their siblings. The counselor will need to adjust the questions on the board according to the children's ages. This game also opens the door to learning about family dynamics and history.

INTERVENTION 13: TRAVELING FRIENDS

Rationale

Children experience loss of belonging, comfort, security, familiarity, and a sense of power and control when they are faced with having to relocate. This loss revolves around a change in the child's home, school, and circle of friends—and possibly a change in family structure if the move is associated with the parents' separation, divorce, or remarriage.

Children often do not get the opportunity to say goodbye to friends and things that were a huge part of their lives and provided them with the sense of belonging they so desire. Friendships are especially important to children and adolescents. Children need to be given the opportunity to physically bring a part of their past with them so they will not forget their previous relationships. "Traveling Friends" not only gives children a chance to say goodbye to their friends during the game's gathering stage, it also allows the opportunity to explore the feelings associated with the goodbyes experienced during the counseling sessions.

Materials

A scrapbook that can be decorated, a disposable camera, plastic ziplock bags, colored paper, various coloring media (crayons, paint, markers), glue, scissors, and other art supplies as needed (such as stickers or ribbons)

Description

To allow for maximum creativity, during the first session in which this activity will be presented, the counselor sets up the activity with very little direction. The counselor gives the child a few plastic bags in which to collect items and a disposable camera to take any pictures the child would like to include in the "Traveling Friends" book. The child takes photos of whatever he chooses, then brings them to the next session if he desires.

Child: Mom and Dad say that I will make new friends at my new school, but I don't want new friends. I like the friends I have now.

Counselor: You would like to be able to take all the friends you have now with you to your new school.

Child: Yeah, but I know I can't.

Counselor: It's not possible for you to take your friends with you to your new school. There may be a way we can take a part of each of them with you.

Child: Parts of them?

Counselor: We could make a "Traveling Friends" book.

Child: That sounds kind of neat. What kind of stuff would I put in it?

Counselor: Your "Traveling Friends" book can contain anything you would like to remember about your friends, such as addresses and phone numbers, e-mail addresses, your best memories, places you liked to go, things you like to do together, whatever you want to remember about your friends. I have a disposable camera here so you can take pictures if you like.

Child: Oh, cool. I'd like to do that.

Counselor: You may even want to have them each give you a little something that you can take with you to remember them by.

Child: Some of my friends have already given me stuff.

Counselor: How terrific that you already have things you might want to put in your book!

Applications

This technique is useful with children ages 9 to 12 and with adolescents. It is helpful in assisting children in attaining a sense of closure prior to the move. During the information-gathering stage, this activity engages children in conversation with friends regarding the move. The gathering stage of this technique may also be a wonderful way to increase parents' awareness of the impact of the transition on the child, if the child desires to share the book with his parents.

INTERVENTION 14: ALL MIXED UP

Rationale

The "All Mixed Up" story is a starting point for the counselor to initiate a conversation with the child about the loss of a special person. It sets the tone for the child to express the feelings she is having—sadness, anger, confusion about what is going on, loneliness, worry, and so forth—and then, with the help of the counselor, feelings of relief and even happiness. When a child has witnessed, or read about, a scenario like the one in the story, in which such communication takes place and feelings are accepted, the child is more likely to attempt telling what she is feeling.

Materials

None

Description

This story tells of a boy and his favorite art teacher, who is absent for the majority of the school year. No one tells the boy why she is absent or where she has gone. He has various ideas about what has happened, and then he overhears some teachers talking. The teacher dies, and the boy eventually talks to his mom, who helps him make sense of his feelings. Because he can't send her a card, the boy draws the art teacher a special picture.

The counselor can start out by saying how the story made him feel, then may describe a similar real-life experience. The child may then feel comfortable enough also to share his feelings and tell a story. The counselor should reflect the child's feelings and follow the child's lead, always being accepting of the child's feelings.

Applications

This type of story is useful with children who may be experiencing grief or loss in many ways, whether as the result of a move, the loss of a pet, or the death of someone close. It is helpful for the child who may not be comfortable expressing her feelings. It is also extremely helpful for an adult who is not sure how to initiate a conversation about a death or other loss. This story could be the start of many conversations between the adult and the child, sharing feelings associated with various losses.

All Mixed Up

Sammy is a second grader. His favorite class is art class. Sammy loves art class because he likes to draw and paint and make things with his hands. Sammy really likes his art teacher. One of the reasons he likes her so much is that she lets the kids listen to music in class. She lets them choose what to listen to. Sammy's favorite station is Radio Disney. Sammy likes the way his art teacher tells him that she thinks he is special because he is so creative and lets him know that she cares a great deal about his work. Sammy knows this is true because he does not like to read or do math, but he loves to draw. One day, about halfway through the school year in the wintertime, Sammy went to school. It was art day, so he was excited. However, his regular teacher was not there—the class had a substitute teacher.

Week after week, his favorite teacher was not there. Sammy still liked to draw, but it was not the same without his teacher. Christmas vacation came and went, and still his teacher did not return. No one told him why. One day, Sammy heard some teachers talking in the hallway, and they said that his art teacher was very sick, and they were not sure if she was going to make it. "Make it where?" Sammy asked himself. He asked the substitute where his art teacher was, but the substitute said she did not know, except that his art teacher would be back soon. "When is soon?" Sammy thought to himself.

Well, soon it was springtime; the snow had all melted, and the flowers were beginning to pop up out of the ground. Sammy still had art class, but not with his favorite teacher. He was beginning to wonder if she would ever come back. He was angry that she had left without saying goodbye to him, but at the same time he worried about her. Sammy again heard some teachers talking in the hall, and they said she had passed away. "What does that mean?" he said to himself. Did she pass his grade and move to another one? He decided he would ask his mom when he got home.

Sammy went home and talked with his mom. She explained that "passing away" means that she died. Sammy's mom asked how Sammy felt. He did not say much because he was so surprised by the news and upset that he did not know she was sick all this time. He wished someone had told him so he could have sent her a card. Sammy's mom told a story about how she once had a favorite teacher, too, and how that teacher moved when she was in fourth grade, so she did not get to see the teacher anymore. She told Sammy how she missed her teacher a lot, that she was sad when the teacher left, and that she cried.

Sammy felt good inside that he finally had someone to talk to about missing his art teacher. Although he was sad that his teacher had died, he was glad that he had memories of her and had learned a lot of ways to do art. He will think of her whenever he does his artwork. Sammy talks about his feelings with his mom when he feels like it. Sammy's mom helped him make a picture for his teacher. He knew he could not give his teacher the picture because she was dead, but he also knew that he could make it special for her and that she would have been proud of the way he did it.

Sammy is now in fifth grade, and sometimes, when he is working on a drawing or sculpture, he thinks of his teacher, and the thought makes him smile inside and out. He feels especially close to her when he is drawing. Sammy is thankful that he has his mom to talk with about his feelings. He is glad that his mom shares her feelings, too. He continues to talk to his mom about things that make him feel all mixed up.

INTERVENTION 15: THE STORAGE BOX

Rationale

Building trust with children who have witnessed domestic violence between their parents is difficult due to the secrecy surrounding the abuse. Children may be hesitant to discuss their own losses because of this secrecy. They are also afraid, thinking maybe they caused the problems and if they don't say anything, the problem will go away.

Children in counseling may have difficulty understanding the emotional loss they have suffered due to their parents' domestic violence. They do not realize that they are also victims of domestic violence. Encouraging children to express their feelings about their parents' fights can help them learn to trust adults.

Materials

A plastic bucket, markers, stickers, paper, and colored pencils

Description

This activity plays out as illustrated in the following dialogue:

Counselor: We are going to play a game today to help you understand that you are not to blame for your parents' fights. It's called "The Storage Box."

Child: How do you play?

Counselor: You are going to take a plastic pail and make your very own storage box. You can decorate it any way you want. The storage box is a safe place for you to put your stories and your feelings. On the paper, we will write down those stories and those feelings. Then you can pick one of those papers, and we'll talk about how you feel.

Child: Can we do this now?

Counselor: Let's get started.

NOTE: Allow only 15 minutes of the session for decorating the bucket.

Child: I'm ready to start talking now.

Counselor: Go ahead and choose something from your storage box.

Child: I picked "frightened."

Counselor: It makes you scared when your mom and dad fight.

Child: I hate it when they fight. I try to be quiet.

Counselor: You don't want anyone to hear you. (The conversation continues.)

After the session, the child places the feelings in the storage box to be used in later sessions. No one but the child and counselor will know what is in the box. Until the child is discharged from counseling, the storage box will remain in the counselor's office in a safe place. Children and adolescents benefit by knowing they can trust the counselor to keep their feelings safe.

Applications

This technique would be helpful with adolescents who have taken responsibility for their parents' arguments. These parents may have told their adolescent not to tell anyone outside the home about bruises, broken bones, screaming, yelling, and so forth.

INTERVENTION 16: ONE DAY IN TIME

Rationale

Students with cognitive impairments often have difficulty comprehending or perceiving the actions or intents of family and peers. They often internalize what others say or do and think negatively of themselves. They deal with many losses—the same losses as their peers without disabilities—but they often have difficulty verbalizing their feelings and thoughts due to speech, language, or cognitive processing problems. This activity allows the counselor to understand what a student is feeling and what has upset the student without direct questioning. It gives students the power to convey their thoughts and feelings in ways in which they are comfortable.

This activity is designed for high school students ages 15 to 17 who have cognitive disabilities that cause them to function more like children ages 10 to 12. It can also be adapted for other ages and populations. This activity does not limit students to just talking. They are encouraged to respond to the sentence stems by writing, listening to music, and drawing.

Materials

Paper, markers or crayons, a CD player, a variety of CDs, a radio, headphones, and magazines

Description

Before doing this activity, the counselor makes a number of "One Day in Time" pages. Each page should include the title of the activity and the following sentence stems:

> If I were a color, I would be. . . . If I were a song, my lyrics would say. . . . If I looked in a mirror, I would see. . . . If I could change one thing, it would be. . . . If I could talk to one person, I would say, . . . The counselor introduces the activity in the following way:

Counselor: We are going to begin to write a book about ourselves called *One Day in Time*. You will be able to write, draw, color, create song lyrics, and create collages. As we meet, we will continue to add pages to your book, and at the end of our counseling together, I will have the pages bound and laminated in a book that you can keep for as long as you want.

Child: Why are we making books, and what are they supposed to be about?

Counselor: I know how much you like art and music. I also know that you like to share stories of things that happen to you. Sometimes it is helpful to create things that show how we feel instead of just talking about them. I would like for us to make a book that reflects who you are and the experiences you go through over time. You might enjoy looking through the book later on, and you will have something that records your memories.

Child: What do we do?

Counselor: You answer one or more of the questions on the page. You can choose to use words, colors, drawings, magazine pictures, symbols, or whatever you like when you respond. You can use the radio or CD player if music inspires you. You can write lyrics or poems. You may be as creative as you want to be.

Child: Do we do this every week?

Counselor: You can actually complete a page whenever you want. If you are feeling down about something or excited about something, you may want to create a page. We can also create pages when we meet together, if you'd like.

Child: Do I have to show you my page?

Counselor: If you would like to talk to me about your work, please feel free. If you don't want to, that's okay, too. I will never ask you to share your page with me if you don't want to.

Applications

This activity would also be useful for any older children or adolescents who have difficulty expressing themselves verbally. It gives them the freedom to create and express themselves without the restrictions of language. It also allows them to have a keepsake by which to remember their counseling experience.

INTERVENTION 17: WHEN DOVES FLY AWAY

Rationale

Children who experience loss through death have difficulty understanding the death and how to deal with it. Often, children are expected to respond in certain ways. By scripting their own stories about their loss, they can reflect on the person they lost as well as their perceptions of what happened when the person died. A counselor can learn a lot from the child as author about the child's feelings and thoughts and perhaps the family's rituals. In telling their experience and feelings through stories, children may be able to work through their grief in ways they might not otherwise have done.

Materials

An age-appropriate children's book about death or another type of loss; paper and pencil; markers or crayons; index cards; possibly a computer, depending on the age of the child

Description

In this activity, the counselor reads a children's book about loss to the client. While reading the story, the counselor reflects on what is written and asks questions about the content to gauge the child's under-standing of the story and learn the child's feelings about the situation. When the story is over, the counselor reviews the story and discusses what it was about, emphasizing the concept of beginning, middle, and ending. Having a discussion about the loss in the story may help the child generate thoughts and ideas from her own perspective.

Counselor: We are going to write our own book about [whatever the loss may be]. You get to decide how the story will go and make pictures to go in it.

The child can brainstorm ideas, feelings, or memories on index cards and then place them in an order that makes sense to her. The counselor can reflect on the feelings and memories the child shares, which may elicit further thoughts and memories. The child can draw pictures to go with the story, or insert family photos, and the counselor can then transfer the story narrative to the picture pages. Giving the child lead phrases to complete can help her identify and communicate her feelings. Examples include "I wish . . ."; "I hope . . ."; "I remember . . ."; and "I felt . . ."

Applications

This technique would be helpful for any child or adolescent who has experienced any type of loss. For a younger child who may not have writing skills, a storybook of pictures may be appropriate, allowing the child to tell the story through pictures. The exercise is also useful for the counselor who has little information regarding the child's history and family. Through the child's story, the counselor can learn about the rituals and beliefs surrounding the loss. The activity can be completed in one session for a brief storybook, or it can be worked on over many sessions to allow the child to thoroughly build on the story.

INTERVENTION 18: THIS IS MY HOME

Rationale

The impact of moving, a common loss shared by many children, is often minimized by adults. Through this activity, the counselor will be able to honor the losses that come with moving, and the child or adolescent will be able to share aspects of that loss. The activity gives the client the opportunity to share life outside the office with the counselor and feel listened to and understood.

Materials

Paper, markers or crayons, stickers

Description

The counselor can use this intervention as part of an individual, group, or family session. It allows for client and counselor to connect through visual, auditory, and kinesthetic modes of communication. The following dialogue illustrates the process:

Counselor: I know you just moved here from the city. Could you take me on a tour of your home or apartment?

Child: Well, I don't live there anymore.

Counselor: What I mean is, can you draw what your home was like and then show me what was important to you about it?

Child: This is going to be hard.

Counselor: You're not so sure about this.

Child: I guess I could draw my room. I mean, my old room.

Counselor: Okay, and then you can show me where things were and what you could see, whatever you feel like drawing. You sound like you miss your old room.

The counselor and child continue to engage in this discussion. The counselor might encourage the child or adolescent to pick one room and ask, "What would your room say about you?" There are endless variations of this activity. The client's direction and verbalizations should indicate to the counselor whether to continue with the activity, augment it, or move on.

INTERVENTION 19: MAKING MUSIC

Rationale

This activity-based intervention is intended to allow children and adolescents an opportunity to use sound to communicate feelings and thoughts about loss and grief. No verbalization is required by the client.

Materials

Anything that can make noise (drumsticks, bells, empty egg cartons, whistles, kazoos, and so forth)

Description

This intervention allows for client and counselor to communicate without being limited by verbal expression. It can easily be augmented for use in groups. The process is as follows:

Counselor: You have not talked about your poppy since he died last month.

Child: I know.

Counselor: I was wondering if you could use the instruments in this box to make sounds that show what it was like seeing him sick and then having him die.

Child: Will you do it, too?

Counselor: If you lead.

The counselor and child continue the intervention. The counselor might ask if the child or adolescent could also pick one instrument to tell a story about the deceased. There are endless variations of this activity. The counselor should follow the client's lead in continuing the activity, augmenting it, or moving on.

INTERVENTION 20: BUBBLE LAUNCH

Rationale

This intervention is intended to give children and adolescents an opportunity to say goodbye.

Materials

Bubble solution and wand, paper and pencil

Description

The counselor engages the child or adolescent by giving examples of some of the emotional responses the child might be feeling in connection to the loss. The counselor then helps the client construct a statement to say goodbye and to write the statement on a piece of paper. The client decides whether she or the counselor will read the statement aloud, and then, after the statement is read, blows the bubbles to honor the loss.

INTERVENTION 21: COPING SKILLS INVENTORY

Rationale

When counselors define loss broadly, as we suggest, it becomes obvious that clients have suffered (and survived) many losses before the initiation of the counseling relationship. This intervention focuses on strengths and coping strategies that the client already possesses.

Materials

Paper and pencil (or computer and word-processing software, if available)

Description

The counselor invites the child or adolescent to discover significant losses, prior to the recent loss, that he has survived. Together, they construct a list of coping skills. The child or adolescent then evaluates how the skill worked and whether it would be useful to begin or continue using it in the present situation. This activity could be used as a homework assignment or in a group setting as well as in individual work.

INTERVENTION 22: GOODBYE LETTER

Rationale

The purpose of this intervention is to allow the client an opportunity to say goodbye to a person, place, or thing. Opportunities for goodbyes are limited by circumstances often out of the control of children and adolescents. This intervention gives the client the experience of control as well as a chance to say goodbye.

Materials

Paper and pencil (or computer and word-processing software, if available)

Description

Little preparation is required for this activity, aside from having the materials readily available. The counselor engages the client about a recent separation or loss and then gives the client an opportunity to write a letter to say goodbye.

Counselor: It must have been hard to have your puppy get sick and die.

Child: Yeah.

Counselor: You never even got to say goodbye.

Child: Nope.

Counselor: I thought maybe we could do that today by writing a goodbye letter to your puppy, Max. I'll start it for you: "Dear Max: . . . . " What next?

The counselor and child continue to engage in this intervention. With some creativity on the counselor's part, countless variations of this letter could be employed. The counselor should follow the client's lead to decide whether to continue the activity, augment it, or move on.

INTERVENTION 23: SNAPSHOT

Rationale

This intervention gives children and adolescents an opportunity to create the family of their fantasy and simultaneously mourn the loss that is the reality.

Materials

A large sheet of paper or poster board, pictures or photos of family members, magazines, glue, and paper (Additional materials may be added as needed.)

> **NOTE:** The counselor may also have the client use dolls or figures to illustrate the ideal and real families.

Description

Using the art supplies and photos, the counselor leads the child or adolescent in making a family portrait of the way she *wishes* her family would be. The more detail, the better. Prompts from the counselor could include "Do you want your dad right there next to your brother?" and "Whoa, your mom is squished between you and your sister." After ample time is allowed for the client to refine the wished-for family, the counselor then leads the client to represent, on another sheet of paper or poster board, the way things *really* are and talk about or play out the discrepancies. This intervention can be modified for use with children, adolescents, groups, and families.

References

American Academy of Child and Adolescent Psychiatry. (1998). *Children and grief* (Facts for Families Fact Sheet No. 8). Available from http://www.aacap.org/publications/factsfam/grief.htm

American Psychiatric Association. (2000). *Diagnostic and statistical manual of mental disorders* (4th ed.). Washington, DC: Author.

Axelson, J. A. (1993). *Counseling and development in a multicultural society* (2nd ed.). Pacific Grove, CA: Brooks/Cole.

Axline, V. A. (1969). *Play therapy* (Rev. ed.). New York: Ballantine.

Ayash-Abdo, H. (2001). Childhood bereavement: What school psychologists need to know. *School Psychology International, 22*(4), 417–433.

Brown, F. (1988). The impact of death and serious illness on the family life cycle. In B. Carter & M. McGoldrick (Eds.), *The changing family life cycle: A framework for family therapy*. Boston: Allyn and Bacon.

Brown, L. K., & Brown, M. (1996). *When Dinosaurs Die: A Guide to Understanding Death*. Boston: Little, Brown.

Burton, L. (1995). Intergenerational patterns of providing care in African American families with teenage childbearers: Emergent patterns in an ethnographic study. In V. L. Bengston, K. Warner Schaie, & L. Burton (Eds.), *Adult intergenerational relations: Effects of societal relations* (pp. 213–248). New York: Springer.

Buscaglia, L. (1982). *The fall of Freddie the leaf: A story of life for all ages*. Thorofare, NJ: Slack, Inc.

Candy-Gibbs, S. E., Sharp, K. C., & Petrun, C. J. (1984). The effect of age, object and cultural/religious background on children's concept of death. *Omega, 15,* 329–346.

Carroll, C. (2000). *Drugs in modern society* (5th ed.). New York: McGraw-Hill.

Corey, G., Corey, M. S., & Callanan, P. (1993). *Issues and ethics in the helping professions* (4th ed.). Pacific Grove, CA: Brooks/Cole.

Cunningham, L. (2004). *Grief and the adolescent.* Available from http://www.smartlink.net/~tag/grief.html

Cytron, B. D. (1993). To honor the dead and comfort the mourners: Traditions in Judaism. In D. P. Irish, K. F. Lundquist, & V. J. Nelsen (Eds.), *Ethnic variations in dying, death, and grief: Diversity in universality* (pp. 113–124). Philadelphia: Taylor and Francis.

Emswiler, M. A., & Emswiler, J. P. (2000). *Guiding your child through grief.* New York: Bantam Books.

Erdman, P., & Lampe, R. (1996). Adapting basic skills to counsel children. *Journal of Counseling and Development, 74(4),* 374–377.

Erikson, J. M. (1985). Sources of lifelong learning. *Journal of Education, 167(3),* 85–96.

Eyetsemitan, F. (1998). Stifled grief in the workplace. *Death Studies, 22(5),* 469–480.

Fitzgerald, H. (1992). *The grieving child: A parent's guide.* New York: Fireside.

Fox, S. (1985). *Good grief: Helping groups of children when a friend dies.* Boston: New England Association for the Education of Young Children.

Fredlund, D. (1984). Children and death from the school setting viewpoint. In J. L. Thomas (Ed.), *Death and dying in the classroom: Readings for reference.* Phoenix: Oryx Press.

Fry, V. L. (1995). *Part of me died, too.* New York: Dutton Books.

Gifaldi, D. (2000). *One thing for sure.* Lincoln, NE: iUniverse, Inc.

Gilanshah, F. (1993). Islamic customs regarding death. In D. P. Irish, K. F. Lundquist, & V. J. Nelsen (Eds.), *Ethnic variations in dying, death, and grief: Diversity in universality* (pp. 137–146). Philadelphia: Taylor and Francis.

Gilbert, R. B. (1995). Protestant perspectives on grief and children. In E. A. Grollman (Ed.), *Bereaved children and teens: A support guide for helping professionals.* Boston: Beacon Press.

Ginsberg, H., & Opper, S. (1969). *Piaget's theory of intellectual development.* Englewood, NJ: Prentice Hall.

Glass, J. C., Jr. (1991). Death, loss, and grief among middle school children: Implications for the school counselor. *Elementary School Guidance and Counseling, 26*(2), 139–149.

Goldenberg, I., & Goldenberg, H. (1997). *Counseling today's families* (3rd ed.). Pacific Grove: Brooks/Cole.

Goldman, L. (2004). Counseling with children in contemporary society. *Journal of Mental Health Counseling, 26*(2), 168–188.

Gorman, R. M. (1972). *Discovering Piaget: A guide for teachers.* Columbus: Merrill.

Goss, R. E., & Klass, D. (1997). Tibetan Buddhism and the resolution of grief: The *Bardo-Thodol* for the dying and the grieving. *Death Studies, 21,* 377–395.

Greenstone, J., & Leviton, S. C. (2002). *Elements of crisis intervention* (2nd ed.). Pacific Grove, CA: Brooks/Cole.

Hagman, G. (2001). Beyond decathexia: Toward a new psychoanalytic understanding and treatment of mourning. In R. Neimeyer (Ed.), *Meaning reconstruction and the experience of loss* (pp. 3–31). Washington, DC: American Psychological Association.

Imber-Black, E. (2005). Creating meaningful rituals for new life cycle transitions. In B. Carter & M. McGoldrick (Eds.), *The expanded family life cycle: Individual, family and social perspectives* (3rd ed.; pp. 202–214). Boston: Allyn and Bacon.

Ishiyama, F. I. (1995). Conflict issues and counseling implications. *Canadian Journal of Counseling, 29*(3), 262–-275.

Ivey, A. E., & Ivey, M. B. (2003). *Intentional interviewing and counseling: Facilitating client development in a multicultural society* (4th ed.). Pacific Grove, CA: Brooks/Cole.

Jacobs, L. (1992). *Religion and the individual: A Jewish perspective.* New York: Cambridge University Press.

James, J., & Friedman, R. (2001). *When children grieve.* New York: HarperCollins.

James, R. K., & Gilliand, B. E. (2005). *Crisis intervention strategies* (5th ed.). Belmont, CA: Brooks/Cole.

Kauffman, J. M. (2001). *Characteristics of emotional and behavioral disorders of children and youth* (7th ed.). Upper Saddle River, NJ: Merrill/Prentice Hall.

Klass, D., & Heath, A. O. (1996). Grief and abortion: *Mizuko kuyo*, the Japanese ritual resolution. *Omega, 34*(1), 1–15.

Kleinman, A. (1986). *Social origins of distress and disease: Depression, neurasthenia, and pain in modern China.* New Haven, CT: Yale University Press.

Kowalski, G. (1997). *Goodbye, friend: Healing wisdom for anyone who has ever lost a pet.* Walpole, CT: Stillpoint Publishing.

Kübler-Ross, E. (1969). *On death and dying.* New York: Macmillan.

Landreth, G. L. (2002). *Play therapy: The art of the relationship* (2nd ed.). New York: Brunner-Routledge.

Mack, C., & Smith, T. (1991). *Separation and loss: A handbook for early childhood professionals.* Pittsburgh: University of Pittsburgh Press.

Maslow, A. H. (1987). *Motivation and personality* (3rd ed.). New York: Harper and Row.

Maxmen, J. S., & Ward, N. G. (1995). *Essential psychopathology and its treatment* (2nd ed.). New York: W.W. Norton.

McEntire, N. (2003). *Children and grief* (Report No. EDO-PS-036). Champaign, IL: ERIC Clearinghouse on Elementary and Early Childhood Education. (ERIC Document Reproduction Service No. ED475393)

McGlauflin, H. (1999). *Supporting children and teens through grief and loss.* Boston: Beacon Press.

McGoldrick, M. (Ed.). (1998). *Revisioning family therapy: Race, culture, and gender in clinical practice.* New York: Guilford Press.

McGoldrick, M., Hines, P., Lee, E., & Preto, N. G. (1986). Mourning rituals. *Family Therapy Networker, 10*(6), 28–36.

McGoldrick, M., Schlesinger, J. M., Lee, E., Hines, P. M., Chan, J., Petkov, B., Preto, N. G., & Petry, S. (1991). Mourning in different cultures. In F. Walsh & M. McGoldrick (Eds.), *Living beyond loss: Death in the family* (pp. 176–206). New York: W.W. Norton.

McGoldrick, M., & Walsh, F. (2005). Death and the family life cycle. In B. Carter & M. McGoldrick (Eds.), *The expanded family life cycle: Individual, family, and social perspectives* (3rd ed.; pp. 185–201). Boston: Allyn and Bacon.

Metzgar, M. M. (2002). *Developmental considerations concerning children's grief.* Available from http://kidsource.com/sids/childrensgrief.htm

Miller, S. I., & Schoenfeld, L. (1973). Grief in the Navajo: Psychodynamics and culture. *International Journal of Social Psychiatry, 19*(3–4), 187–191.

Moloye, O. (1999). The philosophy of upgradeable cosmos: The essences of "omo" (children) in Yoruba ethno-cosmology. *Western Journal of Black Studies, 23*, 58–69.

Morrison, T. (2000). *The bluest eye.* New York: Knopf.

Mullen, J. A. (2003). *Speaking of children: A study of how play therapists make meaning of children* (Doctoral dissertation, Syracuse University, 2003). *Dissertation Abstracts International, 64*, 11A.

Nader, K. O. (1996). Children's exposure to traumatic experiences. In C. A. Corr & D. M. Corr (Eds.), *Handbook of childhood death and bereavement* (pp. 201–220). New York: Springer.

Neimeyer, R. (2001). The language of loss: Grief therapy as a process of meaning reconstruction. In R. Neimeyer (Ed.), *Meaning reconstruction and the experience of loss* (pp. 324–331). Washington, DC: American Psychological Association.

Piaget, J. (1970). *The science of education and the psychology of the child.* New York: Grossman.

Rando, T. A. (1984). *Grief, dying, and death: Clinical interventions for caregivers.* Champaign, IL: Research Press.

Reeves, N. C., & Boersma, F. J. (1990). The therapeutic use of ritual in maladaptive grieving. *Omega, 20*(4), 281–296.

Robinson, T., & Howard-Hamilton, M. (2000). *The convergence of race, ethnicity, and gender: Multiple identities in counseling.* Upper Saddle River, NJ: Prentice Hall.

Romanoff, B. D. (2001). Research as therapy: The power of narrative to effect change. In R. Neimeyer (Ed.), *Meaning reconstruction and the experience of loss* (pp. 311–323). Washington, DC: American Psychological Association.

Rosenblatt, P. C. (1993). Cross-cultural variation in the experience, expression, and understanding of grief. In D. P. Irish, K. F. Lundquist, & V. J. Nelsen (Eds.), *Ethnic variations in dying, death, and grief: Diversity in universality* (pp. 13–20). Philadelphia: Taylor and Francis.

Salvador, R. J. (2003). What do Mexicans celebrate on the Day of the Dead? In J. D. Morgan & P. Laungani (Eds.), *Death and bereavement in the Americas: Vol. 2. Death, value and meaning series* (pp. 75–76). Amityville, NY: Baywood.

Scheper-Hughes, N. (1985). Culture, scarcity, and maternal thinking: Maternal detachment and infant survival in a Brazilian shantytown. *Ethos, 13*, 291–317.

Schaffer, C. E. (1988). Therapy: Critical issues for the next millennium. *Association for Play Therapy Newsletter, 17*(1), 1–5.

Schoen, A. A., Burgoyne, M., & Schoen, S. F. (2004). Are the developmental needs of children in America adequately addressed during the grief process? *Journal of Instructional Psychology, 31*(2), 143–150.

Shaw, H. (1999). Children and grief: How parents can help in times of loss. *Parent and Preschooler Newsletter, 14*(2), 1–2.

Sheehy, N. (1994). Talk about being Irish: Death ritual as a cultural forum. *The Irish Journal of Psychology, 15,* 494–507.

Silverman, P., & Worden, J. W. (1992). Children's understanding of funeral ritual. *Omega, 25,* 319–331.

Sommers-Flanagan, J., & Sommers-Flanagan, R. (1995). Intake interviewing with suicidal patients: A systematic approach. *Professional Psychology: Research and Practice, 26*(1), 41–47.

Steinberg, L. (1996). *Adolescence* (4th ed.). New York: McGraw-Hill.

Stern, M., & Newland, L. M. (1994). Working with children: Providing a framework for the roles of counseling psychologists. *The Counseling Psychologist, 22*(3), 402–425.

Sunoo, B. P., & Solomon, C. M. (1996). Facing grief: How and why to help people heal. *Personnel Journal, 75*(4), 78–89.

Terr, L. C. (1995). Childhood traumas: An outline and overview. In G. S. Everly & J. M. Lating (Eds.), *Psychotraumatology: Key papers and core concepts in posttraumatic stress* (pp. 301–320). New York: Plenum.

Thomas, P. (2003). *The skin I'm in: A first look at racism.* New York: Barron.

Thompson, C. L., & Rudolph, L. B. (2000). *Counseling children* (5th ed.). Stamford, CT: Brooks/Cole.

Trozzi, M. (1999). *Talking with children about loss: Words, strategies, and wisdom to help children cope with death, divorce, and other difficult times.* New York: Penguin Putnam.

Truitner, K., & Truitner, N. (1993). Death and dying in Buddhism. In D. P. Irish, K. F. Lundquist, & V. J. Nelsen (Eds.), *Ethnic variations in dying, death, and grief: Diversity in universality* (pp. 125–136). Philadelphia: Taylor and Francis.

Vargas, L. A., & Koss-Choino, J. D. (1992). *Working with culture: Psychotherapeutic interventions with ethnic minority children and adolescents.* San Francisco: Jossey-Bass.

Vernon, A. (1993). *Thinking, feeling, behaving: An emotional education curriculum (Grades 7–12).* Champaign, IL: Research Press.

Vernon, A., & Al-Mabuk, A. H. (1995). *What growing up is all about: A parent's guide to child and adolescent development.* Champaign, IL: Research Press.

Weaver, T. (2002, July 23). Children's suicides catching experts by surprise. *The Syracuse Post-Standard,* pp. A1, A6.

Webb, N. B. (Ed.). (2002). *Helping bereaved children: A handbook for practitioners* (2nd ed.). New York: Guilford.

Webb, N. B. (2003). Play and expressive therapies to help bereaved children: Individual, family, and group treatment. *Smith College Studies in Social Work, 73,* 405–422.

Weidman, H. H. (1975). *Concepts as strategies for change.* New York: Insight Communications.

Wikan, U. (1988). Bereavement and loss in two Muslim communities: Egypt and Bali compared. *Social Science and Medicine, 27,* 451–460.

Wikan, U. (1990) *Managing turbulent hearts: A Balinese formula for living.* University of Chicago Press.

Wilhelm, H. (1989). *I'll always love you.* New York: Crown Books for Young Readers.

Wittbold, M. K. (2003). *Let's talk about when your parent is in jail.* New York: Rosen Publishing.

Wolfelt, A. D. (1991). *A child's view of grief.* Fort Collins, CO: Companion Press.

Worden, J. W. (1991). *Grief counseling and grief therapy: A handbook for the mental health practitioner.* New York: Springer.

Worden, J. W. (1996). *Children and grief: When a parent dies.* New York: Guilford.

Wortman, C., & Silver, R. (1989). The myths of coping with loss. *Journal of Consulting and Clinical Psychology, 57,* 349–357.

About the Authors

Jody J. Fiorini, Ph.D., is an assistant professor at the State University of New York College at Oswego, School of Education, Counseling and Psychological Services Department. Dr. Fiorini teaches courses in multicultural counseling, counseling theory, research, measurement, and program evaluation; psychopathology, professional issues and ethics; and a variety of clinical training courses. She is credentialed as an Approved Clinical Supervisor and a Nationally Certified Counselor through the National Board of Certified Counselors. Her professional background includes her work as a disability services provider and advocate and as a mental health counselor in private practice. In her clinical practice, Dr. Fiorini specializes in working with individuals with disabilities and their families and working with adolescents and adults who have experienced loss. She is the author and coauthor of several book chapters and other publications related to helping counselors work more effectively with clients with learning disabilities and attention-deficit/hyperactivity disorder as well as those who have experienced grief and loss.

Jodi Ann Mullen, Ph.D., N.C.C., R.P.T., is a professor at The State University of New York at Oswego, Counseling and Psychological Services department. She is the program coordinator of the Graduate Certificate Program in Play Therapy. She teaches courses that prepare community and school counselors and school psychologists. Her professional background includes counselor education and preparation, supervising counselors and play therapists, and clinical practice. She is a National Certified Counselor and Registered Play Therapist. Her professional research and writings have centered on counseling children and adolescents, play therapy, and clinical supervision. She is the author and coauthor of several book chapters and other publications. Dr. Mullen maintains a small private practice where she specializes in counseling children and adolescents.

Feb 27/08